OXFORD EXAMINED

Oxford Examined
Town and Clown

with very best wishes

Richard O. Smith

Signal

Signal Books
Oxford

First published in 2015 by
Signal Books Limited
36 Minster Road
Oxford OX4 1LY
www.signalbooks.co.uk

A catalogue record for this book is available from the British Library

ISBN 978-1-909930-35-3 Paper

Cover Design and Art Work: Korky Paul © 2015
Cover Production: Tora Kelly
Typesetting: Tora Kelly
Printed in India by Imprint Digital

CONTENTS

INTRODUCTION

Hi. I'm Richard. I'm OK, thanks. You? Good.

They say potential book buyers make their decision after reading the first two paragraphs of the Introduction – and I've already used one paragraph to say "hi". So I'd better not take connecting slow trains to get to the point. As I have several great stories to tell. They're all about Oxford and here's the important thing ... oh, that's the second paragraph ended. Goodbye then.

That's better – it's just you and me now – the clever readers who'll enjoy this book, appreciate its wit; even spot the semi colon (mis) usage. Unlike those fickle flickers lacking the required attention span to read a tweet to the end who departed after the second paragraph, you recognise this is a crafted book. And here's what it's about and why I wrote it (I know you'll like it – you've got good taste)…

Oxford Examined is a humorous book about every aspect of Oxford life. Why do we need another book about Oxford? Because although there is a bookshelf- buckling amount of titles written on Oxford there are not many funny ones. And since I'm a professional comedy writer + I love Oxford = this book.

I moved to Oxford 25 years ago. Although I was architecturally star-struck by the buildings, it was not love at first sight. My affection and affinity for Oxford grew slowly, resulting in a deeper relationship than one based purely on looks alone – though Oxford still looks beautiful (not bad given that it's over a thousand years old). Oxford is supposedly divided into Town and Gown. In fact, Oxford is supported by a tripod of Gown (the University), Town (the city) and Tourism. (About 9.5 million tourists visit Oxford each year spending £770 million.)

Though I always defined myself as belonging to the Town tribe, I found it surprisingly possible to glide into the Gown side and also experience the Tourist perspective (sometimes I still feel like a tourist in my own city). Turns out the demarcation lines are not etched as deeply as some lazy prejudices would have us believe.

I learnt this when an *Oxford Times* editor gave me a brief to experience every quirky side of Oxford I could discover and write about my experiences in the *Oxford Examined* column for the multi-award winning *Oxford Times* magazine supplement *Oxfordshire Limited Edition*. This brief issued me with a border pass enabling me to cross between the frontiers of Town, Gown and Tourism. However...

Appointing me to write this column was a callous act. Why? Because I don't like embracing change – it's usually smelly and has bad breath. And change is rarely marked "good change" or "bad change" to help you choose in advance. But the workplace world advocates, promotes and cheerleads for change. Managers, supervisors and editors insist on everyone gleefully adopting change, dealing with change, groping change hungrily in the stationery cupboard of corporate advancement.

That's why they thought it would be funny to appoint a change-avoider to undergo numerous Oxford-related adventures – issuing me with a different monthly assignment that required a radical change to my environment. Plus a permanent eviction from my comfort zone.

Hence each month I would be given tasks such as conducting a walking tour for Greek tourists, meeting Kate Middleton, gate-crashing Encaenia, allowing Oxford University psychologists to experiment on me with a radical new treatment and visiting the 11th dimension with an Oxford mathematics genius.

The consequences of all this unwelcomely encountered change form this compilation of my best *Oxford Examined* columns herein. These despatches from the frontline of change, ducking the bullets of progress, result in a victorious great leap forward for understanding how malleable those dividing lines actually are between Oxford's Town, Gown and Tourism trinity. This is a book about Oxford experiences, interacting with its people more than its buildings or history. Which in itself represents a change from most books about Oxford.

Needless to say, I still don't like change.

LITERARY

THE BOOKSHOP APPEARANCE

A publisher has ordered me to speak at a bookshop event. I am no longer with this publisher hence our relationship is somewhat fractious. It transpires that they are not happy with me for leaving them – especially for a new, younger, more attractive publisher half their age. However, there are the three children to think of – which in a publishing context means the three books I authored for them, including a moderate bestseller. Although we don't have to stay together for the sake of the books, some contact is necessary. This is why I am spending a Saturday afternoon at a well-known bookshop in Oxfordshire.

Only when I arrive at the store do I discover that I am not there to speak. Instead I have to do an author signing. I have done these before and it mainly involves sitting self-consciously behind a desk for four hours whilst shoppers formulate increasingly creative ways of avoiding eye contact.

The manager greets me, pointing out competitively that last weekend's in-store author "sold many signed books". He then gestures towards the door where a tiny table has been positioned. I shoehorn myself between the available four inches of space separating table from chair pinned against a bookshelf. The automatic shop door opens every few seconds dispensing an icy blast of rain-sodden wind. Dependent on whether the doors are shut, the shop climate oscillates between cactus-wilting heat and Arctic storm.

After twenty minutes sitting at my table, alternating between fanning myself and shivering, I encounter my first customer interaction. A man approaches me. I lift up my signing pen expectantly. "Excuse me, mate," he begins, "are you an author?" I am sitting underneath an enormous sign proclaiming "Author here today" next to a pyramid formation of my books. "Yes," I reply confidently. "Good," he says, "can you direct me to where the Horror section is?"

Everyone else ignores me for the next hour, so I decide to interact with the passing footfall. "Hello there, Sir. Do you like reading?" I enquire; I receive a look in return that communicates, "I've already killed today. Don't make me kill again."

A teenage girl approaches me. "You're like the actual author of this, yeah?" she asks, evidently weary of deceitful author imposters at book signings. "Yes," I respond. "Cool," she says. "Can you sign it to Darren?" "Of course," I reply flattered, inadequately disguising the shock that someone is actually buying one of my books. "Darren's an unusual name for a girl," I say. "That's my brother's name," she replies, leaving the phrase, "Obviously I'm not called Darren you moron," left unsaid but not unimplied.

She then presents me with a £10 note. "You need to pay at the till." "But there's a queue," she reasons then departs, causing the shop doors to open, and my working conditions are temporarily akin to those of a North Sea trawlerman. I approach the counter and hand them the £10 note. "Please can you take for this book? A girl left me the money." "You should have asked her to pay at the till," the cashier informs me sternly.

Two middle-aged women enter. Instead of bounding past my table like everyone else over the previous three hours, they immediately brake hard in front of me. The taller one has puffy red eyes and has evidently been crying. "We've come to buy your book." I want to hug them and pant, "Thank you, thank you," but instead struggle to remain cool. "We've been to see *Testament of Youth*. I enjoyed the film so much," she says between sobs. Given she's been crying like a grieving widow at an onion factory, I wonder out loud if "enjoyed" is the most felicitous word selection.

A man enters laden with photographic equipment. "Can I take your photo?" he enquires. Wow, I'm going to be papped. I feel temporarily giddy with fame. A professional snapper has come specially to photograph me! "Someone from *Emmerdale* is opening a new pound shop in the precinct. Then I spotted you. What's your name?" he asks, getting out a notebook. There are still 39 books piled on the table – each one displaying my name.

After three hours I receive a call from my wife. "How's it going?" she asks. "I'm at the book signing." "Well, I'd better let you go as you must be very busy." "Yes, very busy," I confirm. Which is true – I've still got half a newspaper to read and I haven't even started the Easy Crossword yet.

Then it dawns on me that my position near the entrance doors is deliberately advantageous for the shop. Two teenage boys pick up confectionery items and head not towards the till but the door. Until they see me staring at them, whereupon they swivel and replace the chocolate bars. I may not have the physique or wardrobe of a crime fighting superhero, but I temporarily feel like one.

As my fourth and final hour begins, a woman arrives holding hands with her two daughters. The younger one is pulling like an Alsatian determined to unshackle herself from a lead. The oldest girl must be about eleven. "Annabel wants to be a writer, don't you Annabel?" Annabel doesn't look so sure. "Her English teacher says she has a remarkable talent for expression. She really is quite the literary genius." It's funny; I've never met a genius, but I've met an awful lot of their parents. "Tell him about your book idea."

"Can we go to Primark now, mum?" suggests Annabel. "That's an original title - I like it," I respond. Annabel gives me a look that unambiguously communicates, "Look, we all know we're not going to buy your dreary book, that my mother is a prat, and the only reason I'm prepared to be seen alive in public with her is that I've been promised a Primark shopping trip. Which you are currently delaying me from." The younger daughter then yanks her mother with a force that nearly topples her over. "We're going now, girls," announces their mother, deludedly believing she has orchestrated the decision to depart as her two pulling daughters glide her out of the shop like she is on roller skates. Needless to say, they don't buy a book. I worry that the store manager will be unimpressed with my measly sales compared to last weekend's author.

Thankfully I sell a respectable eleven books in the final hour. Two women nervously purchase *Fifty Shades of Grey* from a shelf opposite. Both feel obliged to inform me, a complete stranger, that "It's not for me". "How have you done?" asks the manager afterwards. "Not as well as your last author," I say embarrassed, "How many did they sell last weekend?" "Oh, he did really, really well. Sold four copies."

The Literary Agent

A few weeks ago I had a book published about inept criminals engaged in award-winning stupidity. Some people even bought it. Perhaps some shoplifted it, got caught, and will appear in *As Thick as Thieves* Volume Two.

I have had books published before and now know the usual procedure. You spend between one and two years writing a book and usually manage to finish it just before it finishes you. Then, after much anticipation and fanfare, they are launched. Whereby six copies are sold – all to your closest friends. The fact that you expected to sell seven means that an unfortunate by-product of your book being published is that you now only have six friends. Oh well, one less birthday card to buy next year.

Then no one else buys your book. Ever. Occasionally – albeit a lot less occasionally than authors would admit publicly – writers check their Amazon sales listing. This enables you to establish that you have just written the 4,985,673rd most popular book in the UK at present.

Though this does not stop people encountered socially from responding: "Oh, you're an author. You must be loaded, like that J K Rowling". Yeah, exactly like J K Rowling. Apart from in every way possible.

Then one Saturday morning I check whether I have yet crashed through the coveted Top 5 (million) chart position and discover I am suddenly residing in the Top 500. Later I am Amazon's official No. 1 Bestseller in their Humour category. Take that, Miranda Hart, Bill Bryson and David Jason (or, as I now call them, "numbers 2, 3 and 4"). One reviewer brands me "The English David Sedaris". This historic moment is marked by Amazon sending me a tiny yellow rosette with the caption "Amazon No. 1 Topseller" – a virtual one, obviously. Presumably there being no tax on virtual rosettes. J K Rowling must have been sent one of these – now I have my first thing in common with her.

Needless to say, authors receive a specially diminished royalty of around 4p per copy for Amazon sales. Even though I genuinely calculated that one week before Christmas last year I earned £9000 for Amazon – which, after tax, equates to…£9000! Phew, satire!

Hmm. This is all on the suspicious side of odd. Say what you want about *Take A Break* magazine – and you'll probably get sued – but they have a print circulation of over 700,000. An outstanding distribution figure in 2014 – or any other year you want to randomly pick in history. They ran a surprise two page feature on the book, causing the sales surge and vertiginous chart position.

Suddenly, my voicemail light flashes from literary agents keen to introduce themselves. Consequently I travel to London and meet a bigwig literary agent who represents household names. The receptionist scowls at me for being nine minutes early. Begrudgingly, they make me a coffee. It's an instant coffee. Giving anybody an instant coffee is the way the refined middle classes tell someone to "**** off!" Then another author arrives, whose face I instantly recognise from TV. "Thank you for being so early," the same receptionist says. They make him a coffee on a machine the size of, and as noisy as, a small van. Hmm.

The literary agent comes to reception, completes a showbizzy air-kiss greeting to the Very Famous Author and then asks me to follow him to his spacious office.

There I am introduced to Arabella. When I arrive she is already present in the top corner of the room, like the crop sprayer in Hitchcock's *North By Northwest*. Extremely tall and worryingly slim, she wears a short skater skirt. Viewed from the side, she resembles a flagpole at half-mast.

Arabella sits in a corner, with her back to me, and starts slowly pecking at her keyboard. She is clearly planning on being ignored for the duration of the meeting. That's her game plan, at least.

The agent enlightens me about what agents do, explaining that in the unlikely event of any money being left after they have deducted their fees, percentages, expenses and necessary whatevers, then I will receive it.

"So, what is your next book project?" I have been anticipating this question, and pitch away like a *Dragons' Den* participant. "My next book is going to be titled…" Then freeze. "Yes?" he encourages. I am so nervous I actually have to look at my notes, to remember the title of my next book. My envisaged J K Rowling-can't-compete-with-that blockbuster. "I'm out!" would be the collective *Dragons' Den* decision by now. (Note to producers of *Dragons' Den* – dragons live in a lair, not a den.)

Aided by my notes, I pitch away. Every five seconds Arabella locates another character on her keyboard, and hits it with her right index finger. There is an identifiable type of young female, posh and affluent who prefers saying "ya" to "yeah", that seems only to work in two employment fields: publishing and art galleries.

This, I realise just in time, is the subterfuge cover Arabella deploys. Authors presumably often underestimate her importance, but fortunately she has a visible 'tell' whenever you say A Good Idea. Occasionally during my pitch she will turn around and reward me with 0.3 seconds of eye contact, then do likewise to the agent.

Departing the office I deliberately take a route past Arabella's workstation. Her computer screen is covered with random keystrokes. She was only pretending to type. She is hired to listen and monitor more intently in the day job than most GCHQ staff. And she is obviously the one who determines whether the literary agent will represent me or not.

Sure enough, it is her, not the agent, who calls the next day. They want to see me again in a couple of weeks. I will know upon arrival whether they will represent me - by the receptionist's coffee.

THE ROSE GARDEN ROOM

I am lost and late. This is one of the more displeasing twin combinations it is possible to experience in life, up there with hungry and dieting, old and tired, and Ant and Dec.

I am looking for The Rose Garden Room. Five minutes ago I came to the conclusion, not unlightly given the previous fifteen minutes of fruitless searching, that such a named room does not exist. Much earlier – so much earlier geologists probably have a different name for the era - I had arrived in an Oxford college arrogantly optimistic that such a room existed. But seven U-turns, four dead-ends and three retraced staircases back to my starting place convince me there is no such room. I feel suspiciously like one of those apprentice builders who is told to go to the depot on their first day and request a tin of tartan paint.

A helpful Oxford porter had patiently told me where the Rose Garden Room was located, but after the second mention of "take a left", "then another left" and "thirteenth right", I had lost concentration.

In order to locate the venue I decide to apply logic and search for a rose garden, assuming one must be within the vicinity of the eponymous room. Clever, eh? Nope. Turns out they never promised me a rose garden – just a room named after one.

Reaching the point where I wish I had paid more attention to Bear Grylls survival videos since I am beginning to fear for my survival in this rugged terrain of, ahem, college grounds, I grieve my loss of civilisation and wonder how I will ever find my way back to it. Then a formally attired waiter passes me carrying a tray of rattling wine glasses – suggesting I am probably not yet beyond the mapped world.

Soon I am joined by two other perplexed people – here to attend the same seminar but now reluctant adventurists also lost and seeking the likely mythical Rose Garden Room. Our party of displaced refugees soon grows. Bonded by our disorientation we swap stories, mainly beginning with, "it's not this way" and "definitely not there". A passing stranger is sought, stopped and duly interrogated. He has no idea where the Rose Garden Room is either. Or why I am the fourteenth person to have asked him the same question in the last ten minutes. Curt and speaking with an astringent German accent, his reply borders on being rude. I suppress a retaliatory mention of the war.

I decide to abandon my party of lost fellow room seekers. Admittedly it's a gamble, but Stanley didn't find Livingstone as part of an organised tour group, nor Livingstone discover the source of the Nile on an ABTA-affiliated package holiday. After a few minutes, my sense of isolation fermenting, I spot another human. A girl, maybe in her late teens, steps out of the darkness and crosses my path. She is visibly rushing – proven by the fact both her long dark hair and coat belt are flowing behind her like a motorcyclist's scarf. But I have to risk bothering her in case she knows the room's location. I am unpleasantly late and fear the other search party may have already found the room, occupied the chairs and drunk the promised wine. "Excuse me, I'm so sorry to trouble you…" I begin. She is polite and smiles softly. "I think, though I'm not sure," she errs humbly, "it's this way. I'm going there too, later."

She gestures towards a corner building – one that I had passed twice already over the previous twenty minutes. There I spot the provost sticking a makeshift sign over an existing brass plate declaring "examinations". As soon as he steps back to admire his sign sticking skills, I read the unambiguous words "Rose Garden Room". Trust yourself! I didn't need the others to succeed, they just held me back.

I enter the room to find everyone else already seated. Worse, they greet me with a traitorous look for abandoning them earlier. Furthermore all four wines bottles are now empty. This is particularly grating given it's my favourite type of wine: free wine. I pour myself a disappointing orange juice and sit next to a dark-haired girl.

"Hello," she greets me, "we both found the room, then." It's the helpful girl from earlier.

A speaker rises and begins to talk about Evelyn Waugh. Apparently Waugh ended his Oxford tenure without a degree. Maybe it was because his exams were in the Rose Garden Room and he couldn't find it.

Afterwards we are chatting about Waugh's depiction of Oxford. I mention the rampant snobbery of *Brideshead Revisited*, hiding the fact I've only seen the TV series but not read the book. An academic opposite me opines that Waugh's playful portrayal of existential angst masquerading as satirical intention is contrite. A don nods agreement and gives the word "prestidigitation" a rare conversational outing.

"There are some Sir Alastair Digby-Vane-Trumpington characters to be found unexterminated in Oxford today," guffaws a portly man before rocking backwards and forwards with laughter. At his own joke.

An ageless woman looking magnificent in a timeless black dress accessorised with a kindly smile senses my discomfort at this impenetrably highbrow literary reference. She explains selflessly that he is referring to Evelyn Waugh's debut novel set in Oxford's fictional Scone College. She asks me which Oxford college I attended. "I didn't," I reply. Awkward. "It's okay," I say to fill the deepening silence, "it could have been worse. I could have gone to Cambridge."

Dangerously I want to contribute to the conversation on Waugh. "The scout in *Brideshead* was played by Bill Owen who portrayed Compo in *Last of the Summer Wine*." "I didn't know that," says one of the academics, kindly. They didn't know that I failed my English O Level either, but are now beginning to suspect.

A don asks the dark-haired girl an invasively personal question about her family relationships. "I think I'll save it for my book one day," she replies graciously – cleverly removing the poisonous bit from the conversation.

Then a middle-aged man joins our group. "This is another of the Waughs," reveals the woman. I look impressed. "Oh yes – one of *those* Waughs. The really famous Waughs," she elaborates. "Wow," I say, "the brothers who captained Australia at cricket?" The woman in the black dress laughs heartily before explaining my reference to the dusty don who made the Scone College joke. One all.

The girl who aided my search for the room is revealed as Evelyn Waugh's great-granddaughter. The middle aged man is introduced as Waugh's grandson.

I mentioned the Waugh but think I got away with it.

THE PRIMARY SCHOOL INCIDENT

Tough on education. Tough on the causes of education.

I think that was the government's education policy during my school years. But those schooldays feel an increasingly long time ago. I am getting older and have just approached a crossroads in my life - specifically where the B4493 joins the A4130 Didcot road. We are not yet late, but entering the uncomfortable possibility of lateness. Insulating myself against the likelihood of tardiness ensures I am absurdly early for most appointments. That's the way I like it.

But today a police diversion is in place near Didcot. When my driver enquires why, the police curtly inform him, "It's an incident". He asks them, "What sort of incident?" They elaborate by restating: "It's an incident." That clears that up then.

So why am I currently stuck at a crossroads near Didcot with an information-constipated constable? Like a lot of things we do in the 21st century, it started with an email. I was asked if, as an author, I would speak to the assembled pupils of an Oxfordshire primary school.

The previous school I addressed was Magdalen College School who achieved the best A-level results in England last year. They billed me in their Arts Festival brochure as speaking on "Oxford Ecccentricity". That's right – count those c's in "eccentricity". Odd, as I don't usually associate that school with three C's – although that would get you into Cambridge.

Author visits can be inspiring. Philippa Pearce's visit to my primary school seared an affection for the written word on me still traceable decades later. Unbeknown to the ten-year-old me, Philippa was a bona fide literary A-lister – author of indisputable children's classics *Tom's Midnight Garden* and *Minnow on the Say*. She gave the advice: "Writing is a bit of constructive woodwork. You are a cabinet-maker." I remember this distinctly, wondering if I should be taking woodwork instead of English as a subject if I wanted to express myself as a writer.

Upon arrival I am taken to the staff room. This is the room that I only accessed as a child after being extremely naughty. Hence I used to hang out here a lot. I recognise the amount of coffee that would stock a Starbucks for a busy Bank Holiday weekend. Only the heaped ashtrays are missing from my childhood memory of school staffrooms. A friendly woman greets me by saying she is halfway through my latest book, "And loving it and I hope you'll do a reading." This concerns me slightly as I wonder if she has yet reached the dirty bits. She apologises for her unpunctuality, but explains, "There's been an incident on the roads."

From there I am led to a classroom where an audience of children are patiently awaiting a speaker. They are gathered around a table containing an impressive model of a Spitfire. A whiteboard declares: "Spitfire talk". I stand in front of everyone wondering if they know what I know – which is absolutely nothing about Spitfires. My presence is devitalised by the arrival of a Spitfire expert who is the grandfather of a school pupil. Apparently he is due to speak before me.

He gives an interesting talk about the Battle of Britain, carefully avoiding technical words. Thereby ensuring – unlike the working model aircraft he has brought along – that he is incapable of going over the audience's heads. Until the Q&A starts. One child, no older than ten, asks: "What advantages did the Spitfire Mark Eight's new cut-back rear fuselage design offer over the Spitfire Mark Seven?" Understandably flummoxed, he flounders like a salmon on a riverbank.

This reminds me of an anecdote I was once told by a teacher – serving as a parable warning educators to dumb down to kids at your peril. An embittered primary school supply teacher held up a picture of a cow to her new infant charges. "And what animal is this?" she enquired. No hands were raised. This surprised her, given she planned further animal pictures becoming progressively harder as she revealed each subsequent photo. One pupil asked if he could take a closer look at the photo. Given no one else appeared forthcoming with an answer identifying the animal, the teacher permitted the child to stroll to the front of the class and examine the bovine image. "I know what it is now," chirped the child with regained enthusiasm. "Good," said the teacher, allowing herself to think, "finally we're making some progress and not before time." "So," reiterated the teacher, "What animal is it?" "It's a Holstein Friesian steer," replied the child.

Then it is my turn to speak. All month the school had reassured me they were equipped to provide me with PowerPoint facilities. The day before the talk this is reaffirmed. When I arrive they are surprised to discover I require PowerPoint facilities - for the presentation I have meticulously invested the last 48 hours constructing. Audiences – even ones aged between eight and eleven – will forgive most things with a speaker, but never a lack of preparation.

Getting a computer connected to a basic projector necessitates going headhunting at NASA to recruit the specialist expertise. After ten minutes a nine-year-old strolls purposefully to the front and suggests we run something-I've-never-heard-of to reboot the I-don't-know-what in order to rectify the too-technical-to-remember. We – or rather he – runs these procedures and the thing awakes from its lengthy lazy slumber.

Teachers are obliged to perform a daily confidence trick of maintaining the pretence that they know more than the children. He repeats back as many of the acronyms and words expressed by the nine-year-old as he can recall. Like me, this might be the first time he has heard them.

Midway through my talk a boy falls off his chair and laughs. I note it is reassuring to see young people reviving the spirit of that old Norman Wisdom slapstick standby. Unsurprisingly, only the adults in the room laugh at this reference.

The kids are a warm audience, both interesting and interested. These are the cute ages – still sweet before the souring teenage years arrive with curdling hormones.

On the way home we join the diversion queue again and stop at a red light next to a policeman. My driver winds down the window and asks: "Has there been an incident?" "Yes," replies the policeman with a disconcerted look of "how could you possibly know that?!"

THE LITTLE RED RIDING HOOD STORY

Always ensure you understand the question before preparing an answer. Being a freelance writer means working on my own most days in solitary self-employment. There are disadvantages to this lifestyle – the workplace Christmas Secret Santa is rubbish. I also have to deal with distinctly strange work-related questions.

Like the other day, when a producer asked me to find out: "How old is Little Red Riding Hood?" I expect you to answer this question accurately before the end of the column too. See if you can work it out.

Technology ought to render this question less of a challenge nowadays. Supposedly gone are the days of sliding fingers down indexes in hushed libraries. Yet my research assistant Mr Google denied me any sort of definitive answer – mainly because the stories never seem to state her age. Moreover we are often more indebted to illustrators than authors for our shared visualisations of characters from classic children's stories. Think *Alice in Wonderland* to prove that point.

I check a book retained from my childhood that contains the Little Red Riding Hood story. Never once does it even hint at her age. More detailed library research reveals storytellers have imagined her age ranging from three years to late teens. A Little Red Riding Hood in her teens is older than most would consider the story's central protagonist, although that would make her the original teenage hoodie. Which renders the story impressively modern – even before we consider the cross-dressing wolf.

"Oh, what big hands and feet you've got!" "Yes, that detail does often give away us transvestites."

"What a deep voice you have!" "Okay, I've been on the fags but I'm trying to give up."

"Oh, what big ears you've got!" "I assume Gary Lineker doesn't read that line to his kids."

"Oh, what big teeth you've got!" "Yeah, it's all about picking on physical attributes with you, isn't it? I'm sure you're, like, contravening a bullying charter?"

Ultimately a woodsman appears and rescues Little Red Riding Hood. The fact that he does this while possessing "a big chopper" in the Brothers Grimm version of the fairy tale is of course a comedy open goal. And also dates the story to the 1970s when that style of kids' bike was fashionable.

In my third hour of searching I continue to discover there is no consensus for anything approaching a definitive age. Continuing forensic research leads me to the story's source.

Little Red Riding Hood, Mother Goose, Cinderella, Puss in Boots and *Sleeping Beauty* may be seasonal staples for our nation's Christmas pantomimes. [I'll pause to allow you to shout, "Oh no they're not!"] Surprisingly all these entertainment standards were created, or heavily shaped, by a late 17th-century Frenchman. That's right: that most British of traditions, the pantomime, is basically French. *Zut alors*!

French writer and Académie Française member Charles Perrault (1628-1703) is credited with having invented the modern fairy tale tradition, importing aspects from ancient fable and pre-existing Nordic folk tales.

His original re-telling of *Little Red Riding Hood* (Perrault's pen conjured the character and imagined her defining red hood) was loosely based on a 900-year-old Nordic tale. It certainly favours an older heroine – Little Red Riding Hood appears as an adult woman. Pre-dating the Brothers Grimm version of the story by a hundred years, it dates from 1698.

Go to a pantomime, read to children, recall being read to yourself – if it was *Little Red Riding Hood* then your exposure was unarguably to Perrault's creation.

Grimmer than the Grimms too – featuring some rather traumatising violence in the original story. After the carnivorous wolf has consumed grandma, he salivates over his next red meat snack. In a clever attempt to buy herself time, Little Red Riding Hood announces she needs to go outside to pee. The wolf, being typically French, suggests she relieves herself on the floor instead – what is it about the French and their reluctance to use proper plumbed-in toilet facilities? Once outside she flees then returns with the woodchopper. Before getting his lupine head chopped off, plotting baddie the wolf moans that his last meal, a distinctly grandma-flavoured snack, did not taste nice. Because it was a bit bony. And probably needed more garlic.

The story jolts with modern sensibilities. Moralists saw nothing wrong with the wolf being violently decapitated with a swinging axe. Though the RSPCA may be less impressed.

21st-century attitudes may recoil at an eight-year-old girl announcing she is going out for the day on her own. It seems slightly incredible that her mother would reply: "Yeah, I'm cool with that – walking all day through the thick, dark, dense, pathless forest plagued by wolves with a basket of smelly food to attract them will be fine." Even in the Grimm version, the child's basket is filled with cake (acceptable) and bottles of wine (unacceptable). She's basically an under-age booze mule. And couldn't grandma move to somewhere a bit more central than the middle of the forest?

Aware that I have not yet emailed a definitive answer to the question the producer set several hours earlier, he phones me. "So," he begins impatiently, "have you found out how old Little Red Riding Hood is yet?" "Yes," I lie, thinking I can get away with the average age. I have painstakingly calculated with actuarial formulae that her mean age is exactly eight years. It took me nearly that long to work it out.

"I think she is eight years old," I proffer in a voice freighted with as much bluffed authority as I can muster. This prompts a sufficiently long silence to necessitate a checking "Hello?" from me. "I'm still here," the producer replies. "That answer does conflict a bit with our research," he elaborates. "How old did you discover she was?" I ask with sincere curiosity. "316 years old," he answers.

"Yeah," I confirm, "created in 1698, so she's definitely 316 years old." Like I said, always make sure you understand the question.

CULTURE

The Avant-Garde Concert

I am here in an attempt to become more heliotropic towards culture. Starting by using words like "heliotropic" (it means turning to face sunlight – like a sunflower head).

The man currently on stage knows that word. If you requested a "pretentious, over-intellectualising art commentator" from a casting agency, you would be delighted when he turned up. Wardrobe would kit him out in the exact clothes he is wearing tonight: unnecessarily long scarf and top button done up, somehow without resulting in the look of a nerd. He speaks, spurning pronouns such as "I" and "you" in favour of "one". Brian Sewell would implore him to speak earthier; Will Self would impel him to simplify his vocabulary.

I am attending a concert billed to last eight minutes – disappointingly there's no interval. It is part of a modern art installation. As a dedicated philistine and experienced ignoramus I don't understand Modern Art or how, if say, some bloke has nailed an orange to the wall it constitutes art and sells for £1.2 million.

He is interviewing an internationally revered artist who has digitally slowed down an eight second recording of a thunder clap into an annotated eight minute musical score. The artist and expert begin by informing us they will be "throwing a net through the constellation of ideas". Or, as everyone else calls it, having a conversation. The phrase "interaction with post-modernism" pops up a lot. Most of the audience regret not drinking more in the bar beforehand. Two questions are then taken from spectators. The first is probably the best question I have ever heard, even by Oxford's standards: "Are you able to communicate with a mirage?" before the questioner checks, "is that too unformulated as a question?" The artist assures her it is not unformulated.

Then six formally dressed musicians ascend the steps onto the stage of the prestigious Jacqueline du Pré Music Building in the grounds of St Hilda's College. There are five men (trombonist, flautist, three violinists) accompanied by what appears to be the World's Most Beautiful Woman on cello.

Standing tall in a sophisticatedly cut dark brown evening gown, she is wearing stiletto heels that end in a sharp shiny spike, replicating the thin metallic prong on the base of her cello. Accentuated by the sunken neckline of her dress, she possesses an elegant long swanlike neck, mirroring her cello's neck. A lengthy mane of straight hair is tied tightly into a thin long ponytail draped down her back, resembling her horsehair bow. Basically she has physically transmogrified herself into her instrument, in the way that some owners resemble their dogs.

Purposely picking up her bow, she positions herself on stage directly opposite me in the front row. Then immediately proceeds to open her knees. My wife instantly checks the direction of my gaze is dutifully averted. Fortunately I am staring with laser-locked precision at the potted foliage on the side of the stage. "Nice bush," I remark to my wife, for which I receive a sharp elbow to the ribs.

Whenever spotting a cellist or a double bass player, I have a pathological compulsion to announce two things. Starting with, "Look everybody, a midget with a violin!" before recounting the quote made by conductor Sir Thomas Beecham when chastising a cellist in his orchestra with, "Madam, you have between your legs an instrument capable of giving pleasure to thousands, and all you can do is scratch it!" For this my wife opts to break another two ribs – one for each comment.

However, this cellist, aka The World's Most Beautiful Woman, emits an air of resigned superiority, as if saying, "I am aware everyone watching me agrees I am beautiful," before sighing, "but you have to look this good to get away with the indulgence of taking a cello onto public transport. Can you imagine the hostility I would get taking this thing onto a crowded bus or Tube if I wasn't beautiful?"

The conductor then taps her baton signalling the performance is to begin. It is horrible. The closest comparable sound is eight minutes of going over stones with a flymo. It is the musical performance alluded to between Acts One and Two of stage play *The Ladykillers*.

Midway through this terrifying dystopia of avant-garde freeform noise pollution, the cellist quickly reaches towards her music stand and turns the page of the score. Nice touch. As if to say, "Look, this is a composition and has a properly written score with crochets, quavers, Pringles and everything."

Eight minutes later the torturous tormenting is terminated. I scan the audience. Most have their arms tightly folded or hands in front of their faces, all with looks of abject flinching horror, like they had just been mistakenly shown an eight minute porn film instead of the planned video presentation at a school parents' evening. A tiny laugh leaks from me, badly disguised as a cough. My wife responds by breaking another rib.

For seconds the musicians remain seated, looking like they might play something else. Something proper. Maybe containing melody, harmony, structure or pulse. Or preferably all four. Had they bashed out a quick Agadoo in this context comparable to the preceding eight minutes it would have sounded like the artistic pinnacle of all human expression.

Instead the five male musicians quickly depart in formation. The cellist remains on stage eccentrically removing her shoes while the audience applaud. She holds them aloft, presumably communicating, "I know that performance was rubbish, so let's applaud my shoes instead – they really are fabulous, aren't they?"

Rubbing my ribcage, I exit into the foyer where copies of the piece are optimistically available for sale. Someone my wife knows who helped organise the event recognises us. "Did you enjoy it?" she asks. We answer honestly, identifying an aspect of the show we appreciated. "Yes," she responds suspiciously as if just cracking a secret code, "a lot of people have said they liked the cellist's shoes." At this stage the cellist walks through the foyer; all heads turn towards her heliotropically.

THE BECKETT PLAY

I infrequently frequent coffee chains as I'm a freelance writer struggling to afford life's savoured luxuries like avoiding Council Tax arrears.

I am here because I have a voucher. It is within the prescribed five day window of legal opportunity. They check the date. It is only valid for use before 11am. They check the time. Then the serving girl requests back-up. Another girl wipes her hands on her apron, crucially abandons her beverage-making station and comes over. She advises inputting various codes into the register. None work. The queue grows. Finally, another green-aproned lady is summoned, necessitating her to relinquish her post taking customer orders. She has a gold star on her badge – instantly identifying her as a workplace swot.

The entire coffee chain's division of labour has ceased, tools downed like a 1970s British Leyland factory. Brought to its industrial knees not by Bolshevik militants but by my attempts to get 50p off a still astringently priced coffee. I sense my popularity waning proportionally to the queue's growth. A cacophony of audible tuts emanates from behind me.

All three staff anxiously enter codes into the register and tensely await the outcome, like bomb disposal experts making crucial colour choices. Finally the voucher code is accepted; I claim my partially reduced drink as the tutting becomes so prevalent it sounds like human beatboxing.

Unable to risk a desired visit to the sugar station in case of reprisals from the pre-caffeinated mob of tutters, my lack of sugar will be compensated by the sweetness of paying 50p less than the tutters for my latte. I scurry upstairs to escape any possible pursuers. This results in around 50p worth of expensively foamy coffee sloshing over the sides of my mug.

Through the café speakers American megastar Ariana Grande serenades me with "This Weekend Love Me Harder". Sorry love, but it's Oxford v Stockport County this weekend.

A twentyish woman sits down at a table immediately in front of me and unfolds a laptop. She then approaches me. "Excuse me," she says in a soft American accent. Initially I fear she will ask me to leave the coffee shop since I am the only one present contravening the café's evident All Customers Must Have A Laptop policy.

I feel my entire body conduct an electric charge of anxiety. I am about to indulge in stranger interaction. Approaching strangers tend to ask me for only four things: the time, directions, money and an explanation for why I am standing in their garden attempting to hide behind a holly bush. Admittedly that last one has only happened once.

Then I recall there is also a fifth thing strangers will ask for: the rarer request that leaves you experiencing a frisson of pride.

"Please can you look after my stuff?" she asks. "Wow," I say internally, basking in my approved selection as a guardian of her stuff. She could have asked numerous people in the coffee shop, but I am the selected custodian of stuff. That's right, chatting table of expensively dressed women opposite – you were considered yet collectively deemed untrustworthy compared to me: the stuff trustee. I am overseer of her stuff. Her appointed apparel attendant, wares watcher, possessions protector, materials minder, scarf safeguarder, glove guardian, laptop lookout.

She is wearing black jeans, black shirt, black sweater, black jacket, black scarf and black hat with matching gloves. I am impressed at her dedication to avoid separating her washing cycles.

"Yes, of course," I reply, my brain too swollen with pride to adequately work through the full repercussions of the contract I have just entered into. What if she fails to return promptly? I'm due to meet someone here for an interview.

She leaves me in charge of her jacket, hat and gloves. I also have temporary custody of a bulging rucksack (you can probably guess her chosen colour). And a laptop (also black, obviously).

No one tries to take her stuff. Instead an acquaintance of mine spots me. "What are you doing here?" he asks. Other than responding that I am sitting down and drinking coffee – two deductions that an admiring Dr Watson is unlikely to request further explanation from Sherlock – I struggle to answer. Compared to the other coffee shop patrons we are both dressed shabbily.

After ten minutes she returns with a drink. Apparently quite a queue had built up – for some reason. Her coffee is predictably black. She turns to me and sweetly smiles a "thank you so much." My companion is coffee-chokingly impressed that a beautiful twenty-something with an intriguingly exotic accent has interacted with me and clatters his spoon onto the table in surprise. I can see curiosity powering his thoughts like a battery. "What's she thanking you for? How do you know her?" I answer his questions in order: "None of your business, not going to tell you." Unfortunately this serves to heighten not quench his curiosity.

There is still no sign of the person I am supposed to meet. "Who you meeting?" asks my acquaintance – clearly believing he has immunity from the rules of grammar. Given he is already more curious than a cat detective with a magnifying glass, I decide to answer his latest question fully.

"A bloke called Goddard about a possible freelance job but he appears to have stood me up." Then I realise something aloud. "I'm waiting for Goddard." Nothing. I order my brain to re-scan my last remark; "Yes, it's still clever – try saying it again," my brain reports. So I repeat my utterance. "I'm waiting for Goddard." "Yeah, you said that." "Like the Beckett play," I elaborate. "What play?" "Never mind," I advise, "let's not waste our time in idle discourse." Nowadays Godot would have just sent a text: "Soz late, traffic murder!!"

Suddenly he shouts, "Oi, someone's nicked my scarf!" That's what happens if you don't appoint a guardian of your stuff. "No, it's okay, it's here."

"Let's go." "We can't." "Why not?" "We're waiting for Goddard."

Goddard never arrives. "Shall we go?" I ask. "Yes, let's go." Neither of us move. Girl From The Blackstuff removes her sweater, revealing a surprising glimpse of an unsurprisingly black bra.

"Sorry I'm late," says an arriving Goddard, "for some reason a huge queue had built up."

THE MUSIC CONTEST

"Do different things. Step out of your preferred tastes. Be open to new experiences." My wife is relaying self-help advice, before firmly adding, "No, that does not mean you can start an affair!"

Although she appears to be life coaching me, I suspect this is so she can get the house to herself. So out I go to a children's music competition at a school in Headington. Mercifully, not all music contest formats have descended into adopting X Factor's default maleficence.

This is to support my friends' son whilst simultaneously proving my capability to do new things. Which should qualify as pushing Mick Jagger over onto a pair of chickens, i.e. killing two birds with one Stone.

A Chinese girl kicks off the solo piano competition by playing a Beethoven sonata well enough to be recognisable until it all goes a bit Les Dawson. Another entrant's callous parent sniggers, and I am surprised to experience a swelling of parental protection towards a stranger's child: "Oi!" I feel like shouting at the sniggerer, "she's just played three note-perfect minutes of Beethoven. Can *you*, eh?!"

The next pianist's forced facial contortions relay how intensively she is 'experiencing' the music. Either that, or it's a badly wired electric piano. Whatever the cause – undiluted emotion or unearthed wiring – the face-pulling continues unabated. Occasionally during some high octave flourishes she flounces her hair for emphasis like the pendulous ears of resident Muppet pianist Rowlf the Dog. None of this added physicality risks upstaging the dazzling standard of musicianship.

Another 16-year-old strides confidently to the piano stool. Although wearing mouth braces, she enunciates clearly, "I will now play a piece by Bach." Fortunately, her Bach does not turn out to be worse than her bite. Cascading notes bond invisibly to form a collective whole of astounding beauty. When the music finishes I instantly grieve its disappearance. Should she ever need to redirect the attentions of a hot guy from a blonde alpha female one day, then she just needs to play the piano for four minutes; although taking pianos on dates could admittedly prove cumbersome.

My friends' son Jem appears. He's told to introduce himself. Sensibly these junior musicians stick to announcing the name and composer of the piece prior to sitting down purposefully at the piano stool. Given it is a music competition, I would relay an invented tragic backstory about my parent's dying wish for me, their left-behind penniless orphan, to win the Headington Music Festival Under-17 Category Class 12 (Solo Piano) thereby completing my 'journey'.

Jem plays Chopin and enables the piece to bloom. Notes trill out, swirling straight into my emotional receptors. Later he complains abstrusely about technical errors, but I only hear staggering musicality. I don't want to know the science behind a rose or how the sun works – that would somehow be reductive, dilute its mysticism and diminish the magic.

There is a slight delay. I contemplate approaching the piano and announcing to the assembled audience: "My name is Richard. The piece I will be playing is by the composer John Cage and titled 4'33."

Instead another teenage pianist gamely plays a piece that is generally competent, apart from some crashing discords. I don't recall Brahms being this avant-garde. One passage sounds like removal men dropping a piano down a ninth floor stairwell

Then it's The Results Show. Geoffrey is the avuncular adjudicator. I like Geoffrey. And he knows his semiquavers from his half eaten wotsits, his crotchets from his pringles.

Tonally, it is rewardingly different from most Reality TV judges' disapprobation. Instead of berating the contestants ("You are a pathetic insult to humanity. What you did for four minutes on that piano is worse than the collective crimes of the Khmer Rouge") Geoffrey is encouraging. Dutifully ensuring everyone receives an individual written report, he enables the teenagers to feel rightly fortified by encouraging acknowledgment of their efforts, coating the dispensed medicinal criticism they need to swallow in order to get better.

The next competition category is piano duets for under-8s. Given their slender ages, it is surprising their chosen tunes are blues music. Are 7-year-olds ready to draw from a sufficiently deep dark well of life experiences gone irretrievably wrong by the age of 7 to sing the blues? How many woke up this morning and discovered they had serious woman troubles? Who knew Muddy Waters lines like "That woman ain't going treat me mean no more" were referring to mummy neglecting to pack Dairylea spreadables into a lunchbox?

Two tots play a ragtime blues duet. Then another diminutive duo beat out primal jazz rhythms. One of the talented infants stops playing. Sitting transfixed, paralysed like a suddenly distracted squirrel, he allows his companion to carry on with just the bass notes. Well, Jelly Roll Morton once remarked that the way to play true jazz is to lose that fancy right hand. The music of early 20th-century New Orleans' brothels fills the opulent surroundings of a 21st-century Oxford private girls' school.

Their efforts are staggeringly good for children so young. I couldn't play music like that until … well, I still can't. Though we didn't have a piano at our school; it was used by the teachers to barricade themselves into the staffroom during pupil sieges.

Don't today's teenagers have a bus stop to vandalise? Presumably a side effect of BT phasing out phone boxes in the mobile age is that teenagers now spend time practising Schubert rather than wrecking telephone booths.

Entering the school canteen for refreshments, I notice a walled partition of chairs separating music festival attendees from lunching boarders. Fleetingly, I accidently catch the eye of a sixth form boarder on the other side of the Berlin chair wall. She appears to be carving herself another slice of roast peacock. Across the division I nibble hesitantly on an unbuttered economy-range bread roll and help myself to more tap water. She gives me a look I interpret as, "If only your parents had been more successful, perhaps worked a bit harder?"

One of the contestants puts down her tray near me alongside her stunning late-40s mother, who I immediately notice is not wearing a wedding ring. Which is the point when I recall my wife's second directive.

THE FILM PREMIERE

I am at a Leicester Square film premiere. Furthermore I am on the carpeted side of the barriers, and no security men are approaching me with the obvious intention of removal. This has never happened before. An A-lister walks along the line of waiting media. Countless cameras flash like lightning.

Assembled TV crews, photographers and reporters shout at me. They are all trying to get my attention. Although this transpires to be because I'm blocking their shot of actual celebrities.

An anxious publicist in heels so high they are on the cusp of where shoes become stilts announces: "This is the principal screenwriter." I stand next to her, attempting a look that balances modesty with flowering pride. I achieve neither. "Who is he?" demands a reporter. "Who is he?!" she echoes indignantly, as if the Pope had just failed to recognise the Virgin Mary. "Is the Pope a Catholic?" she asks (though recently that's become somewhat debatable). "He's the principal screenwriter." I thought we had already established that. Then I realise she doesn't know my name. Up on tiptoes to match her vertiginous heels, I whisper my name through her enormous hair.

"What's his name?" insists a presenter from underneath an aggressively trendy hat no-one over 25 could ever get away with wearing – or, frankly, want to. "He's Richard D. Smith." "No, I'm Richard O. Smith," I clarify. "Oh," she says. "Exactly," I repeat, "O." No-one looks impressed. Most reporters just check their phones. "He's one of the writers," she says again, like an angler determined to make one last cast into a dry river bed.

This is the premiere of comedy animation movie *The Unbeatables* starring Rupert Grint, Rob Brydon, Anthony Head, Ralf Little, Alistair McGowan, Peter Serafinowicz, Eve Ponsonby, *Match of the*

Day commentator Jonathan Pearce and, er, former BBC Radio Oxford presenter Malcolm Boyden. Malcolm clearly has a very good agent. The film's lusciously detailed animation took seven years to draw. Taking seven years to complete any project – surely that's a homework deadline missed? – doesn't fit with modern profit practices and belongs unapologetically in the 'labour of love' category. An ethos that attracted me to the project in the first place.

Originally an Argentinian film, its director had bagged the 'Best Foreign Film' Oscar for his previous movie *The Secret in Their Eyes*. This explains why the only TV station keen to interview me at the premiere is Argentinian. "Have you been to Argentina?" asks a microphone-brandishing Latino woman. "No, not yet," I answer flustered, hoping the questions will soon become less Argentina-fixated. "What part of Argentina would you like to visit?" she asks.

Unsurprisingly writing new lines to fit existing lip-syncing was like a punishment out of Greek mythology. But the film contained such a superb weight-bearing storyline to support its wonderful characters that I was prepared to put in the required hours crafting new jokes with my comedy chisel. Then repeatedly panel-beat lines to fit the characters' mouth movements. The movie is packed with double-yoked jokes, i.e. unexpurgated dual interpretations slipped past the censors like a mazy winger's run avoiding the censors' tackle. We are granted a U certificate. In the UK film certification ranges from 18, 15, 12, PG, U and even WR (the latter stands for "Suitable for Wayne Rooney").

During one radio interview a presenter asked the film's Oxford-based producer Victor Glynn and me if it would have been easier to write the dialogue first then shoot the lip movements rather than vice versa, thereby depicting us as Laurel & Hardy standing next to a smashed piano scratching our heads. "Yes," we assured him, "we had thought of that." But director Juan José Campanella had insisted the original should be shot in Argentinian Spanish. Definitely not English. No way Juan José.

Then came the reviews. The dependable *Radio Times* loved it, describing the film as: "The witty script and banter makes for some very funny moments, while the digs at the excesses of modern football will ring true to followers of the Beautiful Game." Other reviews were laced with positives. However a lone critic provided a mystifying one star review. I discovered that most of the films he reviews receive one star; I could enable him to see considerably more than one star if I ever met him in a CCTV blindspot. Friends counselled me not to take it personally. After all, he probably doesn't like films – hence working as a film reviewer must make him permanently furious, like someone allergic to cats working in a cattery.

My hometown newspaper was sufficiently impressed with my involvement in a movie that they dedicated their entire front page to it. Unfortunately they described the film's leading actor as "Harry Potter star Rupert Print." Quite a bad misgrint!

Yet the story of *The Unbeatables* lends itself perfectly to being told in the format of a novel. The commission to write the novel of the film was the job I really wanted - and thankfully landed after doing more weaselling and badgering than most weasels and badgers manage in their day jobs. Writing the novel of the movie permitted considerable expansion of the characters and their adventures, allowing more room for interplay and raising the GPM (gags per minute) ratio.

People rarely use the expression "the movie was better than the book". Yet the truth is they are different entities – that's how it should be. There is more space for subplots and amplitude for attitude. Hence we discover in the novel what happens to some of the characters after we leave them in the movie. Plus in novel the story ripens into more of a satire on contemporary football. Indeed, there are a few dubious off-the-ball challenges on the ethos of the modern game.

The Unbeatables novel references real football clubs Arsenal, Barcelona, Chelsea and Oxford United – obviously Barcelona are flattered to be listed in such exalted company. As well as fictionalised teams Dynamo Bikelight, Wet Spam United, Buy A Lebkuchen and Deportivo Wanka. In fact that last one – a Peruvian first division side – genuinely exists. South American football can be hilarious!

THE STUDENT PLAY

My wife and I, along with the other sixty people present in the room, have just walked past a naked man. We are now collectively staring at him as he lies fully conscious but unblinkingly motionless on a rug. All our seats have been positioned to face him.

Everyone is being very grown up about it. Except me. I want to call out: "Well, you've got to admire his balls." Later a middle-aged lady behind me remarks to her companion, "Good grief. It's been a long time since I saw one of those," before concluding with nostalgic ruefulness, "they're not as big nowadays as I remember." In his defence, it is quite a cold room.

It's true that we were warned. We are seated in a small theatre contained within an Oxford college. A laminated A4 sign in the auditorium warns the production contains "nudity, strong language and scenes of a sexual nature". And it's a good job that it does – otherwise the two 16-year-old girls sitting next to me almost certainly would not have come.

The naked man is a Christ Church English student. He is playing one of the lead characters in an Oxford University undergraduate production of David Hare's play *Plenty*. There is Plenty to admire here (see what I did there? Oh never mind…) Particularly in the lead actress Gráinne O'Mahoney who is currently reading English at New College. Describing herself as "a first wave gingerist", her acting shines like her magnificent red hair – glittering in the darkness as she inhabits the contradictions of her character Susan stomping through the stilted era of post-War Britain. Given Meryl Streep portrayed the character of Susan in the subsequent movie version, these are big kitten heels to fill. But she fills them adequately, whilst the audience fill their boots with some of the play's scrumptious wordplay. Moreover the play requires Susan to speak almost continuously for the two hour running time.

During the interval my wife ponders aloud, "I don't know how she remembers all of her dialogue." "She probably doesn't," I conclude unfairly, given we are completely unfamiliar with the script. The person two rows back certainly knows Gráinne is on book throughout. Given how loudly he repeats to his companion that he was once in the play himself. But tonight he is playing a different role: Annoying Boastful Man in Theatre. Regrettably it's a part with a lot of lines. And he is very convincing in the role. "The play is about knowing your place," he thunders.

Two male undergrads are conducting a conversation behind me in the interval. "Have you read the whole book?" "I don't read books. I've read the Wikipedia page." "You don't read books?" he questions. "Not a whole book. Besides," says the loudest one, "depends on how you define book." I'd define book by something that really hurts when I beat you over the head with it to make you shut up.

"The second act confirms what I was saying about knowing thy place," bellows Annoying Boastful Man in Theatre. Does it? It certainly confirms you're an annoying... "The play's all about knowing your place," he reiterates as he pushes past me without an "excuse me" on his return from seeking interval refreshments.

The curtain rises on Act Two. Or it would, if they had a curtain. So we just imagine. An actress appears in pretty white lingerie and writhes on a table directly in front of me. My expected enjoyment of this scene is sabotaged by my wife's disapproving sighs.

The script's constant moving between eras and countries is confusing. The technique is benevolently described as cinematic. I'd describe it as closer to hallucinogenic. Besides, 'cinematic' is surely best left to the, er, hmm ... if only there was an indication in the name, oh yeah ... cinema. In the cinema the production can be as 'cinematic' as it likes. Significantly, the subsequent Meryl Streep and Charles Dance movie version dilutes the weirdness by opting for a more linear narrative approach. Regrettably the play does not and on a small stage with a limited props budget it is hard at times to make sense of where and when the action is supposed to be unfolding.

Here's a précis of the two-hour play. It's France 1943. Under a mackerel sky. Someone buys an ice-cream in Argentina in 1973. Damn this post-war Berlin. Then we're in a London flat with the Persian ambassador in the late 1960s. A man wanders on and tries to sell Susan five hundred cheese graters. Still under a mackerel sky. "I know my place," says Susan ruefully. France 1943 again. Curtain.

It's one of those plays that, in the absence of a curtain at a student theatre, you only know has finished because the lighting/tech gallery applaud loudly to signify "that's all folks". The New York Times described the original Broadway production with the line: "A list of the evening's casualties would include at least three lives, the egalitarian ideals of a generation and many of the conventions of a narrative play." Ouch.

The play is an allegory for the decline of the post-War ruling establishment's influence. Contained within it is Susan's mental breakdown – a one-size-fits-all metaphor for how inner feelings can affect the outer world. Susan's ballsy intelligence is portrayed as an uncomfortable fit for the times.

We trundle out of the auditorium. "Darling, you were wonderful," says an undergraduate girl to one of the cast. They embrace like wartime lovers reuniting dockside after enduring years of enforced separation. The actress receiving the embrace only had three lines.

The undisputed star is Gráinne, maintaining the Oxford tradition of a breeding ground for actresses. Rosamund Pike, Kate Beckinsale, Emilia Fox and Emily Mortimer all progressed from treading the boards at Oxford colleges to treading on red carpets at Hollywood. I'm hoping that Gráinne will deservedly become a famous actor one day too. Then I can bore everyone loudly during future theatre intervals with my revelation that I once saw here playing to sixty people.

Ninety-eight per cent of the departing audience exit through a door that takes them back into college. I leave through a separate door for Town not Gown and end up back in the street next to some overflowing bins. I know my place.

UNIVERSITY

THE ENGLISH STUDENT

Sarah is not acting like a student at all. Firstly, she arrives exactly on time – not even marginally late. Then she proceeds to be serene not shouty, immaculately mannered instead of self-absorbed, personable not pretentious, and sober rather than unconscious on a night bus. Although it is only 2.30pm. "Really appreciate you being up this early," I greet her. "Very funny," she replies through smiling rather than gritted teeth, unwilling to nibble on any dangled bait about student stereotypes. Keble student Sarah has kindly consented to reveal what the current crop of Bright Young Things are getting up to at Oxford University.

But aren't students like foxes? An increasingly urban pest emitting nocturnal noise and mating on your bins? Not all, it transpires. To me, devoid of any academic qualifications, Sarah represents the apotheosised chosen ones: someone currently studying English at Oxford. Only 0.000000001% of the world's population, I calculate, get to achieve this. That's an equivalent probability to marrying Ulrika Jonsson.

So, in today's student life, how much sex, booze, drugs and *Countdown* are involved? Turns out that there is very little *Countdown*. More on the other unholy trinity later. Instead, I proffer the real questions that matter about student life.

"How many traffic cones have you got in your room?" "None." "Any road signs?" "Sorry, no. But I did once spot my friend wearing a traffic cone as a hat." Already we've managed to confirm one stereotype. I'm surprised Oxford students traditionally enter the media or banking professions after graduation, since working for Highway Maintenance would surely constitute their dream job.

"How many books have you read in Oxford?" "A shockingly low number!" Sarah admits. "Reading lists dictate I should be reading five or six books a week!" Surely impossible, unless movies exist of each one? "I don't read everything from cover to cover, so a lot of skimming inevitably goes on backed by reading synopses and criticism. Although I read prologues, introductions and summaries, I try to approach the subject afresh and form my own ideas."

I am keen to know how she copes with the Oxford year being crammed into just three terms, everything compressed and compacted into mere eight-week segments. "Very difficult. For the first two weeks after each term I go home and literally sleep. The exhaustion and realisation you don't have to do this intense work anymore lasts for that long. It is difficult to adjust but important to balance two different social circles."

"Is Old English compulsory at Oxford?" I ask. "It is not mandatory, but most colleges would study Old English. I found it initially overwhelming then began to love it. Great translations help, but learning it enables you to get closer to the originals than relying on analysis."

An English student's typical week involves one tutorial, endearingly known as "tutes", with a one-tutor- to-two-students ratio, supplemented by a class. Classes would usually have four or five students. These are probably different ratios to the University of Scunthorpe (formerly Scunthorpe Polytechnic, formerly an all-night garage). Then Sarah is expected to write one or two 2,000-word essays a week, sometimes supplemented by a commentary piece. Lectures are optional. Remarkably, Oxford rejected English as a degree subject until well into the 20th century.

"Any species that relies on only eating one foodstuff is vulnerable to extinction i.e. pandas only consume bamboo and koalas exclusively eat eucalyptus. Would students survive if the company that manufactures Pot Noodles went bust?" I ask. Sarah's dolphin-blue eyes arrow me a look which suggests this may not be a problem at her college which serves Formal Hall most nights.

There are wonderfully Wodehousian abbreviations that Sarah confirms are still surviving in common usage in Oxford parlance: "tute" (tutorial), "pidge" (pigeon hole) and "plodge" (Porter's Lodge). To be fair, townspeople use abbreviations too: we routinely say "students" instead of "bloody students".

I ask how aware she is of any Town and Gown divisions. Thankfully, there are no negatives to report. Instead we expose a Brookes v. Oxford University thing, "Which I wasn't aware of until shocked to be told by some Brookes students," thereby disassociating herself from any perceived prejudices. Once a Brookes student meticulously detailed the modular structure of his course to justify its academic worth – in a nightclub! I think she nodded politely right up to the point when she lost consciousness. Interestingly, Sarah confirms that inter-college rivalries are relatively frivolous nowadays; Oxford students' true contempt being reserved for deserving recipients "The Tabs" (Cambridge).

"What's your weekly student alcohol unit intake?" I enquire. "Varies, but it doesn't help that some college bars provide lethal cocktails with names like Quad Vod." As the title implies, this is a cocktail created with a sensible quadruple vodka base that Amy Winehouse would probably have condemned for promoting irresponsibility.

She has an enviable proclivity for going out at midnight. That's right – when most people of my age have already drained their cocoa, unslippered their feet and turned off the light on another day, the ultra-cool people like Sarah begin contemplating a night out. "What time do the clubs close?" I ask. "3am," I'm informed. "Yeah, too early!" says Sarah with a this-really-needs-addressing tone.

"How much student budget is allocated to buying giant Rizla papers?" "Probably less than one in ten Oxford students smoke – hopefully drug use is falling out of fashion."

"What time do you get up?" "Very early!" she announces confidently with the accompanying mannerism of someone who is about to enjoy detonating a shock: "9am!" We are not conversing in front of a live studio audience, so no one laughs.

Newshound Sarah is Deputy Editor of the rather excellent The Oxford Student newspaper and President of Oxford Media Society. An Oxford student recently wrote in the Telegraph that some undergraduates are obsessed with pulling multiple partners.

"How common is that type?" I ask. "Not very common. There are a few like that, but I believe it happens less in Oxford than elsewhere," she confirms. We discuss the fabled "walk of shame" – supposedly an early morning dash back to college after a one-night stand without being seen. Any time before 11am should avoid detection – only Sarah will catch you if returning at 9am. St Hugh's and Wolfson are traditionally considered too geographically remote to receive any such conjugal visits – presumably their lack of carnal distraction translates into obtaining better degrees.

I ask a succession of short questions, combing her for insights, until she sagely espouses the perspicacious line "We're not really here for the degree", recalling her aunt's advice "to get a 2:1 as that shows you've done the work, but also had time to experience Oxford." Clever.

THE ENCAENIA CEREMONY

Let's face it, most of us don't get to attend Royal Weddings or State Openings of Parliament. The only Oxford contender for such an illustrious establishment occasion is Encaenia, where Oxford University flexes its colourful pomp and celebrity connections. But not many Oxonians get to see this annual ceremony either, and that includes a significant portion of those actually sitting inside the Sheldonian Theatre. The sightlines of the Sheldonian are poorly designed, and since most of the seats are backless, and allow for exactly 3cm of leg room, I wondered what cowboy, fly-by-night, cash-only architect put up that building. Er, turns out to be Sir Christopher Wren.

I'm attending Encaenia to see what happens at the culmination of the University's year and to witness Aung San Suu Kyi receive her degree. This involves ignoring a woman repeatedly kicking me in the back; she's constantly apologising, but it's not really her fault that she has legs – a realisation Wren could surely have factored into his design.

Most of us don't speak Latin either. Yet almost the entire ceremony is stubbornly conducted in Latin. Once, as an emotionally unripe adolescent, I found myself sent on a teacher's errand to the school secretary's office. Finding it surprisingly unoccupied, I spotted the school's public address microphone. Devoid of doubt that this was not A Very Good Idea, I switched it on and orated to the entire school: "A message for those currently studying Latin: you are wasting your lives!" Double detention failed to infringe on that doubt.

Yet throughout Encaenia Latin remains the spoken language. Occasionally a pocket of robed intellectuals will guffaw with unnatural laughter – principally to point out they get a joke and thus understand Latin. Fortunately for those who don't converse in dead languages, there is an English translation benevolently provided in the programme. This enables me to comprehend Chancellor Chris Patten's speech that introduces each worthy recipient of an honorary degree. When forced to translate the word "Internet" into Latin, I suspect they are clearly beginning to cheat and make words up.

And yet that is a resentfully churlish response, because surely the whole point of Encaenia is to celebrate pomp and tradition. It is not necessarily elitist to add a sense of theatrical ceremony to proceedings every so often. After all, no one attends weddings and then chastises the pomp: "I don't know who she thinks she is, wearing that long white gown and carrying a posy. What a pompous elitist."

Six officials known as "bedels", sporting regulation silly hats, are given the job of escorting each honorary degree recipient towards the Chancellor. Each bedel carries a four foot mace for this job; presumably they are expecting trouble when covering the ten metres between the Divinity School and the Sheldonian.

The first of this year's honoured is Aung San Suu Kyi. She is the new Nelson Mandela; the next Gandhi. She's a politician people genuinely love. This must irk Nick Clegg, who might want to consider being imprisoned without trial for twenty years too – really Nick, you should try it. Ms Suu Kyi ascends the steps to receive a tubular black scroll containing her degree. Forget any perceived stuffy formality – the crowd, mainly attired in academic gowns, then goes proper mental. Applause fills the theatre for two full minutes.

Inevitably the next honorand is like the band who have to follow the Beatles. I think she had something to do with MI5, or it could have been MFI – my Latin is not that good – but hardly registers on the clapometer. Compared to Aung San Suu Kyi, her applause is akin to that expected for a double fault at Wimbledon. Though in 1907 Mark Twain and Rudyard Kipling received honorary degrees at Encaenia and clocked up an astonishing ten-minute standing ovation, even though both were out the back smoking when the bedel went to fetch them. Perhaps he got to use his mace on them. It was a triumph for Kipling, but had it been a disaster, I'm sure he would have treated it in exactly the same way.

Then John Le Carré is inducted in his real name David Cornwell rather than his nom de plume – which must cause complaints at book signings. Next up are the American historian Drew Faust, Sony Chairman Howard Stringer, Charles Taylor (there is an awkward moment while I await the ex-Liberian leader recently imprisoned in The Hague for war crimes, but thankfully this is Charles Taylor the philosopher) and physicist William Phillips. The final recipient, attending in a wheelchair, is Henry Barnett. Unlike many typical Oxbridge academics, he was born in a brothel in Newcastle upon Tyne. Surprised me, too. He pioneered the discovery that aspirin could protect against arterial corrosion, and first revealed that several strokes are caused by narrowing arteries, not previously attributed cardiac activity. This reinforces my belief that Oxford awards honorary degrees to authentic achievers, rather than some less salubrious universities who may possibly be snaring the odd vacuous celebrity for a photo call by dangling a free degree. Though I soon learn that "friends of the University" in an Encaenia context prompts Thesaurus to offer the equivalent word "donor".

Then something remarkable happens. A gowned figure appears on a side balcony and asks the Chancellor in Latin for permission to speak English. He immediately uses this granted privilege to insult the Chancellor. He's the Public Orator and his job is to lance thoroughly the proceedings' pomposity. And here's the surprising bit: he's actually funny – certainly pitch-perfect within the context of an Oxford University event. He has proper written jokes. And proclaims that this year's Encaenia is almost certainly the largest global audience in history for an event in Latin. "Eat your heart out, Cicero," he proclaims. Then he delivers an anti-Cambridge Nick Clegg joke that receives a round of applause. I catch saintly, hagiography-inducing Aung San Suu Kyi laughing at Nick Clegg.

She steps forward to the podium and speaks about her humble bus journeys along Banbury Road, recalling how once she and an undergraduate friend had simultaneously fallen victim to the fashion of ripped-knee jeans, and then discovered they possessed different shaped knees: rounded and pointed. This, in the classic Oxford tradition, raised the question of "why" their knees were different, prompting a subsequent desire to fill that knowledge void. The woman behind me in the backless Sheldonian seats definitely has pointy knees.

Then the Nobel Peace Prize winner joins the ceremonial exit procession. Outside I hesitantly step back into the mundane, monochrome world, feeling like I've been an extra on a movie set, still in awe of Aung San Suu Kyi's sacrifice in standing up to oppression. I don't need to understand Latin to understand that. Qui tacet consentire (who is silent gives consent).

THE OXFORD UNION EJECTION

The Oxford Union, oft perceived as stuffy and in dire need of opening a window to let the 21st century blow in, was recently animated by scandal. These scandals characteristically involve inviting controversial speakers. Who then get cancelled. A few years ago they invited serial Holocaust-denier David Irving; although personally I have always denied the existence of David Irving. Jordan once appeared at the Union and spoke for only seven minutes – less time than Kermit the Frog managed, and he's not even real.

The people who run the Oxford Union do not like journalists. They even pronounce the word "journalist" with the same emphasis a keen gardener might place on the word "greenfly". Keen to convey through this column the experience of attending the Union, and hopefully expose a few shallow buried truths and myths in the process, I contact the Union to arrange admission.

Initially they appear receptive towards my honest intention to demonstrate the Union's inclusivity, as well as their better known exclusivity, by revealing the lesser reported facts that members of Brookes and even non-collegiate left-wingers Ruskin College are permitted to be Union members. Hence I am invited to attend a Union talk. Until I arrive, at which point they refuse to let me in – with unexpected malice.

"No journalists – you can't come in!" scowls one of the door apes. "But I have a written invitation," I bleat in a voice far too high-pitched to garner respect. Another more senior door ape is summoned and equally relishes the opportunity to dismiss a journalist. "I've been specifically invited by the Union to show you're an inclusive, not exclusive, organisation." To which they unthinkingly reply: "You can't come in." This is baseline irony. Chapter One of "Irony for Beginners". The Oxford Union, supposed powerhouse of intellectualism, formers of future governments, fail to spot this.

They threaten to summon "The Librarian". Trembling, I wonder what she's going to contribute other than 'Sssshhh!' In fact The Librarian is a confusing student post because the Union owns a large library, whose actual librarian is called Librarian-in-Charge. She decrees "No journalists!" like a general ordering minions to shoot a captive.

Months later I see my nemesis, overdressed and seated ridiculously on her throne like Lewis Carroll's The Red Queen. One disadvantage of refusing to meet a journalist is that you cannot recognise them when they go undercover to penetrate your institution.

The press officer turns up and nobly begs for my admission. He is refused. Spotting he is an honourable man surrounded by mainly dishonourable ones, and suffering because of his association with me, I graciously decide to leave after half an hour being stuck outside the building like a dog visiting the shops. Annoyingly the speaker I don't get to see is actor Michael Sheen. Even more annoyingly, I now cannot use the line "Mr Sheen gave a polished performance."

A few weeks later, I try again. This time the Union assures me I will get access. Everything is confirmed, then re-confirmed. Arriving early, I approach the entrance. "You're not on the list!" "I was assured I would be, but fortunately I have an email invitation." "Doesn't matter, you're not on the list," is the iniquitous response. Another official is summoned who bats away my legitimacy.

Four undergraduate girls arrive. Fumbling in purses to produce their Union cards, one is mortified to discover she left it in another bag. Providing her membership details, flashing her Bod Card to confirm ID while her friends vouch for her, she offers to go to the Union office to confirm her membership. Nevertheless she is not let in. On the edge of tears, she is instructed to go back to fetch it, knowing full well the event will be over by the time she returns.

There are rows of empty seats inside. I've accessed Israeli embassies in war zones where security was less tight than this. Perturbed to learn of my repeated entry refusals, a helpful former President quotes me the Union's own rule: "Any correspondent of any journal may, unless the Standing Committee shall otherwise determine, sit on the Press Bench if holding a Press Ticket."

Another term, another attempt, another legitimate access invitation is invalidated by officials. Clearly I need to go undercover, so conduct a covert operation – akin to reporting from inside North Korea rather than St Michael's Street. A month later sympathetic Union insiders riskily gain me access. People were smuggled out of East Germany with less effort. Inside at last, the only forty-something sat nervously undercover among undergraduates, I fail to spot what they are so keen to hide.

The debaters are outstanding. People stand up, walk to the front and contribute to an "Emergency Debate" offered by the President, speaking brilliantly with effortless erudition for and against a motion. They are staggeringly confident, strutting like a bear who just mated with the sexiest bear around. There's a rugby club arrogance without rugby physiques, and it dawns upon me that this is where the kids who aren't good at sport go. This is their competitive place to shine. Their standard of erudition is dizzyingly high, and their efforts are garlanded by adulation from the crowd.

Mid-debate, the President – seated on his central throne, bestridden by the opulently dressed Treasurer and Librarian sitting either side on their own thrones – requests speakers from the floor. These range from 18-year-old fully formed Cabinet Ministers to a floorshow for nutters. A man with a vast umbrella on a cloudless evening then speaks at length about nothing of any relevance to anything; he's either drunk, requires sectioning under the Mental Health Act or is a serving MP. Then the final debaters lock existential horns, with such adroitness, verbal aptitude and proficient articulacy that you wonder how glossophobia ever got to be so common. This is how Oxford got to rule the country.

In conclusion, this house believes that an Oxford Union debate is a must-see part of the Oxford experience. Unfortunately, they won't let you in!

THE HOLDING OF BIG BALLS

The problem with the University of Life is that the lie-ins are rarely as long as those at conventional University. Enrolment still saddles students with corrosive debt for years afterwards, yet you're unlikely to be home in time for *Countdown*.

Everyone seems to live outside college at the University of Life too: I haven't experienced a scout cleaning my room since Bob-A-Job week ended, though I do share with traditional university graduates a disinclination to cook. While discussing the theme of students' culinary abilities, anyone else wish to see the BBC, after *Young Masterchef*, commission *Student Masterchef*? "I'm going to be doing two courses, Danny. Firstly a tarragon chicken starter then, controversially I know, a spicy beef bad boy ... so I'm just going to pop the kettle on, and they'll be ready in three minutes once I've peeled off the foil lids and stirred."

The University of Life route continues to disadvantage its students once they've graduated. Casually announcing "I'm going to take a gap year" once yoked into the working world is considered socially unacceptable. Yet after three years spent at actual university consuming heroic quantities of subsidised alcopops and converting sweaty energy into spreading STDs, it's apparently perfectly acceptable to announce: "I like so need a year off now." A year off from what? Texting your friends, playing X-box and unnecessary use of the word "like"?

Living in Oxford does inevitably expose oneself to the perennial inspiration of learning: the pursuit of excellence for its own sake, philosophical fragments fermented into potent whole theories, pretentious casual deployment of the word 'solipsism' in conversations at parties without immediately prompting other guests to announce they're departing in search of dips, walking the same ancient streets strewn with spires' shadows once trodden by Halley, Wren, Wilde and Rachel Riley. (If you don't see Oriel alumna Rachel Riley daily, or even know who she is, then you're probably not currently enrolled in the University of Life.)

Another disadvantage of University of Life graduation is that I missed out on having any balls (I'm a busy man, so please supply your own punch line – quickly, before my wife does) to attend. College balls festoon Oxford with a rare opulence incongruous to everyday utilitarianism, though it hardly drains Oxford's seeping pools of perceived privilege. I once travelled on a Cowley Road bus with tuxedoed men while ladies rejected empty seats, preferring to stand and avoid creasing magnificent gowns. It's good to see people making an effort when they go to Tesco.

Cambridge University recently published an article concluding that "only a small minority of current undergraduates have direct hands-on experience of holding balls". I assume the report's author is now Julian Clary's head writer. Their point was that balls take a lot of organising and ... well, er ... balls. Big money is required.

After a hard day spent protesting against graduation taxes, a contemporary student would need to find £150 a ticket. Teddy Hall recently cancelled a ball, citing poor tickets sales—students supposedly rejected its cheapness, opting to attend bigger, better balls attracted by delivered promises of gluttonous hedonism.

Such aggressively expensive prices retain the capacity to polarise students. Whereas some Oxbridge scholars wouldn't jeopardise their dignity by bending over to pick up £150 if they dropped it in Turl Street, others would expect that to last them a term. Hence there is a longstanding tradition of crashing balls.

St Hilda's was viewed for decades as the ultimate ticketless crasher's prize. Given that it was formerly the last all-female Oxford college, perspective male crashers acted like foxes attempting to enter a chicken coop. Fortunately the college often invested in security to curtail such vulpine threats, and regularly nailed barbed wire alongside the Cherwell bank on ball night. A boatload of intended crashers fatefully discovered that barbed wire is invisible in the dark when they arrived in a rowing boat, and were apprehended by hired security after their cries to be untangled from the wire were intermittently audible above the hired band. One student unconvincingly attempted to pass off the resultant grazing as "Hildabeasts are such animals".

Gatecrashers, also known as "ball breakers", were out in force this year. Exeter College fleetingly provided the rare sight of crashers climbing the ramparts of its medieval college walls; they were intercepted by security, who resisted pouring traditional boiling oil on them. Crashers often purchase black tie outfits and stepladders – money that may have been better spent on ... oh I dunno ... a ball ticket? Some colleges offer legitimate tickets to University of Life alumni (i.e. the public) on eBay for charity – one formerly wealthy man paid £6,000 to attend St John's Ball in Cambridge this June – only he didn't mean to: pranking friends used his laptop whilst he was asleep!

A popular crashing technique is to impersonate staff. An undergraduate once gained entry by dressing up as catering staff – only to be forced to work in the kitchen all evening by a terrifying sous chef swearing like Gordon Ramsey with a stubbed toe.

However, matriculating into the University of Life can also provide occasional opportunities to attend posh functions equivalent to college balls. One corporate event I attended provided a Wild West rodeo theme complete with working mechanical bull - rendering it a refreshing change to see a bull dispensing managers all day, rather than vice versa.

I've stayed on as a post grad at the University of Life to do a Masters in Disappointment, followed by a PhD in Hard Knocks & Advanced Setbacks; currently I'm studying for a second degree in Abject Bitterness (with Honours).

THE SWEARING SEMINAR

We are assembled inside a prestigious Oxford college. Our lecturer is eminent philosophy fellow Dr Rebecca Roache, who has tutored at some of the world's top universities (and also Cambridge).

As Dr Roache steps up to the raised podium a hushed reverence descends. The seminar room houses a collection of encased ceramics illustrating the college's august haughtiness. Oil paintings redolent of the institution's timeless dedication to highbrow scholarly pursuits, serve as a backdrop. "Good f***ing evening," she begins.

Within the oak-panelled serenity of St Cross College expressions blush on the portraiture of those ancient fellows lining the walls, as Dr Roache reveals her first slide: "Is there anything wrong with this f***ing question?" Her second slide bears the message: "Is this one any f***ing better?"

Only the second slide contains asterisks covering the offending and shocking letters like a stripper's nipple tassels. Instinctively we laugh. Swearing while presenting academic research papers is simply not something you ever expect to see in Oxford – like a cyclist stopping at a red light. Dr Roache is an engaging speaker and delivering a lecture on society's uneasy relationship with swearing; questioning as a philosopher why mere words can ever be taboo.

Dr Roache likes swearing. You probably guessed that already. But she does not like asterisks. She relishes showing slides of shocking words with modesty-clinging asterisks removed – enjoying her disburdenment of the symbol. But don't asterisks protect children from seeing swearwords? She postulates there is no evidence that swearing is damaging to children. It used to be damaging for me – I got a clip round the ear from my mother. Unsurprisingly, research into whether children are harmed by swearing is rare. But she distinguishes between the moral and legal argument, rightly pointing out that language possesses a capacity to provide more offensive words than swearing.

Slurs, slanders, threats, racism and libels all constitute an illegal use of words – but it is not against the law to swear.

She is speaking about the social acceptability of swearing at St Cross College. St Cross appears an appropriately named college given how permanently cross everyone seems to be here – tonight everything is "f-this", "f-that" and "f-you". But she is here to make an intellectual argument. "If we banned swearing who would the victims be?" asks Dr Roache from behind her sturdy podium emblazoned with Oxford University's Latin motto. She then quotes obscenities that are commonly said in France – if you pardon her French.

This is unlike any academic talk I have previously attended. For starters, it's really interesting. Plus our speaker has dispensed with traditional academic dress. Exchanging gown for jeans and a satchel spray-painted a dazzling gold, her outfit is augmented by a pair of the most intimidatingly high-laced shiny airwear boots since the reign of the 1970s bovver boys. Remember the bovver boys? The implication being that the bovver boys were too busy kicking your head in to address the fineries of correct spellings. In academic circles she resembles a punk on dress down day.

Her presentation is spicily seasoned with countless swears – she cusses like a docker who has just hammered his thumb instead of a rivet. My mother would have popped out two minutes into the lecture to fetch some caustic soap to give her potty mouth a good scrub.

The Spectator creatively described swearing in an 1870 editorial as "the italics of the vulgar". Yet Dr Roache evidently does not believe swearing belongs to the linguistically impoverished nor signals a poor command of language.

She has found an ally in Stephen Fry whom she quotes: "The sort of twee person who thinks swearing is in any way a sign of a lack of education or a lack of verbal interest is just a f***ing lunatic."

"We trade off the intended benefits of swearing. But can it really be claimed to be offensive?" she poses. Often we swear as an intensifier of language or a discharger of emotion. She believes the current intolerance of swearing constitutes a restriction on language and that the offending potency of these words should be downgraded

Her final slide asks: "Any f*****g questions?" There are plenty. When asking a question I am expected to say the taboo words out loud. Like the inverse of every classroom culture around the word, our lecturer will challenge us if we do not swear. However, I discover that referencing a swear word without the conviction to repeat it necessitates uncomfortable linguistic contortion. "When using the er … um … f-word…" I say unwisely. My cowardly balking ensures a chastising glare. It requires a conscious determination to swear. No pixelating asterisk adumbrations permitted here.

"So why are so many swear words genitals-based?" I ask, "given that people are really fond of genitals and would definitely miss them if they were gone?" "A very good question," Dr Roache replies – on probably the only occasion all night she manages to string together four words without including any of the four-lettered variety. She provides the intriguing answer that when we refer to genitals or acts of copulation (which most swearing alludes to) we are offering a shocking unwon intimacy, like calling someone by their first name whom you don't know.

One man in the audience shares the fact he was chastised by his puritanical parents even if he substituted the moderate "swear" word 'sugar' for 's**t'. "Both words were considered exactly the same in our home," he recalls. I definitely wouldn't have a cup of tea at his house.

Dr Roache believes denying swearing constitutes an obstruction of language. She's clearly a language libertarian, furious "that it is possible to be sacked from certain jobs for swearing," before ruefully adding, "though thankfully not from my job!"

She cites an academic research paper that shows the public appraise politicians more positively if they swear (Butler & Fitzgerald, 2011). But she dismisses *Guardian* writer Rachel Holmes' evaluation of swearing "being simply impolite" as "prissy b*****ks". Which I'm sure Rachel Holmes would consider being simply impolite.

Nearing her conclusion, she shows a slide quoting an old *Guardian* style guide stating that newspapers should never print a swear word. Quite f*****g right.

THE FINALS STUDENT

Finals. Just the name conjures up the ultimate image of termination. The End. La Fin. Like those two words that appear at the end of a film, announcing that your time of escapist make-believe — safely cocooned from reality — is over.

Which is not unlike discovering, with Finals marking the culmination of a student's time in the Dreaming Spires, that Oxford is not real either. And now you have to exit the cinema into the glaring unforgiving light of the authentic world, leave Oxford, go home and pack for confronting humdrum reality.

But what are Oxford Finals really like? What happens in those seven or eight exams compressed into a fortnight that every student has spent, or supposedly intended to have spent, focusing their previous three years towards with laser-guided precision?

We have all seen those students dressed in sub fusc (the formal clothing worn for examinations) swarming towards the Exam Schools in the High Street, assembling on the raised steps outside like black migratory birds. Some wear a bafflement of colour-coded carnations.

Well, those tri-coloured carnation traffic lights can be explained. Wearing a white flower in your gown's buttonhole signifies your first exam and you are about to pop your Finals cherry. Pink indicates that this particular Finalist belongs to the most common group of his/her species — taking any intermediary exam in the Finals sequence, while red signifies your final Final.

I ask St John's College Finalist Lizzie Porter how the tradition started. She said: "The one I have heard the most is that it represents blood in your arms. You start off with white arms, then after writing for days your arms grow redder, until the end when — it is more a metaphorical description — all the blood drains into your writing arm, hence red."

Other explanations are available.

Given that few students write with anything other than a laptop these days, how do they adjust to two weeks of anachronistic penmanship?

"I had done most of my revision in ink to practice, as I knew this was going to be a problem," explained Lizzie. "That doesn't stop your hand hurting like mad during the exams."

Former President of the Oxford Union Isabelle Westbury also took her Finals this summer — an experience that was sufficiently traumatic for her to declare: "To my future self, so as never to forget what this feels like: Finals are awful. Awful. No wistful nostalgia. Do not even think about it."

Finalists must wear their sub fusc gowns and bow ties. "You do feel a bit of a twerp walking through town in sub fusc, but there are so many people doing it in exam periods that you get used to it," Lizzie said. "Although I am vehemently opposed to school uniforms, I actually do not mind sub fusc — it means the exams are compartmentalised in my mind, and when I put those clothes on I switch into exam mode."

How strictly enforced is the dress code? "Very!" Lizzie confirms. "There is always someone inspecting us as we go into the exams to make sure we are appropriately attired. At the end of one exam there was an announcement to remind us about socks, as some candidates had been 'infringing' the dress code with non-conforming socks!"

And those exam questions can be a tad tricky. An actual Finals question Lizzie encountered this summer reading French: "Does Montaigne teach us how to die?" Another question asked: "Are André Gide's works narratives of crisis?" Personally, I would go for a stab-in-the-dark "yes" to that one — or rather "oui" if I wanted a First.

I know only two facts about André Gide — he married his cousin (true). And (thanks Wikipedia) that he spent two months filling in at makeshift right-back for Stockport County. This is unlikely to gain me a 2:1.

Gide once famously remarked: "One does not discover new lands without consenting to lose sight of the shore for a very long time," and maybe the Oxford experience is just that, being necessarily adrift on the sometimes turbulent seas of intellectual pursuit.

Unsurprisingly, such approaching Finals apprehension commonly manifests itself in anxiety dreams. "I dreamt frequently that I had to catch a train to get to my exams, and I would miss it," Lizzie recalled. Others report dreaming about receiving Finals results that are meaningless — opening envelopes containing random numbers or pictures.

Then there are the ritualistic post-Finals "trashings". For those unfamiliar with Oxford parlance, this is the explanation for spotting highly-dressed people covered in foam and pancake batter. Brasenose College has made super-soaker water guns available for student hire in an effort to channel trashings towards less destructive modes, believing a water fight on college property will cause less staining than some other materials hurled in a celebratory capacity. One girl this summer was pinned to a quad lawn while her friends painted her face completely green. They mistakenly used indelible ink. Probably necessitating a cover story: "Yes, I am an alien."

Trashings got out of hand in the 1990s when Townspeople were caught in the crossfire, often receiving an egg to the forehead on their way home. This led to accusations of criminal assault and controversy when it was inferred that Gown was able to act with impunity, whereas if a homebound commuter had decided to empty a bag of flour and a dozen eggs over a member of the University, they could reasonably expect to be telling a courtroom about it a few weeks later.

Nowadays, trashings are supposedly confined to backstreets. I ask Lizzie for any trashing stories. "A good one is where friends sellotape two cans or bottles of something into the finisher's hands." I assume this is handy, as you never have to remember where you put your drink down — until you have finished, at which point you must drunkenly spend ages frustratingly unable to put the empties into the bin.

At least I can now tell people the only reason I do not have an Oxford degree is because I wore the wrong socks.

FOOD AND DRINK

The Chip & Porn Reader

I have a female friend.

This simple sentence supports a surprisingly radical concept. Given mankind's social ascent since, anthropological wisdom surmises, we collectively departed Africa 70,000 years ago (clearly our ancestors rejected all those unblemished blue skies, and considered it worthwhile to walk 4,000 miles across mountain ranges in search of general greyness and drizzle), evolving humanity has achieved notable landmark accomplishments: the wheel, Bronze Age, moon landings, ITV2+1. Yet are we insufficiently evolved to fully permit cross-gender friendships?

Luckily my female friend is securely married and possibly pregnant – which I helpfully remind her of, as I selflessly confiscate her white wine. However, there is still an unspoken lingering guilt about our meeting in an Oxford bar. This really shouldn't be the case: why feel guilty when you haven't done anything? That's like refusing the dessert menu but still counting the calories – though looking at my friend, she hasn't scanned a dessert menu for years, subscribing to the I-feel-guilty-because-I-ate-a-blueberry-2-days-ago brand of female irrationality.

She speaks about her fears for a possible child: "How can I protect any offspring against the really terrible people in the world? Like those who exploit sick people."

"You mean like Frankie Boyle's tour promoters?"

"No. I mean if I had a daughter, and then she got involved in pornography or something."

Now it's my turn to feel guilty. To be fair, I've never understood the perceived male obsession with porn. If you're feeling hungry with no immediate prospect of a meal soon, how does watching footage of other people eating help? And why do seemingly all hotels pimp nefarious adult channels, charging lonely business reps to watch films featuring people experiencing a far better time in a bedroom than they're currently having?

The food arrives, and in spite of deliberately rejecting the chips from her order, she starts to pick at mine. "If you wanted some chips, why didn't you order some?" I retort. "It's okay, I'm happy to just eat your chips." "Good decision. 'Cos that's clearly making me happy too."

In order to distract me, she asks a question about Oxford's past. It's a good question, though clumsily phrased: "You know that bit of Oxford where those posh buildings are ... the one where the students get given their degrees? The Sheldonian?"

Being an Oxford tour guide, it would be worryingly inept if I replied "no".

"No."

"You must do, at the end of Broad Street, with those other old buildings."

"Oh yes, sorry - I was distracted by having to guard my chips." Glancing down, I see her retreating fingers triumphantly holding another successfully captured chip like an opponent's queen in a chess game. I'm now holding my fork menacingly above the plate, gripping it like a medieval yeoman holding a pike, stabbing chips and impaling stealing hands with equal alacrity.

"Ouch – that was my finger!"

"Sorry", I lie.

I chivalrously push a few chips towards her – mainly because I'm no longer sure if they're covered in ketchup or blood.

"Well, I was wondering what was situated there before some of Oxford's defining buildings were erected."

The answer reveals that 17th-century Oxford also encountered problems with pornography. A coffee house named The Turk's Head stood on the edge of Broad Street, and proved extremely popular with students. So suspiciously popular was it that the University proctors investigated and discovered that coffee was the coffee shop's second biggest selling commodity behind pornography. This is impressive business acumen, given it was still 200 years before the invention of photography. Displaying Town's utter subjugation to Gown, several University proctors and bulldogs returned a few hours later and, rather than merely closing down the coffee shop, opted for a more permanent solution, and promptly demolished it. Thus creating some prime land for Oxford University to build on.

My friend's husband arrives in the pub and remarks that his wife's finger is bleeding.

"Oh, you know what it's like – having to put your wedding ring back on in a real rush!"

Awkwardly, only I laugh. Worse, I made the comment.

"Hmmm. What were you two talking about?" he enquires.

"Porn, mainly – and why you men are so obsessed with it," she stirs.

Now it's his turn to look guilty, a cue he takes, blushing like a lighthouse on a moonless night. He looks suddenly anxious, like a man who's just realised that he's left porn in the DVD player. I can't watch a fellow man drown while standing idle on the riverbank of smugness, so I toss him a conversational lifebelt.

"Do you know how Oxford University got the land for the Sheldonian area?"

He takes up the offer to hear about The Turk's Head, whilst his wife takes up the opportunity to steal my remaining chips.

Still feeling hungry, mainly due to losing more chips than a bankrupting casino visit, I suggest, "who wants to order chips?"

"I'll have some chips please" the guilty husband says, firstly to me, and then again a few minutes later to a returning waiter.

"None for me, thanks" says his wife. "Oh, but can you bring me an extra fork please?" I think I've finally realised why men don't have female friends.

THE SUPERMARKET QUEUE

With the predictability of leaves falling in autumn, another year's batch of freshers have hatched at Oxford. Even those residing on high ground in the North are described as having "come up to Oxford" in prevalent local parlance for uncertain etymological reasons. Many realise their immense fortune to be here – others just realise they have an immense fortune, and behave like a 1920s aristocrat with a teddy christened Aloysius.

While the overwhelming majority apply themselves to academic endeavour, others opt to behave jejunely. Obviously, and I'd like to make this point irritatingly clear (phew ... wipes imaginary sweat from forehead in gesture of relief), most freshers demonstrate their capability to be credible human beings. However, there are a rare exotic few who display award-winning levels of arrogance.

For an example of the latter category, you needed to be in Sainsbury's Westgate branch during Michaelmas Term. It was a rainy day, with my mood decidedly unenhanced by contriving to leave my umbrella on the bus that morning. Indeed, my mood had been further polluted on the wet walk to Sainsbury's by enduring endless pavement-blocking students and their fresher banter (for any undergraduates reading, please note that "I was so drunk last night" does not, in itself, constitute an anecdote. Thank you.)

While innovative computer activated "Slow Down" signs now flash speeding drivers, I'd like to see similar automated signage rolled out across Oxford's streets for mobile phone users and student conversations, triggered by breaching a pre-set acceptable volume level by flashing "Now shut up" or "Zip it, gobshite".

Supermarkets are bizarre havens from reality, intentionally removing themselves from time and daylight (windowless, no clocks). Late at night the only justification to enter such drearily soulless environments is if you plan to free the staff.

Having grabbed a few necessities I approached the checkout. Hardly anyone appears happy in a checkout queue: a line of joyless souls trundling slowly forward resembling a prison exercise yard. I joined the shortest queue – which turned out to be quite a different entity to the quickest queue, as there was an altercation ahead at the checkout.

"I think not, woman!" declared a plummy voiced Old Twatonian fresher. The rampant pomposity of the statement, intonation and election to deploy "woman" as a pejorative term shocked the queue. A sudden shower of silence blew coldly across the shop, only the perennial "bleeps" now audible. "This lager was half price. Are you aware what a half is?" Well he would be if he could ever view a scan of his brain. Clearly this Bullingdon Club President-in-waiting wanted to be noticed, something he managed with his visibly dripping sense of entitlement. There were other clues: an anachronistic jacket and he's probably the only teenager in Britain to own a cravat. Accompanied by friends, one of whom was a female at least attempting to look uncomfortable (her soul may be redeemable if help can reach her quickly), they pushed a creaking trolley filled with essentials for a nutritious student diet: 48 cans of supermarket own brand lager, 12 wine boxes, 6 champagne bottles and one packet of Maltesers.

Presumably the Maltesers were for sensibly lining their stomachs before consuming the contents of their mobile off-licence.

"I'm sorry, Sir" (he so didn't deserve the "Sir"), returned the cashier, "but our system isn't showing it on offer."

"I know how to read a price sign!" And then he delivered the line that no fresher should ever orate: "I AM AT OXFORD UNIVERSITY YOU KNOW!" Oh, we know. The red nuclear button had been pushed. The spirit of 10 February 1355 reignited; Sainsbury's was becoming the 21st-century Swindlestock Tavern.

You could imagine him back on an estate where it's a twenty-minute drive from front door to gate, and shaking a small trilling bell whenever he wanted staff to remove the tiny black specs from his kiwi fruit. This was a level of Oxford poshness almost wholly vanished, only reachable via books and costume dramas, yet which had somehow survived here in an air pocket of excess. Though that particular luxury liner had long since hit the iceberg of meritocratic modernity.

"Then I suggest you check the shelf!" he thundered, as if he was back in the nursery and nanny was attempting to point out that maybe he shouldn't open a fourteenth consecutive bag of sweets – so he was going to have her sacked.

Ping! Our checkout number lit up. Cue much sighing and agitation amongst the queue. "I can wait all day!" Not with me clubbing you over the head with a fire extinguisher, you can't!

A supervisor eventually drifted over, a pale smile not yet completely filed away by daily exposure to recalcitrant customers. "I'll show you the sign, you pointless oik" (he didn't actually say the last three words, but they were clearly inferred by tone). Off they went to check the sign.

This was getting interesting. Customers from other shorter queues were now migrating to join our longer queue. Nobody wanted to miss Return of the Supervisor. Surely this was not an insuperable dilemma: quick observation of the displayed shelf price would declare a winner. And one immensely humiliated loser. Everyone hoped Spoilt Fresher would be humiliated. Morphic resonance ensured the entire store was aware. Silence descended throughout. Even the checkout bleeps, unrelenting for years, finally fell silent like the guns on Armistice Day.

The tension was longer and more dramatic than a Reality Show winner's announcement. If England and Germany contest the 2018

World Cup Final, it goes to penalties and we must convert a final spot kick to win 10-9, the tension cannot be stronger than this. Only this time we could share in the collective harmonious joy of the right outcome for once.

The Supervisor returns. "Well?" his friends communicate by looks alone. In the quietest voice he had probably ever used in his life (i.e. everyone else's normal speaking volume) he muttered, "the sign was for above." Only the girl showed signs of hosting an uncomfortable new feeling called embarrassment.

Outside it's raining harder, but it's ineffectual in spoiling my mood. I pass Spoilt Fresher mouthing as loudly and unashamedly as before, as his entourage slowly push their laden groaning trolley. He isn't helping. Redeemable Girl finally snaps: "Shut up. SHUT UP! S-H-U-T U-P!!!" I have an idea for a sign that could have saved her that job.

THE COOKERY SCHOOL VISIT

The English love filtering activities by class. Sport is regularly attributed class designation, i.e. tennis = middle-class, polo = upper-class, greyhounds = working-class, football (1860-1999 = working-class, 2000-present = oligarchs).

The English love filtering activities by class. Supermarket shopping remains a favourite for perceived class stratification. "Put down that papaya now, Arabella!" is a parental chastisement supposedly heard commonly in Waitrose. Lidl's or Aldi's shelves meanwhile vibrate to shouts of "Oi, put down them microwavable burgers now, Duane, Shane and Wayne!" or "Leave the Stella, Stella!"

Aspirational upper-middle classes can often be heard cooing their affection for Waitrose and John Lewis goods – devout in their belief that paying more for something automatically increases its quality. Surely Waitrose will soon be employing nightclub-style door staff to vet potential entrants, "Sorry love, you're not coming in here in jeans - there's a Tesco Extra round the corner for your sort."

Waitrose have nailed their colours of discernment to the upper middle-class (sustainably sourced organic timber) mast by providing free newspapers – but only the broadsheets. Perhaps Tesco can retaliate and offer free tabloids. Costcutter: free top shelf mags. The larger Waitrose stores offer a "shopper advice" corner enabling customers to seek recommendations from a trained staff member. Presumably these dispensed recommendations are usually along the lines of "stop being so poor" or "try and get more successful parents".

Waitrose is class personified. Particularly in its semantics. Only at Waitrose are customers able to read a fast track checkout sign instructing them: "8 items or fewer" as opposed to the grammarian-peeving "8 items or less". Although posher branches will probably display checkout signage declaring: "Quae octo aut minus." (That's one for any classicists in.)

Significantly Waitrose trusts their customers to self-scan, whereas the ubiquitous presence of burly security men in some budget chain grocers broadcasts the impression that they trust their customers to stuff eight items or less down their jumpers.

And yet Waitrose is undeniably lovely. Their products are lovelier than something lovely draped in loveliness. Lovelier than a box of puppies being stroked by Lucy Porter.

Now instead of merely consuming Waitrose food, it is possible to consume Waitrose - The Live Experience. And on behalf of middle-class aspirants everywhere, I briefly left my Oxford council estate to visit. Behind a deceptively utilitarian door just off the perennial roar of the Finchley Road - one of London's unpleasantly busiest roads – exists a portal leading Narnia-like to the scrumptiousness of the Waitrose Cookery School packed with upmarket goodies. Star anise and white coffee blossom scents the stairwell. Exotic, demulcent aromas draw us to the summit where an arriving glass of just-popped prosecco awaits. This place is basically the premier members' club lounge for the middle class. I've never obtained this door code before. I suspected the middle classes had places like this, but they never invited me to their dinner parties to eavesdrop on its potential location.

We are here to learn to cook The Waitrose Way. Preparing a gorgeous Thai dish that only works if we use specific ingredients – coincidentally all available from Waitrose stores.

A forty-something lady in an outfit more appropriate for presenting an award at the BAFTAs than rolling pastry positions herself at the workstation opposite me. Her height is increased twenty per cent by ludicrously high heels meaning she can barely reach down to stir a saucepan from her unnatural elevation. Later she expresses distraught concern that her coconut milk is too creamy. A decidedly middle-class origin of stress, you'd have to say. Our instructing chef Mark assures her it isn't. "It's beautiful," he insists, before coming over all Jamie Oliver and adding the unwise postscript, "a lot like you, darling." Jamie Oliver can get away with this sort of banter. Most men, including Mark it transpires, can't.

"Have you deseeded your cucumbers yet?" he bellows. A wholly original question in most people's lives. I make an observed face at having to deseed a cucumber and waste food. "Cucumbers are 97 per cent water. And the highest water content is in the seeds," he informs us. "Do you want your curries to be slightly too watery?" he asks. Most people react like this would be a terrible thing, something that the government's COBRA committee would be forced to convene to address. I compliantly slice off my cucumber seeds.

Inevitably, cooking by following the lead of an expert renders the experience akin to the *Generation Game*. A culinary virtuoso demonstrates a series of expert manoeuvres that we have to replicate. The group size of around sixteen allows for individual tuition; and it's required by everyone at some stage. Particularly me.

Chef informs us that we must use one banana shallot. On my ingredients list I write down "take one onion". He then insists the recipe specifically requires Jasmine Hom Mali rice from North West Africa (I jot down "add rice"). Next we add Madagascan vanilla-infused demerara ("sugar") and smoked Kashmiri crimson chilli bell pepper ("chilli"). A woman raises her hand and asks which branches stock it. Presumably its availability is included in Waitrose's Essential range. She is told to head for South London. She diligently writes down the store's address.

Then we're shown how to make rice. Really, really nice rice. Rice so tasty I could willingly scoff it unaccompanied with a spoon in each hand for three meals a day. It involves adding jasmine and coconut milk. And doing something I had genuinely not intended to do today: shaving an unwaxed lime.

Culinary ignoramuses like me learn to define correctly that tricky trinity of coconut liquids: coconut milk is extracted from the pressed white flesh, with the fattier coconut cream rising to the top like in bottled milk. Coconut water, meanwhile, is the transparent liquid contained within the shell.

Our instructor gifts us a great tip. Ginger roots are always an ugly shape, nobbled and gnarled, rendering them hard to peel with a knife. Simply use the back of a spoon and scrape. Incredibly the peel is easily removed, and no precious tangy ginger is wasted.

However, the proof of the pudding is said to be in the eating. This adage transpires to be equally true for the main course too. It tastes undeniably fantastic. Waitrose chefs certainly known their onions (and banana shallots).

The Dinner Party

Attractive people intimidate me. Fussed over like a backstage diva, they are showered with accolades and adulation, popularity and sex. They definitely get the most sex. It's so unfair. Whereas most of us get served a cup of tepid instant coffee with gone-off milk, life's baristas serve these people a double shot foamy mochaccino with extra cream and chocolate sprinkles. Then they get a bonus little sex biscuit balanced on the side too. Grrr.

These are my exact thoughts when my wife asks me what I'm thinking about. "Er … nothing," I reply, shiftily. Fifteen years of marriage has sharpened the realisation that truth is not always best expressed.

"Typical. Nothing going on up there. Have you even remembered I'm staying out tonight?" she retorts.

"About that," a sentence recklessly commenced without any idea how it may end, "when I mentioned being alone this weekend, Lucy [*name changed*] invited me to a dinner party". "That's very nice of her," replies my wife. "So you don't mind me going?" "What, like you pose some sort of romantic threat? You with gorgeous, youthful, model-looks Lucy? Ha Ha." Humiliated, I strike back. "Well, you married me!" It's the worst comeback ever, akin to pulling the pin from a grenade and then lobbing the pin at my wife whilst firmly keeping hold of the exploding bit.

Bussing into town I become suddenly anxious that I won't know anyone else present. Fortunately I find both Lucy and the correct street in Jericho at the same time, enabling me to ask her about the hosts. "They both joined Facebook to check what their teenage son is doing, but don't seem to realise other people can read their own posts as they upload comments about naughty things they plan to do in the bedroom with each other!" Lucy explains. "Oh, and they argue. A lot! But you'll like her – she's really pretty, and he's a bit of alright too." Spotting that she's bought a decent bottle of proper fizz, I clasp a concealing palm over the label on mine which proclaims "Blended Wine Product of Kazakhstan".

The hosts greet us, emitting delight at Lucy's gifted bottle and barely concealed shock at mine. Their thoughts are clearly readable: "I didn't know it was still possible to buy a bottle of wine for £1.99."

Both hosts are extremely attractive, so I'm expecting trouble. It arrives before the starter. They immediately depart to the kitchen and commence an argumentative swearfest, creating a kitchen environment where Gordon Ramsay would pop his head through the serving hatch to ask if they could tone down their language. Then pots start being banged in a manner surely too violent for culinary endeavours.

Outside in the dining room a well-dressed man sits next to Lucy and remarks: "Can I just say I really admire what you do. I think society needs to be more grown up about it."

"Errr. Thank you," Lucy replies, somewhat bemused. She works in an office.

"May I discreetly enquire about fees?" he continues.

She turns to the only other person present she knows, who is now emitting an asinine grin and throws him a "what's going on?" look.

"I told him you were a high class escort I'd hired," he replies.

Understandably flummoxed, Lucy returns fire with, "His cheque has bounced, so I'll have to leave," and immediately repositions herself on a safer side of the table.

The hosts' son silently enters the room, snaffles a bottle of wine, then disappears out of the French doors into the garden. Fortunately it is the bottle I brought.

Eventually the hostess reappears, straightening her hair and sweater – a look of calm serenity only slightly undermined by the black panda eyes of running mascara. Then the host departs from the kitchen and any pretence of calm, spilling their argument out into the dining room around the collected guests. "So, what did I miss?" enquires the hostess. Your husband with a hurled frying pan by the sound of it.

"As you may have noticed, we've been having a row," announces the host unnecessarily.

"Really? We'd no idea," we collectively lie. Badly.

"Because my husband is having an affair with a schoolgirl," divulges the hostess.

"She's 26," interjects the host, significantly not denying the affair bit.

"How did you meet?" asks the escort hoaxer with an inappropriate tone of conveyed subtext "respect, well done mate" that risks seriously irritating an already seriously irritated wife. "At the gym," volunteers the host, "when she dropped her newspaper."

"You handed back her *Jackie* comic? Did you help her read the big words?" enquires the hostess. "She's 26," restates the host.

"You should have invited her," says the man who had earlier mistaken Lucy for an escort.

"Good idea," says the hostess, "I could serve her some dinosaur shaped nuggets and Ribena."

"She's 26." You know who said that.

The hostess stabs a fork into her starter like a gladiator making the final kill. Its significance is not lost on her husband, prompting him to proclaim, "I'll go for a walk." A dinner party can never be fairly described as a success when the host is the first to leave.

"Why not visit your tiny tart? You could help with her homework!" she shouts after him. You can guess her husband's response. "She's 26." Told you. He then turns around to detonate the remark: "Well, she's older than your latest gym instructor." I couldn't help suspecting that if they weren't both so attractive, they wouldn't have got into this ménage-à-quatre mess.

Lucy asks if I want to go into the garden for a smoke. This is an honour. I have never been invited outside to accompany anyone for a smoke before as I'm perpetually deemed insufficiently cool and, mainly, because I don't smoke. But exposure to cancerous carcinogens is preferable, and far safer for my health than staying in the dining room that the other guests are now hurriedly abandoning like war-torn refugees.

Lucy's face glows momentarily in orangey incandescence as she stubs the lighter into action. Then an undignified splodge of something unmistakably wet and heavy falls to the ground, narrowly missing her shoes. "Sorry," says the hosts' son, who has just stuck his head out of a tree house to vomit. Either he has already sunk that entire bottle of contraband booze, or just read his mother's latest Facebook update.

"Sorry about this," says Lucy. "Still, you can probably write about it in your column." For an attractive person, she's actually alright.

EPILOGUE

The Dinner Party is the odd one out in this collection and accordingly I very nearly did not sanction its inclusion in this compendium. This is because I have a contract of honesty with my readers. Hence I ensure my stories are uncompromisingly and unblinkingly true. However, this column, although never dishonest in reporting what happened, does permit embellishment. (No, come back … I can explain!) Hopefully the justification is acceptable: namely I had to protect some of the real people's identities.

The story actually took place at two separate dinner parties – one in a restaurant on George Street in Oxford and the other at a North Oxford address as described with a treehouse. The central point to this piece appears to be my bitterness at not being attractive and thus having to exist on starvation sex rations. My own tears of bitterness risk sloshing over the side of the piece at one stage. But they're soon dried by seeing what a life mess being good-looking can deliver to a person. Clearly you have to handle the responsibility of being attractive well. By the way, well done to readers who spotted the visual metaphor representing Lucy and me: her bottle of pricey sparkling champagne, me with my undrinkable £1.99 wino vino.

The real Lucy from the article is traffic-stopping, head-turning, lamppost-butting attractive. She chose the alias Lucy for the column. One of the best conversations I ever had was with her in a coffee shop where we discussed the taboo subject of attractiveness. Columnist Samantha Brick famously got vilified for daring to stick her head above the bullet holed parapet in a *Daily Mail* comment piece several years ago. She subsequently got a barrage of abuse arrowed at her for suggesting that being an enticingly attractive woman comes with complications. As a society we are sensitively preoccupied with spotting prejudices by gender, race, sexual orientation, age, income, nationality, reglion, disability – yet one of the biggest social divides left wholly unaddressed is attractiveness. Expect to have more friends and promotions, earn more money and live longer if you're attractive. Really. Ask an actuary. Preferably an attractive one.

Fascinatingly, the real Lucy told me she once arranged to go on six dates in a day. "Why?" I asked. "'Cos guys kept asking me out, and I'm too polite to reject them all." She also added sagely, "There's no way a man could handle the practicalities of going on six dates in a day." In the end she cancelled one – but she's still right. The multi-tasking requirement for managing five dates in a day is beyond my gender. I can't even manage five portions of fruit and veg a day... not even dates.

I discovered later the hosting couple at the dinner party had a reputation for this sort of thing, and Lucy really was mistaken for an escort. On our way back to the bus stop she confided in me, "I'd have been a lot more offended if he hadn't specifically called me a 'high class' escort."

McBeverage: The Scottish Play

There are many things that people do regularly without ever admitting to doing them: voting Conservative, eyeing waiters' bottoms and eating junk food. Especially the latter: "Me? Oh, I just had some salad"; yes, you probably did, though selectively omitting the salient detail that your salad was snugly contained within a burger so huge that it directly affected the gravitational pull of distant planets.

I recently did one of the above supposedly secret things, and will now stand up and admit it publicly in the gallantly expressed hope that it will enable others to acknowledge they are not uniquely afflicted. Here goes. My name is Richard and I once knowingly stared at a waitress's ... oh-oh, wrong one ... I recently frequented a popular fast food chain. Like most sinners, I harbour remorse and have a ready excuse. Plus, like others who've wandered off from the path clearly signposted "straight and narrow" for a sinful picnic in the long grass of moral ambiguity, it occurred when I was away from home and thus lessened my chances of encountering witnesses capable of recognising me.

I had been at the BBC and the coffee in the writers' room is akin to putting a spoon of river silt into a mug of water. Britain has fought a successful revolution against insipid inferior coffee over the last twenty years, yet apparently the BBC must have remained neutral throughout this conflict. Which is odd, because two of the best things about modern Britain are its drastically improved coffee and Radio 4. Isn't Radio 4 brilliant? If Radio 4 ever dumbs down, then the canary has been discovered dead in the coal mine of British culture. And Britain's coffee is immeasurably superior nowadays. Recently a friend got access to one of those espresso pod machines that George Clooney advertises – and then set about attempting to drink so much coffee in the resultant hope that it would turn him into George Clooney. It hasn't. He may be contacting Advertising Standards.

Encouraged by the *Daily Mail*, some people believe that the entire BBC licence fee revenue enabled Jonathan Ross to live in a solid gold house. In reality, I've had to queue up behind some well-known people at the BBC in an egalitarian manner, all accepting substandard coffee (once queuing in the cafeteria behind the late great Brian Hanrahan whilst he bought a tray of coffees, prior to helpfully returning the empties later: he counted them all out, and counted them all back).

Recently Hugh Dennis and I both handed over £1.80 for something optimistically described as coffee. Yes, Hugh Dennis can probably afford to go outside to a posh frothy coffee dispenser but then he'd have to pay a price far higher than £1.80: enduring every passer-by pointing a finger and camera phone while declaring "it's the dad from *Outnumbered!*" Also, there are no biscuits in the writers' room – they disappeared in about 2008 so that Jonathan Ross could have a sapphire encrusted toilet brush made from a unicorn's tail (I think that was in the *Daily Mail* so it must be true).

Departing the BBC, I pass Rob Brydon in reception. He's quite short in real life, a perspective not helped by two bigger men delivering a huge box the size of a fridge freezer. The box would easily be large enough for Rob Brydon to fit inside; maybe then he could do his little man trapped in a box voice – only for real this time, while everyone ignored his desperate cry for "Help!" thinking: "actors, such show-offs!" I notice he's wisely brought his own coffee.

Once outside, I crave a proper coffee too. Spotting a familiar fast food outlet prominently advertising reasonably priced coffee, I enter their establishment. But there's a delay at the counter. A baseball-capped server is frozen into inaction by an enforced deviation from his script.

A manager wanders over, with the air of someone secure in the knowledge that he'll never be saying "do you want fries with that" in the workplace again, and shoots a hubristic, furtive look at the two protagonists. "What appears to be the problem?"

"He won't have a drink with his Sad Meal," replies the baseball-hatted minion, prior to repeating the flavours like the recited mantra creed of a brainwashed cult: "Cola, diet cola, sprite, concentrated sugar-spiked water with 98 per cent ice…" "You have to have a beverage", confirms the manager.

"Why?" asks the customer, somewhat reasonably in my view.

"Because you want a burger and fries, but with the [lawyers have removed a good joke here] MealTM you get a drink included," adds the manager, helpfully.

"There's coke, diet coke, sprite, diet sprite…" adds the underling, unhelpfully.

"But I don't want the drink", the customer interrupts in a Scottish brogue.

"Alright, I'll have an apple juice."

Both manager and subordinate carp, "We don't serve apple juice!" in perfect stereo, just like Jedward, and equally as annoying. Actually they are more annoying than Jedward. Yes, I am aware that last sentence has never been typed, spoken or imagined before.

"Okay, you win", he concedes like a torture victim about to provide the information his inquisitors require: "I'll have a coke."

"Small, medium, large?"

"Don't care."

"Small, medium or large?" the server repeats constantly and robotically like a computer refusing an incorrect password.

"Medium," utters the customer resignedly.

"To eat in or out?"

"Out," concedes the customer, realising resistance is ultimately futile.

Go on, ask him whether he wants a straw or not. Plastic or wooden tray.

Finally, the queue moves briefly until the baseball-hatted junior screams out, "Sir! You've forgotten your drink!"

"Tell you what – you drink it!" replies the man insouciantly.

With that, I head for the door. An impending alarm will surely be sounding imminently and the store shutters will descend. No one – I mean no one – is going to escape their system. "I think I'll have a baked potato tomorrow," says my famous would-be lunch companion.

Nearby I find a tiny independent café. Their coffee is not only better, but the waitress has a lovely, perfectly shaped, spherical … (pause for comedic effect) …badge; it says "Sarah". Great ass too.

SPORT

THE NATIONAL FINAL

770 people are assembled inside Christ Church to witness the top ten teams in the country. Each team has fought through the eliminators and qualified. For the first time since the UK National Championship's inception in 1975, the final is happening here in Oxford.

Each team has twelve members. Pre-competition they are huddled under a canvass roof to escape the monsoon-like rain, most displaying an understandable nervousness. On the day of the big national final no-one wants to drop a clanger. Especially since they are here to compete in the National Twelve Bell Ringing Contest.

Arriving competitors greet each other. One man is struggling to recall the name of his fellow campanologist. "I knew that face rang a bell," I remark.

I find one of the organisers but he claims to be too busy to speak as he's about to ring. "Ah come on, pull the other one – it's got bells on it," I say. Fortunately nearly all other competitors are willing to speak, even before the bar opens at 10.30am. One of them is Richard Grimmett. Unbeknown to me, he is the Beckham of bell ringing, the Cantona of campanology - the star name in competitive UK bell ringing. He has led his dominant Birmingham band for several years and confides in me, "Bell ringing is as much an art form as a science." He also imparts, "Home advantage is huge." So how will Oxford fare on home quad?

Everyone then packs into Oxford's Cathedral where the Dean of Christ Church welcomes competitors and supporters. I like the Dean. Rumour insists that an aggrieved religious fundamentalist wrote a complaining letter objecting to his holy place selling Harry Potter wands in the cathedral shop. The Dean's reply shared his correspondent's concern about promoting black magic practices but reassured her: "I've tested all the wands, madam, and am relieved to report that none of them work." I so hope that story is true.

The Dean conducts the all-important draw – all-important because it decrees the order in which the teams will ring. This enforces the crucial difference between ringing as early as 11.30am or as late as 4pm; in other words, it decides what time the drinking starts. Cambridge smugly go first – allowing them to hit the bar before midday. Poor Bristol, last to go, has to wait like members of a temperance movement picketing a pub.

York follow Cambridge, booming out the bells across the Oxford skyline before they partake of the extensive selection available in the beer tent. Bell ringers certainly like their ale. Two members of one team confide in me that their job is to watch that another band member does not sample too many fine hoppy brews with citrus back notes before it's time to yank some serious rope. "Otherwise," they remark sternly, "it'll be like Guildford all over again." "What happened in Guildford?" I enquire with genuine intrigue. "No one talks about Guildford," I'm told. "No one."

Each team rings "273 Stedman Cinques". (Didn't Daft Punk cover that one?) This is an intricate piece and explains why campanologists are often able mathematicians who like numbers. However, as a spectator it is disappointing to hear each team ringing exactly the same tune. Imagine how boring the Eurovision Song Contest would be if every entry performed the same song. In fact, imagine how boring the Eurovision Song Contest is when each entry does a different song. Nevertheless, standing in the "designated listening area" (or anywhere else within a two mile radius) it is possible as a layman to appreciate the incredible skill and complexity as the piece builds to a conclusion. It is certainly an inclusive sport – teams feature all ages and genders.

Distinguishing between the seemingly faultless performers is difficult to the cloth-eared non-expert like me. Handily a panel of eight judges and strikeometerists (yes, that's a word) are on hand to evaluate the contestants. Whereas cricket has Hawkeye to intervene in umpiring disputes, Twelve Bell contests have Hawkear. Really, they do. It's a computer graphic displaying strike consistency.

Leeds is the penultimate team to perform. They appear in tracksuits with squad numbers emblazoned on their backs and purposefully stride towards the ringing chamber – which Charles Dodgson aka Lewis Carroll noted in his journal used to double as the college's meat safe. After Leeds re-emerge to race each other to the bar, Bristol close the competition.

Now we shuffle into the Great Hall for The Results Show. Here the adjudicators evaluate each performance. A judge inhabiting the Simon Cowell role accuses Cumberland of "constant compass changes" – the unspoken subtext here being "stick to making sausages". Meanwhile St Paul's Cathedral is praised for "maintaining a strong rhythm". Then tension fills the room like an escaping gas as the winner is about to be announced. The overall winner is proclaimed. Following … an… inevitable … and … overlong … pause.

Birmingham win for the fifth consecutive year. This is not universally well received. I hear tutting – which is as loud as dissent gets in this sport. Only St Paul's have broken the Second City's monopolisation of the title in the last twelve years. Surprisingly, Cumberland come second. Oxford take fifth place. Leeds finish last, somewhat flinching from a judge's "inconsistent and contained numerous faults" summation. But they're definitely the best dressed team. Already teams begin focusing on Norwich 2015 – destination for the next Final.

I check with the beer tent. They only have three pints remaining from thirty barrels. That equates to 2,157 pints sunk with the same metronomic timing as the campanology.

Birmingham jubilantly hold their trophy aloft, narrowly avoiding triumphalism. Then insight strikes me like a bell: the sudden realisation that The Dreaming Spires may be everyone's encouraged perception of how Oxford looks. But what is the defining sound of Oxford? Unquestionably it is the summoning bells housed in those spires. Emphasising their timelessness, two of Christ Church's twelve bells predate the college, being cast in 1410 and moved from Osney Abbey. The 17th-century Oxford antiquarian and diarist Anthony Wood was a keen campanologist. Some say he looked like Cromwell. He's definitely a dead ringer. (See what I did there? Oh, please yourselves.)

THE UNITED CITY OF OXFORD

When writing for Radio 4, I am advised to exercise caution if pitching football jokes. Spurious wisdom dictates that the conventional Radio 4 listener is steadfastly unknowledgeable about soccer and its hired parvenus. Hence an attempted gag about Arsene Wenger would require the additional explanation that he manages Arsenal. And that Arsenal is a football team. And football is a ball-based sport formalised in the 19th century. If a joke requires a series of footnotes,** it's probably going to be about as effective as Emile Heskey* in the box. [*Emile Heskey is a footballer. He falls over a lot. In football parlance "box" is the area near the goal. **You see my point.]

Since Radio 4 and *Oxfordshire Limited Edition* are perceived to share a crossover intellectual demographic, I consider it time someone finally wrote an article without assuming everyone is a football fan. Thus I'll explain football. According to Gary Lineker, "football is a simple game: 22 men chase a ball for 90 minutes and at the end the Germans win." Though that quote should be two words longer, requiring: "on penalties".

With the new football season already commenced on its long journey to culmination in May 2013 (yes, non-football people – they really do have a close season), I decided to measure the optimism at the first home games of the season for the city's two foremost sides City and United. No, I didn't go to Manchester: the City and United rivalry I oversaw necessitated trips to Marston and Minchery Farm.

Football clubs have been fighting off property developers for a surprisingly long time. Chester, Oxford City's first opponents this season, were forced to disband when their ground was suddenly claimed for a housing development – in 1898!

Ninety years later, a similar injustice befell Oxford City, victims of an outrageous act of Town v. Gown hubris when Brasenose – owners of City's former White Horse ground – took this most semi of semi-pro clubs to the High Court, serving them with a sudden eviction notice. Oxford City Council's attempts to mediate were rejected by the college, torpedoing any hope when Brasenose thundered to the *Oxford Mail* in 1988: "the college are sympathetic towards amateur clubs and school teams, but not to Oxford City who are unsuitable and unacceptable tenants." Given the club runs numerous teams for boys, girls, amputees and people with learning difficulties, presumably Brasenose suspected the under-7 girls team were on wages equivalent to Robin van Persie. [Robin van Persie is a successful footballer. He plays for Manchester United. They are a football team.] Destroying

Oxfordshire's oldest football club is about as incendiary as Gown could get – presumably Brasenose's next plans (thankfully thwarted) were to blow up the town's library and railway station. Although the diagnosis was terminal, volunteers refused to switch off the life support machine, fulfilling fixtures on a council pitch at Cutteslowe Park.

City kick off this season on officially the hottest day of the year at their current Marston home of 18 years. Even without the heat, a knackered-looking Chester sub, clearly flagging in the pre-game warm-up, looks incapable of going for more than twenty minutes without a fag break. Unsurprisingly, he doesn't appear in the game. An Oxford defender claps his hands and yells, "let's keep it tight!" Chester then score with their first attack in the opening minute, his advice clearly unheeded. The half-time whistle is blown by surely the world's smallest referee. On pitches where the grass has not been cut for several days, he could disappear from sight. A side-effect of the relentless 30 degree heat is that the dressing room windows are left open, allowing spectators to eavesdrop on the half-time team talk. One manager constantly repeats the same phrase: "put it in the box, put it in the box, your job is to put it in the box". He probably combines football management with the day job of supervising at an Amazon warehouse.

City have a secret weapon – their no. 2 propels impressively long throw-ins, delivered with a physics-bending velocity. On one occasion he hurls the ball across the pitch and straight out of play. "Put it in the box," shouts the manager from the dugout. City lose 0-1.

Over 6,000 turn up for Oxford United's first home game of the season three days later, with visitors Southend looking noticeably weaker than Chester. United relocated to the Kassam Stadium in 2001 – though not because Brasenose sneaked into their former ground, The Manor, during the close season and dynamited it.

Three corpulent blokes in front spend the duration of the match scrolling through their smart phones, only occasionally raising their necks above 45 degrees. One informs the others: "Swindon are 1-0 up." "The bastards," retorts another. "Yeah, the bastards," confirms the other one. Their sizable frames do not curtail regular shouts to fit professional athletes of "run faster – put in some effort you lazy git!" as they unwrap another jumbo sausage roll.

Southend's no. 8 gets himself pointlessly sent-off after only fifteen minutes, rendering his involvement in proceedings over by 8pm. He then sprints down the tunnel like a man desperate to catch the beginning of *EastEnders*.

United's skilful winger Alfie Potter constantly evades Southend's defence with mesmeric hip-swivelling dummies, rendering his marker unable to find him without a sniffer dog. Potter's wizardry will see him cast spells at bigger clubs, and benefit tabloid headline writers everywhere.

United score and the noise rises like a blast of hot air propulsion, as if the stadium is somehow struggling to rise from its tethering foundations. The wave of celebratory noise takes several seconds to decay, and when relative quietness descends, it is broken again by the largest of the three XXXL replica shirt wearers announcing, "Swindon are beating Crawley 2-0." "The bastards," reply the other two in unison. Given clubs have nicknames (Norwich = The Canaries, Luton = The Hatters, Boston = The Pilgrims), I assume Swindon must be nicknamed The Bastards.

As we funnel out of the stadium, someone announces, "Swindon won 3-0". "The bastards," replies a different corpulent man. I have observed sufficient to make three predictions for the season ahead: City will struggle, United will do well and Swindon should seriously consider choosing a better club nickname.

THE RUGBY MATCH

Oxford has a fine tradition of hosting the Welsh. For centuries, until the 1950s, it was said you could always both see and smell a Jesus College student approaching. The college was founded by Queen Elizabeth I's treasurer Hugh Price in 1571 to provide an Oxford education for Welshmen and maintained a tradition of undergraduates wearing a raw leek in their hat band.

Top flight rugby has arrived in Oxford this season, although the non-rugby fraternity may not have noticed this, not least because Oxford's Premiership rugby team is called London Welsh. The name offers an enticing contradiction and sounds like a Ryanair destination ("We have now landed in London Wales"). The club was established in 1895 for exiled Welshmen in London, but they were homeless until

Oxford allowed them to sleep on their couch at the Kassam Stadium. This ground share means London Welsh had a venue graded adequate for promotion to the Premiership, where they have the league's smallest average attendance.

Actually, Oxford may make logical sense as London Welsh's home location since our city is roughly halfway between Wales and London. But the enforced Welshness required for Oxford's rugby fans does seem spuriously weird. Particularly given how the Welshness is camped up. Starting a match with a valley-dwelling Welsh male voice choir performance, cheery mascot Dewi the Dragon then bounces onto the pitch and recurrently gives the crowd a thumbs-up – Welsh dragons seemingly being the only reptilian to have evolved opposable thumbs.

Opposable thumbs are vital on the field of play too: fast handling skills are undeniably impressive whenever a prolonged passing sequence is completed. Noticeable differences to watching football at the Kassam include the teams running out individually (no one boos the opposition) and an unreal – bordering upon downright spooky – descent of silence to allow a penalty kick to be taken. This courtesy is also extended to the opposition. This is rugby's great dichotomy: politeness and gentlemanly respect mixed with violent, hands-in-front-of-face revulsion.

Watching rugby without a commentator renders it unfathomable to the rookie spectator like me attending his first game. At one stage it appears that a Bath forward is being pinned to the ground whilst a home player repeatedly bounces on his chest like a makeshift trampoline. Meanwhile, someone's ear is seemingly being chomped off on the blind side of the scrum, before a player appears to stamp on his head, yet the referee gladly waves play on as being perfectly legal. Until sternly blowing his whistle seconds later, when awarding a penalty for some technical offence like "misuse of a past participle verb tense in the line-out". Mystifying.

Furthermore, the scoring seems to be wholly decided by technical infringements, and for 79 of the 80 minutes playing time the only scoring opportunities are penalty kicks. Which is probably why a game primarily about ball handling is significantly called rugby football. A prospective Bath try is referred upstairs to the additional referee with a TV monitor for review, necessitating a delay so long that maybe the guy was watching the *Eastenders* Omnibus instead. The try is not awarded.

Bath contrive to miss a penalty directly in front of the sticks, equivalent to throwing a stone off a pier and missing the sea. Then London Welsh are awarded three successive penalties. Gavin Henson, perhaps better known as the former Mr Charlotte Church, sends two soaring over the bar and into the car park. Perhaps playing rugby at a ground without a stand behind one set of posts is not an ideal design, unless you own a windscreen repair business. Then Bath score three penalties of their own, nudging them into a 9-6 lead.

Rugby's positional names offer flickers of familiarity to football fans (full back, right wing, outside half). Where the sports divide in terminology is the naming of famous rugby positions (scrum half, tight head) and the one that must cause endless sniggering in the stands on any American tours: hooker. With 15 positions to name, they had clearly consumed all their imagination by the time it came to naming the number 8's position, which is called, er, "number 8". Genius.

The PA announcer consistently announces the score in measured, assured tones prior to dispensing with any perceived sense of impartiality by hollering, "Come on the Welsh!" It is distinctly odd to hear this sentiment delivered in enunciated tones redolent of an uncontaminated Home Counties accent.

Active in stopping the Welsh "coming on" is a terrifyingly muscular Bath no. 11 who possesses long flowing blond Scandinavian locks, yet spends periods of the game isolated on the left wing with his head down, resembling a Viking looking for his lost axe.

London Welsh do a clever line-out ploy where the thrower quickly lobs the ball to the nearest man, who immediately returns the pass, leaving a tiny chink of space along a touchline corridor leading to try-line glory. Unfortunately the thrower is so surprised to receive the ball back, he stands paralysed like a mouse awaiting an eagle's imminent swoop, and four bulky Bath scrimmagers descend upon him. I look away, but hear a horrible crunching sound.

Not unlike accounts of military action, rugby offers long periods of tedium offset by sudden flashes of extreme violence and excitement. The scrum is possibly the most pointless occurrence in sport. Firstly, it takes ages to assemble, and then invariably collapses, necessitating a re-start. Eventually the team that puts the ball in ALWAYS receives possession back. Then London Welsh turn around two consecutive scrums, after the expert next to me comments this will never happen. Another inexpert observation is that there are simply too many players. At fifteen per side, anyone obtaining possession immediately runs into heavy traffic and gets flattened underneath a thirty-player pile. This player pyramid then inevitably collapses, and the concussed participants buried at the bottom hesitantly get to their feet like bears slowly awakening from hibernation. Too often it's a mess without finesse.

With ten minutes remaining, London Welsh bring on a hairy giant sub resembling King Kong, a man definitely capable of ascending the Empire State Building's exterior while swatting at bi-planes. He helps win a penalty, and The Exiles – as London Welsh are suitably nicknamed - achieve 9-9 parity.

Exactly four seconds remain when a Bath forward passes the ball directly to an opponent. The surprised recipient, former Bath player Nick Scott, pirouettes past an opponent then legs it for seventy metres at a speed usually reserved for those being chased by Aldi's security man. The try line is reached and London Welsh win 16-9.

Celebrating, I have succeeded in finding my hitherto unknown inner Welshness.

THE CREW DATE

This month Oxford University felt itself lit by the full glare of the national media again, and no matter how much they tried to cover the camera lens and shield their faces, the story was well and truly out. When the social secretary of Pembroke College Rugby Football Club (PCRFC) clicked "send" on a notorious email – presumably thinking, "This is really funny, everyone will think I'm so hilarious," directing how his team should behave on a Crew Date, the consequences were surely only unforeseen to him. Odd that, as you'd expect someone who is both a student and rugby club member to normally behave so well and un-laddy, wouldn't you? The *Daily Telegraph* was quick to point out its "vulgar subject title" before carefully transcribing its vulgarity, while one national newspaper, accustomed to being professionally outraged, was so appalled by peacetime use of the "vile P-word" that it referred to it six times – like Mrs Slocombe with Tourette's.

The offending email subject header was "Free Pussy". Unusually for a student email subject header, merely adding the word "Riot" would have avoided all this trouble: "Free Pussy Riot" offering solidarity for the Russian political prisoners. Or not, as it transpires, because the message ordered PCRFC to prepare for their forthcoming Crew Date with Pembroke's freshers by picking a hottie, spiking her drink, then using a pregnancy test kit repeatedly until it displays positive.

I know. If any of that's offensive, then surely it's just PC gone mad. Given the glimmering intelligence required to get into Oxford, you do wonder how the email's author thought this might be acceptable. He probably composed his missive then read it back, thinking: "Better just check this is okay as it's being sent from an official Oxford University email account, and going to numerous recipients. Yeah, the subject header is uncontroversial, the stuff about spiking freshers' drinks is mundane enough, the rapey stuff should be okay, impregnating teenagers against their will is obviously fine too … Oh My God! What have I done?! If this ever goes out the consequences will be unthinkable for me and my college. The eternal shame! I've only gone and spelled 'discreet' erroneously as 'discrete'." And he thereby clicked "send". With "discreet" genuinely misspelled as "discrete".

He resigned the next day (good spelling is taken seriously in Oxford), while Pembroke College initiated a damage clear-up campaign to rival the aftermath of the London Riots. A week later, PCRFC's captain resigned too. Followed by the team's temporary suspension, then automatic relegation to the third division.

A statement was hastily written, with his college's gun barrel indent clearly visible on the writer's forehead: "Every fresher girl in Pembroke is quaking in their boots thinking they may be picked" … sorry, that was one of their earlier statements that caused the fuss… "The PCRFC accepts that the email circulated about our proposed Crew Date was entirely misguided and represented a serious case of poor judgement." I haven't checked, but hopefully the reconciliatory statement of apology was not given the subject header: "Free Cock".

Members of the rugby club were reported to have attended "a sexual consent discussion forum at Pembroke" and a compulsory "consent class". But surely consent sets the bar too low. Personally, I would always advise holding out for mild enthusiasm.

Oxford students can now obtain a written permission form for sexual consent. How long does a completed consent form last? Can you turn up at the house of your intended partner five years later waving a signed consent form and say: "I think you'll find this paperwork is all in order. And I've brought my lawyer."

Crew Dates are a longstanding Oxford tradition where a male and a female sports team meet up on a blind group date, consume heroic quantities of alcohol and then 14 hours later queue to receive the morning-after pill. Corpus Christi's netball team is one of the most sought-after Crew Dates, rejoicing in the name CorPussy. They dress as cats, with feline ears and painted whiskers, and have made my time spent at bus stops vastly more enjoyable whenever they tottered past on impracticable heels.

However, the legends of all Crew Dates is Bacchanalia – this is Oxford University's female drinking society. As their names implies, classics fans! For fun they play "Spirit Roulette". This involves blindfolding each other and having six bottles on a table in front of every participant. Three are soft drinks, one is whisky, one is vodka, and other is stocked with a vile brew whose title translates from the original Bulgarian as "Goodbye loved ones". Anyone used to drinking this would spit out industrial alcohol claiming, "Who's watered down this insipid tap water?"

Each girl takes turns to select a blind bottle and down a generously portioned shot. Basically the rule is: if you still register a heartbeat, you're still in the game. The rounds keep coming until the only girl left standing is declared the winner. The girls do this to cleanse their palettes *before* going out. Various male crew daters commented on social media: "Bacchanalia are so sexy it hurts, and they drank us under the table." Their other reviews include such phrases as: "They trashed our bathroom," "Thrown out of college bar for rowdiness and pennying," "After vom-stops en route to college, they all demanded tongue jousting!" and "Best sconcers in Oxford." A sconce is the challenge of drinking a trumpet full of booze to be downed in one. These are not girls to invite to the vicarage for tea.

Bacchanalia and CorPussy Crew Dates have been undeniably responsible for raising many things in their presence, and gender equality is certainly one of them. They prove you can have a salacious agenda and consume an amount of alcohol that makes Smirnoff struggle to keep up with production. And no one gets hurt – livers notwithstanding. The trick, it seems, is not to send offensive emails first.

And if anyone, attracted by Pembroke College's email, is on the lookout for some free pussy in Oxford, then HomesForPets.com are always looking for adopters.

TRAVEL

THE PADDINGTON TRAIN

I am on a train about to leave Paddington, the only occupant of a line of three seats. Similarly, the triple seat facing me also only contains one passenger – a suited man in his late fifties speed-reading an academic book. "Bet he gets off at Oxford too," is my sole deduction, before returning my attention to my noticeably less intellectual reading matter. He is reading about syntactic paradigms, whilst I'm reading about Melanie Sykes getting a new tattoo.

Just as the train doors electronically shluuussh close, a pack of students occupy the four remaining seats in our previously isolated republic of calm. The suited academic and I exchange a fleeting gaze. Two strangers connected by disappointment; brought together by a shared grieving for our lost tranquillity. Our hope of a peaceful train journey now atrophied. Our dared hopes for a journey spent in quiet rueful introspection, beset with reading opportunities, now lost.

The students are noticeably young, brash and loud. They appear to be compiled of two separate girl/boy couples, as if Noah had mistakenly ordered twice for his Ark's breeding pair of "shouty annoying student-types".

"Oxford·is like soooo supposed to be intimidating, ya, but it like so isn't," announces the taller of the two females as we pull out of the station. As becomes quickly evident, she feels the need to announce a lot of things. Very loudly. I consider getting off at Slough and waiting thirty minutes for the train behind. Merely moving to another carriage would not have worked – they would still have been audible. An equally loud brown-haired girl puts on a woolly hat, even though the temperature of the carriage – crammed with people – would be sufficient to cook boil-in-the-bag rice.

Music leaks from the headphones of a passenger two seats away, but even he cannot avoid the tumultuous din of student voices. One informs the entire carriage of the minutiae of woolly hat girl's breakfast muffin preferences ("And I got like only four bits of chocolate in my white chocolate and raspberry muffin…"). This is fascinating stuff, but surely she should retain an anecdote this good until she's interviewed on *Desert Island Discs*. She has probably already announced the information on Facebook and Twitter.

They reveal everything to the train. So loudly that passengers waiting on stations where we do not stop will hear them as we whoosh past their platform. The four are in the Sixth Form at a private school and are coming to Oxford for college interviews, elaborating at length how the college will wither in grateful acceptance of their presence. The two boys forcibly inform everyone on the train: "This college will probably be begging us to study there – so I'm not going to say 'yes' to the first Oxford college to give me an offer."

His male friend agrees. "My sister went to Cambridge. She's given me something we call 'cue card bull'. I just say barely believable bollocks about how it is my destiny to study at Oxford, how I really want to do outreach." All four collapse into laughter at this proposal.

One of the girls, still continuing her compelling muffin monologue ("I had, like, too many raspberry seeds in my muffin…"), then informs everyone throughout the entire train's eight carriages about last month's skiing trip. Although with a voice as loud as hers, the resort was probably closed all week due to avalanche warnings.

"The college dons who interview you can't breathe outside their Oxford bubble," she declares. "I'm like so pleased I plan a gap year to get out of academia. I like so need a year off." A year off from what? Instagramming your friends, pointlessly uploading pictures of yourself onto Facebook and reaching Level 6 of *Grand Theft Auto*?

At Reading a huge swathe of humanity enters our carriage. An immobile man in his seventies stands. None of the students offer their seat. A middle-aged woman does the decent thing, but her offer is courteously declined. The four students are oblivious to the scene.

A woman in her mid-twenties joins our carriage and sits opposite. Clutching meretriciously coloured designer bags, she is wearing all black. Her skirt is so short it is on the cusp of failing to exist. As passengers disembark, she claims both seats next to her with bags. An elderly man asks if he can sit down. She refuses to move the bags – or look up from her texting – and remarks, "There are other seats on the train." Even the four students notice this discourteous conduct.

"Ancient manners is like so important in interviews," hollows Hat Girl. "Yeah," agrees Shouty Boy, "'cos at Young Fogey College they're all living in the past." All four fall into hysterics, repeating as much of the phrase "Young Fogey College" as they can say before laughing.

After a platform wait so long it is likely the station had to build it first, starting with submitting a request for planning permission, we arrive into Oxford. "Just spin a load of bull about upholding proud Oxford traditions, believing that any relationship I have with my college won't be for three years, but for life. You know, all the bull you can deliver while keeping a straight face," advises one of the shouty males. They all nod collectively like chickens pecking feed off the ground. "Oh, and mention your dad is a regular benefactor to his old college – that's a complete lie, obviously, but if they get a whiff of the word 'benefactor' then you're in."

The suited man opposite, whose demeanour somehow manages to pull off an enviable combination of avuncular yet headmasterly, gets down a large umbrella and expensive looking coat from the luggage rack, before speaking for the first time.

"I'll probably see you four later," he says, joining the conversation of the students and matching them for confidence, if not volume. "Err ... hello?" says the taller male student, clearly startled but also dismissively recalcitrant towards a stranger talking to him. "I'm the Principal of [better not say] College, Oxford, a.k.a. Young Fogey College."

Their faces.

EPILOGUE

Occasionally – very, very occasionally – a songwriter will discover a tune, a gagsmith think of a joke, a novelist find a plot, simply by the act of waking up from a dream. The rush is then on to sketch the outline of that idea into a recognisable shape on a bedside notepad before it disappears with the early morning dew. Paul McCartney has spoken of writing *Yesterday* with such serendipity.

However, the chances of obtaining a fully formed column simply by waking up from a good sleep while my subconscious memory has put in an industrious nightshift is never going to happen. But just as rare is having a story like this dropped into my lap.

My day in London had been notable for its stressfulness. All my journeys had been delayed and crowded. The person I was due to meet texted to say he couldn't make it and a writing job I was hoping to obtain did not materialise. In a city of ten million people it is surprisingly easy to feel alone. Then the train back was delayed too, necessitating an anxious wait on a crowded Paddington concourse. When the departure board rolled over the digits to reveal the Oxford platform number, everyone ran inadvisably fast.

Then at the very last moment of a long and disappointing day – two seconds before I completed my circular journey back into Oxford station where it had commenced nine hours earlier – the above happened.

I recall disembarking but remaining at the station for a while, sitting on the metallic Oxford station seats outside a closing newsagents in order to scribble down the dialogue the four students had produced on the journey. I knew it would fade from my memory shortly, overshadowed by the fantastic ending. Already I was aware of the dichotomy that this was a wondrous gift of a story that had just come my way by pure happenstance, but at the same time it inspired a melancholic awareness that I probably wouldn't be witnessing a story this good for a long time. If ever again.

The core details of this story are all faithfully reported. However, some scent-distracting distortions were necessary. The person delivering the line at the end was a very senior University figure from the college, but not a 'principal' – I used that term for both its global recognition factor and also because his actual title would have rendered the identity a lot more traceable. Elsewhere there are only minor factual contortions to preserve anonymity – regardless of whether anonymity was deserved. The woman's refusal to move her bags was so devastatingly rude I included the incident as a shame exercise; one day she'll be old and karma will hopefully arrange for her to be stood up on a train whilst a young women spreads out her designer purchases across two seats.

Perhaps what I like most about this story is its illustration that justice can come from a multitude of unexpected sources. In a way I suppose it's an old fashioned morality tale at heart. And the four students hopefully learned a lot at Oxford.

THE GINGER NUT

The London Underground allows a different functioning code of human behaviour. Once humans have shuffled underground in sufficient numbers, acceptable conduct transpires to be a rather nebulous affair.

This month I had to travel back to Oxford during London's rush hour. The concept of personal space is suspended on the Tube between the hours that constitute rush hour (another nebulous concept), so I had applied extra deodorant as a precaution – a consideration noticeably not reciprocated by the man grabbing the support handle opposite me. Then the train stopped, and even more people managed to board, a bit like those student world record attempts at the most people it's possible to squeeze inside a phone box – only more crowded.

At our next stop, a small oriental man gamely tried to get off, but it was clearly an impossible manoeuvre and he shrugged to his resigned fate as if silently fulminating, "Once again I'll end up at Barnet when I just wanted to pop to Oxford Street."

Elementary laws of physics concluded it was now impossible for more people to board our carriage; at our next stop, another twenty got on. I spotted a sprightly pensioner on the platform taking a run-up like a frightening fast bowler, gaining the necessary propulsion to hurl himself into a non-existent gap. "Mind the gap," I thought.

Between Baker Street and Paddington someone was treading on my foot. It was a woman and she apologised to the wrong man, but he accepted her apology – the apology stealer. She was so close that her hair was flicking my face as the train bumped and jolted along. I think her shampoo had hints of apple blossom. Sharing an uncomfortable intimacy, I couldn't help notice her hair was uncompromisingly ginger, and her feet were much heavier than her slim frame indicated.

Things were getting awkward. There is a lowly class of perverse tube criminal known as frotteurists. These are nasty parasitical perverts, only one rung higher in public estimation than investment bankers, who obtain paraphilic pleasure from rubbing themselves against strangers. Only cats can do this in public without consequences.

I don't know how to distinguish a frotteurist from a rush hour commuter, but presumably you certainly can if unfortunate enough to witness one. They are regularly arrested on the Tube network. Presumably being handcuffed very closely to a police officer, then thrown into an overcrowded cell, is hardly a deterrent for people who derive perverse pleasure from being invasively close to strangers.

Determined not to have my uncomfortable position misconceived as frotteurism, I inched – or rather milli-metred – myself away from the ginger girl, only to find that this was rendered impossible by the pressing barrier of men and women behind me with their noses stuck deep into my hair.

Reaching Paddington, I went a different way along the platform, yet still ended up standing behind her on the escalator. This concerned me, in case she thought I was following her. She glanced at me like I was an unordered side-dish placed before her in a restaurant.

Boarding the Oxford train there were no available seats in the first six carriages, until I reached what a man confirmed was the Quiet Carriage by telling someone on his mobile. I spotted a lone vacant seat – simultaneous to a man approaching from the other end of the carriage. We acknowledged a hundred-yard stare, and mutually accelerated.

So this was why we trained at infant school: those years of competitive musical chairs were purposeful after all. He was gaining and looked odds-on to reach the sole empty seat before me. Then a pensioner placed a bag in the aisle, and the speedier seat-spotter tripped – leaving me as the Devon Loch of last seat-claiming Grand National winners. It was the last space of four around a table.

Glowing with victory, I sat down prouder than a king on a newly claimed throne. I looked up and saw the ginger lady, now starting to wear an expression ordinarily reserved for walking through graveyards at midnight. The coffee cart squeaked past – she resisted ordering a double brandy.

At Didcot Parkway disembarkers created spare seats. I considered moving, but feared this might be interpreted as worse: "Is my ginger hair so repulsive you have to move? You gingerist!" I stayed put.

Eventually we reached Oxford. She exited to the left of the carriage, so I turned to the right. Somehow we both arrived together at the foot of the platform stairs. Nipping to the station's M&S, I spotted her surveying the sandwiches so immediately swivelled towards the exit. But the copper kopf soon overtook me and headed, predictably, in exactly the same direction I needed to go. Glancing at my watch I realised my bus was due to depart Bonn Square in eight minutes.   So I pounded the pavement behind her.

She started to speed up. So I walked faster. She quickened too. I accelerated.

I decided to overtake her – that would prove I wasn't following her. Thanks a lot, brain, for that. When almost drawing level, she increased her speed. Another spurt of acceleration on my part was matched by her. Basically I was now racing a woman through the streets of Oxford to prove to her that I'm not a weirdo. This is a self-contradicting directive – like asking Wayne Rooney to hand in a written transfer request.

Belatedly abandoning my quest to prove my idiocy, I decided to let her go in front – the bus could go without me. At Bonn Square you know who was standing at the same stop. We exchanged looks and I received one that suggests I'm considered weird. Initially I declined joining the queue until someone else arrived, but no one did. As I followed her onto the double-decker, she turned to speak.

"Excuse me," she said, while I braced myself for her to fumble in her bag and spray me with mace – although she was clutching so much shopping, macing me would necessitate first asking if I could hold her other bags while she located the spray. I prepared to defend myself against any forthcoming charges of following her.

"I saw you speaking at a literary festival." Relief poured into my brain. Flooded with assuagement, my frontal cortex couldn't think of anything meaningful to say. Though I silently noted she didn't say I was "good" or "funny", just that she saw me.

She boarded first. Ignoring the empty seat beside her, I now spent the journey ruminating whether I should have positioned myself next to her and chatted. Thankfully she got off before my stop – or that could have been awkward.

I had to return to London a few days later. I went by coach.

The Road Not Taken

I was cycling along the Thames towpath being vigilant for dogs and ducks (and other animals that aren't naturally coupled on pub signs) when a bend in the path suddenly revealed a "Road Closed" sign. This was surprising because it wasn't a road. Several workmen had fenced off the path and were installing the traditional paraphernalia associated with road works: 1 x digger, 2 x shovels and 3 x brimming skips filled with used tea bags. Road works are basically mobile pop up cafés for the working classes – favoured by the alfresco tea drinker; it's only a matter of time before one receives a four star review in *Time Out:* "Delightfully authentic bricolage, detailed perfectly to include chipped mugs and sweary ambient footy banter."

A yellow diversion sign pointed persuasively to the left. This would ordinarily be helpful, yet there was no road to the left. Just thick pathless woodland. So I juddered along off-road on my untrustworthy bike, shaking like an aspiring young actress on a night out with John Leslie, Peter Stringfellow and Silvio Berlusconi, and headed into the woods, the bike's ineffective suspension shaking the fillings from my teeth.

The woods were pleasant, providing an overarching canopy of hawthorn and birdsong. Although it was a big surprise to be in the woods today, there were no teddy bears picnicking. Nor behatted, bowtie-wearing bears planning over-elaborate and impractically complex schemes to relieve naive picnickers of their baskets. But there was a picnic table next to an idyllic stream – a brook so bubbling it would certainly have inspired Tennyson into purposefully opening his notebook - about twenty yards from the route that I pass twice daily on a head-down commute.

Most people power down their existence, going into mental screen saver mode and refuse to have any worthwhile interaction with the world until the duration of their commute is complete. Having tutted at the inconvenience of the diversion, I now pledged to return to this spot – enthralled with the initial thrill of discovery.

This all happened exactly as I described above i.e. it's literally true. But it is also allegorically true – representing a structured heavy-load-bearing metaphor for the restraining influence of choosing familiarity. As those of us who have long since secretly selected security over adventure can testify, the metaphor can support a lot of weight. The road not taken is often perceived to be a scary place – yes, the road we know may be littered with potholes and used syringes, and although desperate for road works we always put them off for feared resultant inconvenience, but it's our familiar road. We are fearful to leave it – hey, we may get lost. Or end up in a slightly worse place. Oddly, once we pass the turning we harshly reappraise the untaken option –

instead of representing lateness and fear, we often harangue ourselves for allowing its secrets to remain unsampled, its views unseen, its lay-bys unpicnicked (hey, I'm allowed one neologism), its potential berries of excitement unpicked. The voice in my head/inner SatNav urges me to "turn around and go back" (though I'm later relieved to realise that voice was a SatNav and I haven't developed schizophrenia). I'll save expanding the analogy for my planned self-help book, provisionally titled *Help Yourself* – although that title could encourage shop-lifting.

Once I cycled along the towpath and passed two girls sunbathing (and here's a detail I left out when recounting that incident to my wife: they were both topless). And utterly gorgeous (OK, two details I omitted). Surprise was the predominant emotion (which in itself, was surprising), and – although you would probably assume otherwise – I really didn't know where to look. The pair of them (the girls, not their … tsk, do grow up!) cheerily greeted me with a friendly "hello". Wanting to appear polite, I reciprocated the greeting while staring straight ahead, which seemed politer than fumbling through my bag for a camera.

Comedic evolution has finally ensured that we no longer find breasts hilarious (from Benny Hill to Ray Cooney, *Carry On* to seaside postcards, all illustrated comedy speciousness); if breasts were as debilitatingly hilarious as former comedy generations considered them to be, then surely women were rendered unable to dress themselves in the mornings for laughing fits. As a child, I distinctly recall my first trip to the theatre when the entire house leaned forward in shared convulsions of laughter whenever a character announced: "I've lost my glasses but can see a young lady holding what appears to be two balloons"; as an eight-year-old I groaned, and thought they really should aim higher.

Since the topless girls weren't about to offer me a roll (really … what did I just say about comedic evolution?) from their picnic, I carried on cycling.

Unfortunately real life rarely replicates the plot of porn movies – which is particularly unfortunate for anyone who trained as a TV repair man on the strength of it.

Cycling ensures that, ideally, I'd prefer two separate bells: one whose ring is universally interpreted as "excuse me", while the other bell signals "you friggin' moron". It was one of the latter rings that

I witnessed a towpath cyclist give a female jogger, significantly after she'd emitted a startled "yelp!" and swerved across his path. Initially I assumed he'd unchivalrously goosed the unfortunate jogger and I'd now become a witness, prior to realising this was unlikely given (a) none of us were Italian, and (b) an actual goose had been startled by the cyclist into flying towards her *derrière*.

Topless sunbathers, diversions into woods and a goose goosing a jogger make a hat-trick of weird sights from several years of towpath travelling, but not, it turns out, the weirdest thing it is possible to see there. That occurred a few weeks ago when a yellow car drove along the route. Thankfully cars aren't allowed on the towpath, so the driver had creatively navigated around this restriction by casually driving in the river. You don't believe me, do you? Luckily, those earlier encounters ensure that whenever I cycle on the towpath, I now always carry a camera.

THE HOLE TRUTH

I've never understood why people use the expression "I wish the ground could have opened up and swallowed me." Usually reserved for footballers missing goals more open than a 24-hour shop, the phrase receives considerable airings whenever social embarrassments are recounted: "...and then I called him Steve but his name is Dave!" Really? Would you genuinely prefer nose-diving into a sudden subterranean abyss to experiencing the consequences of exonerative memory frailty? Had you mistaken a Dave for, say, a Sue, then perhaps absolution would be slower in forthcoming, yet still surely preferable to being hurled into a spontaneously appearing void?

You could always attempt the linguistic equivalent of fumbling in a dark room like a desperate light switch locator, until eventually realising there is no light switch: "...err the Dave I know is very feminine, he could be a lady boy ... not that I mean you look like ... I'll see myself out." This is digging one's own hole.

At least a hole suddenly appearing removes the imposition of having to dig it yourself. That chore is recognised as a punitive gesture: digging a hole for oneself is punishment meted out for a squirming social faux pas – reserved for weapons grade faux pas – the sort of social embarrassment resulting in immediate despatch of an

SAE to the Foreign Legion. Congratulating a corpulent woman on a misinterpreted pregnancy being a common one.

Toss offenders a conversational rope ladder into their self-dug hole and invariably it's rejected, even though everyone else can see the teetering heap of potentially engulfing earth they've just busily piled precariously at the hole's mouth - everyone except the digger, whose view is obscured by being in too deep and about to go deeper: "But darling, surely you're talking about a different Lisa we also know?" "No, it's definitely this Lisa here, the party host, who gave everyone a drunken lap-dance in a bar on holiday. More tea, Lisa's mum?"

Recently, while performing the over-familiar and stultifyingly mundane task of turning into the road where I've lived for the last two decades, I was shocked to discover... [pause for dramatic effect] ... [just a bit longer] ... that the road had suddenly opened up and was about to swallow me. In a startlingly literal sense. There was a huge cavernous hole in the middle of my road resembling a bomb crater. It certainly hadn't been there earlier that morning, otherwise I would have probably noticed when cycling into its deep capacious entrance. Either it had been caused by sudden catastrophic subsidence or else Tony Robinson is getting seriously out of control.

Only frenzied braking preserved my health and (possibly) life, for this was a gargantuan aperture: more black hole than pot hole. I've lived in Rose Hill for many years. To some North Oxford residents, this is equivalent to dwelling in the Sea of Tranquillity – both equally unlikely ever to be visited by the former – though these two places now share an additional attribute: an enormous surface crater.

By the time a van load of authorities arrive, hole tourism has already commenced, with a circle of onlookers collectively assembled around the gaping, yawning void, some dutifully warning the approaching traffic. Collective authority figures in high-vis jackets disembark and conduct huddled meetings until, after an hour, they're presumably ready to confirm that it definitely is a hole we're dealing with here. Yet holes, I soon learn, range in status. Ours is a top category one, with holes graded in size and status from the tiny and unthreatening, to a truly enormous hole (e.g. Swindon). Fences and "Road Closed - Diversion" signs are hastily erected. The hole is quickly deemed sufficiently dangerous to have its own personal security guard appointed. A dedicated team of two arrive, charged with providing 24-hour hole security throughout the Bank Holiday weekend. This involves keeping watch from a parked van, like a cop show stake-out all through the night. Dawn's first light reveals that the security watchmen have been suitably vigilant, since no one has yet stolen the hole.

Capacious cavities freakishly appearing in busy roads is a surprisingly common syndrome. National statistics on spontaneous road holes are difficult to collate, but we do know that there are 4,000 holes in Blackburn Lancashire alone (thanks to the Beatles). One of the security team appointed to guard the Rose Hill chasm had been scrambled from Wiltshire, and he's been professionally securing spontaneous holes for two years now – without ever experiencing a jobless diary day. The largest one he experienced was over sixty square metres. Needless to say, this can get serious. Very serious. Both public and workmen have died in spontaneous road holes. Idiots intent on dismantling safety fencing have been spotted at other sites thus necessitating a permanent security presence; personally, I'd be tempted to allow these people to voluntarily remove themselves from the gene pool by falling in.

A hole of this magnitude can host significant hazards for workmen, who risk daily exposure to corroded severed pipes, collapsing earth, tangled wiring, escaping gas, rodents and Chris Moyles' radio show; there are definitely easier ways to earn a living. Yet they are legally forbidden to mend it until an Assigned Welfare Unit is in situ. Assigned Welfare Units can be assembled in storms, floods, war zones and radiation areas but not, it turns out, during a Bank Holiday weekend. Nowadays, as a visible sign of the deservedly improved conditions road workmen can finally expect in the 21st century, an AWU contains toilet, shower, decontamination facilities and a personal sushi chef. OK, that's not true about the shower.

Later that afternoon I spot my wife purposefully scurrying along George Street, long hair trailing behind her blue dress while consulting a hand-held watch – thus simultaneously resembling two characters from *Alice in Wonderland*. Changing upwards through the gears walking, jogging, running and sprinting, should enable me to reach and inform her that a hazard has appeared in our road and she'll need to take a detour home. I lunge and grab her trailing sleeve: "Our road's got a huge hole in it!" It was not my wife.

I wish the ground could have opened up and swallowed me.

THE 11TH DIMENSION TOURIST

This month I arranged to go on a trip with a recent Corpus Christi maths graduate. Chloe has just gained a First and kindly consented to be my guide, as we embark towards our destination. It's a place few people not pursuing a pure maths degree have visited. We're going on a trip to the 11th dimension.

Apparently pure mathematicians used to work in the 10th dimension, but now Chloe, her mentor Marcus du Sautoy and others routinely explore the 11th dimension. I ask, "Is that a Spinal Tap thing, i.e. other pure maths people study the 10th dimension, but yours goes all the way to 11?" No, it transpires. I ask Chloe if we're ready for her to show me the 11th dimension.

"I'll try. But it's imaginary," she replies.

"Can I have my photo taken in the 11th dimension?" I ask.

"No," she confirms.

"Is stuff cheaper or more expensive in the 11th dimension?" I enquire.

"It's theoretical maths like quantum physics, so things won't be for sale," Chloe elaborates, patiently.

"Really? Surely there's a planning application pending for a Tesco Extra there?"

"Unlikely as that seems – no."

Like most people, I suspect, my dimensional comprehension stops abruptly at four. I know that the 4th dimension is Einstein's special relativity; the 3rd dimension is 3D movies. Two dimensional is a flat drawing, and I can also define one dimensional (the plots in *Neighbours*). Hence I am curious to know what constitutes dimensions 5 to 11.

Fortunately Chloe is one of the best placed people in Oxford to enlighten me. She is one of Professor du Sautoy's protégés conducting the free "Maths in the City" walking tour.

Chloe is 22. That is not a prime number. She will probably prefer being 23, which is a prime. Chloe likes primes. Really likes primes. Her pupils actively dilate when spotting a prime. At the start of her maths walking tour we pass a door numbered 37. Her eyes pop out like a cartoon character, and she emits an audible purr. My wife assumes Chloe must have spotted a hot shirtless guy. It turns out to be another door with a prime number. Later Chloe observes a further prime and gets equally as excited. Her ideal job after graduation ought to be post(wo)man. After she'd rung their doorbells at 7am, blurry-eyed inhabitants would say, "Morning postie, have you got something for me to sign?" "No, just wanted to inform you that your house number is a double integer prime in Fibonacci's sequence. How exciting is that?!"

To be fair, primes are immensely important and are vital for theoretical maths and cryptology, attracting interest and funding from banks and the military.

As a former maths rejecter I found the subject enfeebling rather than enlightening, so I was curious to discover exactly what an Oxbridge maths degree entailed. Most people can imagine the type of studies encountered by someone reading history, English or geography at Oxford, but would struggle to envisage how a pure maths student fills their days.

Chloe agrees with this summation. "It is difficult for maths students, because unlike most other subjects where Oxford is just an advanced progression of what students have been studying before, it is almost a brand new subject starting at Oxford." The transition from predominately applied to pure maths is a journey from the practical to the theoretical, almost the scientific to the artistic. I ask her about the sectarianism between pure and applied maths and which she prefers. "I like pure maths, but I also like applied maths. But I don't know which is better." Surely Harry Hill can help her find out? Fight!!!

If you think Oxford maths students study intimidatingly large numbers all day, then prepare to be shocked when Chloe announces, "I have not used a number for two years" (well, not counting the number she used in that sentence, obviously).

Soon it's time for us to depart for the 11th dimension. That's where the cool maths people will be hanging out. We start with a square Chloe draws on graph paper. We're already in the 2nd dimension. Adding extra right angles creates a cube. Although it's a cube, it's a two dimensional drawing masquerading as three dimensional in my imagination. I can only see three physical sides, yet my mind adds another three. This is imaginary maths made rational. Then we add equivalent cubes by joining additional right angles. Then more. It soon gets difficult, but with an expert holding my hand, pulling me into the 5th dimension, I can see it. And then the 6th. Reaching the 7th dimension, I only stop when my brain runs out of capacity, needs to close and sends an error message. After rebooting my brain, we try again, and I reach the 8th dimension. I'm teetering on the edge of the 9th dimension, and just when my failing imagination causes to me to fall out, Chloe tugs me back inside by reminding me not to think in spatial but in imaginary terms.

We do eventually reach the 11th dimension, although this is akin to taking credit for climbing Everest when another mountaineer has carried you all the way to the summit. Then I descend quickly by falling back to my base camp ignorance. Back in the dimensional foothills (I like the 3rd dimension – it's my kind of dimension and I'm happy to settle here), I am met by a grinning mathematician.

"Did you see it?" she asks.

Shards of effulgent insight had shone through when the thick grey clouds of my momentarily lifted ignorance had allowed piercing lucidity to evaporate my incomprehension. Or something like that.

Then this new knowledge disappears from my grasp like ultra-fine saffron dust trickling between the cracks of my fingers. But for about three seconds I held that insight in my hand; that comprehension was mine. For a fleeting nanosecond I had reached the end of the rainbow, pulled the sword out of the stone, and then the enlightenment crumbled to the dust from whence it, and all things, ultimately came.

I ask to keep the bits of paper as proof that I've visited the 11th dimension – like children's TV character Mr Benn, who always retained one physical, tangible souvenir of his otherwise imaginary trips. She asks me who Mr Benn is. That's because she's 22. Kids today, eh? They don't know anything.

EPILOGUE

This column remains one of my favourites. People still occasionally mention it to me at book signings.

Although they usually visit me with the irregularity of desert rain – or buses whenever I'm late for something – this piece combines two Very Good Ideas for a column: namely (1) the idea of tourism to an unvisited location and (2) scouting a great interview subject that Chloe undoubtedly represents.

The gags in the piece mainly still work – although Tesco probably are not quite so rapacious today. Even they couldn't invade Moscow in the winter. But the unchallengeable truth is the column would stand up – fully erect and comfortable on its feet – without any jokes. This is a deceptively difficult thing to accomplish in comedy – a routine or sketch that would remain interesting even without the gags. I've heard it done on *The Now Show* occasionally, but never regularly.

I was interviewing Chloe in a noisy JCR at Corpus. "Come on," she ordered, "let's go to my room. It'll be quieter there." Somehow she passed a hidden eye-rolling judgement on her lesser mature contemporaries, yet without ever being condescending. Despite her huge talent she was the opposite of arrogant.

I envy Chloe for being so infactuated with her subject – so unshakably sure of its, and thereby her, purpose. Her enthusiasm was sticky too – I attributed my subsequently increased interest in maths directly to her. Though I'm still just as ignorant at calculus (asking me to solve a maths problem is akin to asking a badger to lead a bridge hand), I now accept maths is hugely, cardinally important. Re-reading my interview notes now, I discovered three paragraphs that are out-takes from the originally submitted column. They are reinstated here:

Chloe has pure ambitions for pure maths. "You wouldn't believe the amount of unsolicited emails we received at Oxford from City banks and financial institutions, offering us freebies to meet them." "Like," I suggest, "a drugs dealer driving slowly past a school and offering your first hit of smack for free?" "Exactly", she agrees. "There is no way I'm going over to the dark side."

This committed idealism is a genuinely inspirational antidote to perceived banker greed. See, young people can be great. Admittedly, there's a slight statistical risk that in a few years' time she'll be in Canary Wharf sacking her chauffeur for being two minutes late, but I can't see that. I'd like to check in with Chloe in a few years, and see what theorems she's helped to crack. I'm confident she has remained on the good side, her integrity unblemished.

"I first fell in love with maths when I read Marcus du Sautoy's book *The Music of the Primes*. Everyone else on the school bus was shouting and throwing crisps at each other, but I was lost in abstract mathematics." I think about asking if my wife and I could adopt her, but as she's 22 we may have left it a bit late.

THE BICYCLE ACCIDENT

Last week I was involved in a serious accident. I came off my bicycle, soared through the air like a human cannonball and landed head first on the Iffley Road. Yes, that did hurt. A lot.

Several pedestrians immediately came to my aid and dialled 999. When the ambulance crew arrived roadside they needed to establish my potentially concussive state. The ambulance crew asked my name. "Richard," I replied confidently. Then they asked a second question: "What year is it?"

Typical. They sucker you into a false sense of security with an easy opening question before hitting you with an impossibly difficult follow-up. Eventually, after a lengthy pause that a geologist would consider a long period of time, I replied: "2015?"

As a comedian, normally I would have answered the question, "What year is it?" with a response like: "Well, I saw *Mrs Brown's Boys* on primetime BBC1 last night so I assume it must currently be sometime around 1975?"

The ambulance crew needed to ask me more questions. Answering questions on my surname, address and age is normally my specialist round. If I could play a joker in this round, I would.

I recalled my name and age but stumbled over where I live. "Do you live in Howard Street?" asked a helping member of the public. Even in my shocked and concussed state, I realised this is an inefficient way of determining where I live – going through every street in the UK until I confirm, "Yes, Balloon Street, Runcorn. That's me."

My responses prompted several more tests before they ascertained I could be moved to a waiting ambulance. Nearby a traffic warden viewed the ambulance parked on double-yellows wistfully, like a lion forced to watch tasty humans from behind bars.

"You realise," said the ambulance driver sagely, "that's it's your helmet that probably saved you?" That and an emergency stop by the no. 3 bus driver behind me. No matter how long I live (which, as I was reminded by this experience, is an arbitrary amount of time) I will always hear the sound of those squealing brakes. The ten tonne double decker came to a halt one metre from my spilt carcass. With Cowley Road closed, diverted traffic had doubled Iffley Road's bus count, so this was not the best chosen afternoon to hit a blemish in the road and experience my bike saddle resemble an ejector seat.

Wheeled into the John Radcliffe Hospital, I overhear a medic being briefed by the ambulance crew. "And he was wearing a helmet?" he checks. He gives me a look of approval, with an encrypted subtext: "Well that's saved the NHS ten grand." Not bad for a £17.99 helmet. They evaluate me and decide I am well enough to wait in triage. No helmet and it would have been a different part of the hospital.

An unshaven man in a T-shirt sits next to me. "What are you in for?" he asks, as if we are two prisoners meeting in an exercise yard. I expect his next question to be, "Did you bring any snout from the outside?" "Suspected broken wrist and head injury," I reply, trying to ratchet up my legitimacy to be here. "Me? Arm injury," he reports. As it is his right arm, I can see the urgency – given it is almost certainly his drinking arm.

Even on a Sunday afternoon A&E is busy with incessant arrivals. In the first area where the parading injured register at reception, you have to purchase drinks from a vending machine. Only after you've been processed by a medic are you taken round the corner where the ill patients converge. Here the coffee is free. This is a nice touch – and a definite fringe benefit of being evaluated to go through to the "definitely ill" round.

Eventually I see a doctor. She asks me: "After you hit the road with your head, what part of your body suffered impact next?" This is difficult. "My elbow ... then my leg, no I landed on my bottom next. I'm not sure." I literally cannot tell my arse from my elbow.

"Now," she says calmly, "we need to check if any of the bones in your wrist have been damaged. Does it hurt here?" "No." "Here?" "No." "How about here?" My scream is so loud and elongated that panicking birds ascend en masse from every rooftop in Headington. "I'm going to put down 'yes' for that one."

It has taken my wife's mood twenty minutes from arriving at the hospital to alter from "oh my God I'm so grateful you're alive" to "you really are such a git."

"I'm only going to discharge you from hospital if you're not going to be on your own tonight," says the kindly doctor. She advises certain drugs to nullify the pain. My wife asks if they can give me something stronger. She's hoping for something that will knock me out for the next eight to nine weeks, since in her view my role has become nothing more than a producer of laundry, dust and crumbs.

At home, I pledge never to take my elbows for granted again. Who knew they were required for using a saucepan, cleaning teeth and absolutely everything else. This is the elbows' chance to get long overdue recognition. "Oh, no one thinks we're sexy, do they? Or compliments us. Now – try using a fork without an elbow movement. What's that? Can't reach your mouth? Well, all we ever wanted was just a little acknowledgement, that's all."

They say you have to throw away a cycle helmet after an accident and get a new one. It seems an unfairly undignified end for something that saved me from serious injury. But without a helmet you could be throwing your life away instead.

I want to thank Denise and the other pedestrians who helped me, the bus driver who braked, the ambulance crew, the JR doctors and staff.

CELEBRITY

THE DARA O'BRIAIN DOUBLE ACT

I'm in a BBC TV studio and Dara O'Briain is about to ask me a question. Apparently I'm supposed to answer it. Intelligently. And be interesting. Plus funny. Luckily, I have an off-the-cuff riposte – an impromptu adlib that I wrote an hour earlier during a meeting with the Assistant Producer when we also discussed Dara's extemporaneous question. The only problem is, I have to deliver my "spontaneous" lines in front of the combined glare of studio lights and audience. Unsurprisingly, I am nervous. Just repeating my own name out loud at this moment seems impossibly ambitious.

"We're rolling!" shouts the director. The floor manager mimes a clap and the audience obligingly applauds. Dara speaks to camera: "Here at Science Club, we thought," pronouncing "thought" in that peculiarly Irish way as if the word is devoid of an initial "h", "we would ask our studio audience how they would spend £1 billion on a science project." A student in a glamorous red dress, who has just been literally shoved into shot by the production staff like a piece of livestock reluctant to enter a pen, replies first. A crew member has just directed her to "push them up for the cameras, love". She informs Dara that she would invest the money in particle physics research, though she would probably prefer to spend it on a BBC Staff Sexism Awareness Course.

Then Dara specifically asks me the same question. My heartbeat reaches 200 per minute. "I would invest it turning the Circle Line into the British CERN." Nanoseconds pass, with an initially oppressive silence. Then there is a laugh, and another, until suddenly everyone is laughing.

"Excellent idea," replies Dara. "Although," I add, "presumably there could be no particle accelerating on a Sunday due to engineering works." Now, that was spontaneous. Wow, look at me – I'm riffing with Dara. On. The. Television.

Buoyed by confidence, and like Icarus ascending, I deliver another gag. Unfortunately, delivering gags is unsurprisingly difficult – and missing out a crucial set-up link in the middle renders me humiliated. I am a writer on the series, but currently discovering that being a writer is an entirely separate skill from stand-up.

Thankfully Dara – the effortlessly funny and consummate professional – saves me. He asks, "What's the smallest known thing" – there apparently being no "h" in "thing" either in Ireland – "in the entire universe?" "Is it a quark or a banker's sense of shame?" I suggest to returning laughter. "These are the questions that matter, people. It is a quark – but only just," Dara announces. We get big laughs. And yes, I had written that line an hour earlier too. After the show Dara confirms that my lines were funny. Resisting the temptation to seek constant "but was I really great, darling?" showbiz validation, I experience an overriding sense of relief.

Surely the scientist guy who follows us will struggle to be more impressive? The act that follows me makes a comet. In the studio. Take that, Health and Safety. It's way more impressive than me. Coincidentally, his ingredient list to make a comet (coal dust, dry ice, sand, iron filings and amino acid) is also Heston Blumenthal's favourite pizza topping.

Apart from the occasional cameo by an idiot jester boy like me, the show is populated by proper scientists, rendering it A Force For TV Good. Somehow, and this is the skilful bit, it is also entertaining as well as unflinchingly intellectual. Making it the perpendicular opposite of those old Open University science programmes, and not just by ensuring the presenters have better jackets. Uncompromisingly informative, courageously scientific, yet willingly accessible; this is the distilled essence of Science Club, and why I am proud to be scripting parts of the show.

In an episode about extinction, I write the following line narrated by *Skyfall* actress Helen McCrory: "It's a statistical certainty that humans will become extinct. It's not a matter of if, just a question of when. So stop looking so smug on the sofa." For some reason, although recorded, they edit out the very last bit – i.e. the softening gag. So it ends with me basically telling everyone that they are all going to die! Great. Now I'm like the *Daily Express*!

Significantly, the sofa on Science Club's set contains the arses of accomplished and distinguished scientists, in direct comparison to most TV showbiz sofas which just contain arses. Harsh but true. "So [insert name of latest vacuous celeb briefly anointed by populist culture with a product to plug], do tell us about your newly ghost-written book of barbecue recipes…"

The show's zeitgeist dynamic combines a Manhattan loft set sprinkled with a *Top Gear*-style studio audience of young people looking like they are in a nightclub. I ensure my gurning face appears in shot on a few episodes, to drag down the attractiveness level more towards normality. There is also an added derivative dash of *Later With Jools Holland*, as cameras spin and people jump over cables, enabling a clipboard-clutching Dara to introduce a scientist in a corner with "please welcome Dr Mark and the DNA Extraction Process" (the latter being an experiment, not his backing band). And we have researched proper facts too, such as humans have fewer genes than a banana!

So, have we achieved physics for all? Quite a quantum leap, eh? No! Because a quantum leap is actually so small it would be an unnoticeably tiny jump. This is the sort of detail we have to get right on Science Club. Or else there are letters – well, mainly tweets. Unfortunately, most omit "BBC" from @BBCScienceClub, prompting complaints from a bar in Chicago called @ScienceClub after it received thousands of misdirected questions about quantum physics.

People invariably ask me what Dara is like to work with. My answer is an honest one: he possesses a glimmering intelligence, and can hold conversations at extremely high scientific levels without having to look at that clipboard. He owns a rare ability to recount tricky pieces to camera even when mined with difficult scientific names, whilst adlibbing amusing asides. (Yes, I do want to be invited back for a second series.)

Ahead of the transmission date, I excitedly inform my friends with a breathless enthusiasm to watch BBC2 at 9pm as I will be on TV doing gags with Dara O'Briain. When the air date finally arrives, I remind everyone again. Just to make sure.

The scene where I appear with Dara is completely edited out. Though they keep the bit with the banana – but then again, it has more genes than me. Oh well. That's showbiz.

THE SNOW FALL

The person sitting next to me is shouting at Channel Four newsreader Jon Snow. Unlike most people who shout at the television she receives an immediate answer back from Jon Snow. Because he is physically present in the same room. Then Ben Okri rolls up his honorary doctorate and gets involved in the verbal ruck too. No, it is not a dream.

It is a late Friday afternoon and the sun, evidently intent on knocking off early for the weekend, has allowed drizzle to fall from the prematurely dark sky. Escaping the rain, I am inside one of those wood-panelled rooms so beloved of Oxford colleges, sitting behind two rows of seats clearly marked "Reserved for Fellows". Then a hairy student arrives and obscures the "Reserved" sign by sitting on it.

A gowned academic appears and enquires, "So, are you a Fellow now?" to the illicitly seated undergrad. This is barely code, instantly decipherable as, "Move your skinny, pale student ass now!" Instead of the student's sudden realisation, "Oh, these seats are reserved for Fellows? That would explain the uncrackable enigma of the 'Reserved For Fellows' sign," he fails to pick up on the almost ground level subtext and stays seated in the reserved row.

The gowned Fellow makes a point of surreptitiously kicking him as she squeezes past along the row. "Oh, sorry!" she lies. He is not the only man to receive a kicking in the room as we are about to discover.

Jon Snow has courageously come to the JCR in Mansfield College – which, as many annoyed SatNav users may have discovered, is in Oxford not Mansfield - to discuss male feminism. That's not an oxymoron, like "reality TV" or "polite Frenchman". Men can be feminists too. Yeah, we can. Because Jon Snow says so, remarking that he asked David Cameron recently if he was a feminist, "And eventually he said yes."

Jon Snow espouses an audacious gender theory ascribing predominately male or female personality attributes to individuals. This does appear reductively binary. Snow continues ploughing this lone furrow, devastatingly unaware that he is ploughing in a field where he possesses no expertise. Another gowned academic with curly hair and a gentler demeanour than many in the 98 per cent feminist audience patiently points out in a restrained way that his argument is "b******s".

One contributor stands up and shouts so loudly that the chandeliers start to swing. She was supposed to await the roving microphone girl, but it really wasn't necessary. Her complaint is that women are perennially denied a voice.

The first fifteen people to speak from the floor are female. They all reiterate with confidence the same point: how women are generally more diffident than men in speaking out. This is clearly an irony free zone. I am too petrified to speak, my words ossified in my throat. Plus, I am physically shrinking down in my seat like Alice and her "Drink Me" potion, post gulp.

The Snow plough brakes suddenly. To his credit, and typical of a man who should be garlanded with National Treasure status, he admits his entire premise might be wrong. This temporarily confuses some of his beraters, who were salivating at the prospect of a continued fight. After a brief pause they continue to verbally thump him anyway, regardless of whether the referee has already stopped the fight. "Well," he resignedly harrumphs in belated defence, "I've only had a week to think through this theory, whilst you lot have had an academic lifetime."

Wisely moving away from his binary gender theory, he speaks movingly about his grandfather being a First World War general and about an Old Etonian father who was often distant. Snow endearingly self-deprecates that his family suffered downward mobility: "General, bishop, newsman."

Then he fights back, pointing out that if tertiary education is wholly gender equalised, how come no university offers a degree course in Men's Studies? Good point. "What would be on the curriculum for Men's Studies?" we ponder. "Porn, beer, football and being unfaithful," whispers a giggling blonde undergrad to her friend behind me. Bit sexist. We don't all like football, you know.

Snow casually cites flower-arranging as a typical female interest. This gen(d)eralisation offends an academic in the second row so much she starts fibrillating with rage. Her convulsive shock could not have been greater had Snow casually addressed her as "Professor Sugartits". She does ever so well making her point in public though, with lots of very clever words. Well done. Oh yeah, and she also has a swipe at men for being patronising. As if.

"Well," deadpans Jon Snow graciously in conclusion, "I'll take that message away burning in my ears."

Naively, I never realised before that under the so-called Fourth Wave of feminism men and women are becoming increasingly like cats and dogs. I have always advocated the advice to anyone informing me that "Men are from Mars, Women are from Venus" that they're both definitely from Earth – so deal with it! Personally, I consider myself a member of Team Human. Though surely this doesn't mean we have to conform to one homogenised gender. After all, we acknowledge, allow and celebrate defining differences in cultures, religions, sexuality and nations. Hopefully that's allowed in gender too. Then again I'm genuinely indifferent to Marmite, so what do I know?

Another vocal contributor lets rip under full sail complaining about the word "hysteria". Apparently its etymology stems from the Latin hystericus derived from the Greek hysterikós which defined hysteria as being a uniquely female condition caused by disturbances in the womb. Presumably these were nothing compared to the disturbances inside his house when the author of that particular definition returned home one night from his lexicography job to duck flying plates. Which may have been how the tradition of Greek plate smashing started?

Afterwards Jon Snow is bundled away from hostilities. A few feminists remain in the room making critical comments like plumes of smoke still rising from an empty battlefield.

It was a good event. Much better than a night spent shouting at the TV.

THE LISTENING PROJECT

Everyone in the room is wearing a blindfold. Including the man who is supposed to press "play" on an audio device enabling us to hear a recording. This probably accounts for the delay and fumbling noises, augmented with a muffled "oh bollocks".

The room – the JCR of an Oxford college – is so dark that our blindfolds are mainly redundant. The college appears to be burning the world's only single watt lightbulbs. Through the dimness we earlier made out arriving BBC Radio 4 presenter Fi Glover disrobing from her coat.

Fi positions herself on a flat floor stage in front of the audience sitting on five rows of very low chairs. Sinking into an equally low chair, her petite frame disappears from spectators' view. Anyone hoping to see Fi rather than just her voice will instead have exactly the same experience of listening to her on the radio. Even before we put on the blindfolds.

Fifteen minutes earlier I had arrived to see two volunteers placing blindfolds on empty chairs. "People will think they're marking reserved seats," says one of the volunteers. "No they won't," her colleague assures her. A man arrives and assumes the blindfolds are marking reserved seats. Another couple stride towards the front rows, only to be repelled like magnets sharing the same polarity when noticing the eye masks covering chairs. "They're reserved," he informs his partner.

Several students shuffle into the room. They have no qualms about occupying potentially reserved seats. Three undergraduate girls, noticeably possessing an indestructible self-confidence, sit behind me. One spots her chair doesn't contain a blindfold. "Where's my headband?" "They're not headbands – they're blindfolds. You know, like in *Fifty Shades of Grey*," says another girl mischievously – then blatantly wishes she hadn't when the others arrow her a curious look. Awkward.

The trio appear to be busily engaged in a world record attempt for the most times the word "like" can be used unnecessarily in a sentence. One is wearing a swath of wide-mesh netting draped around her neck as a scarf. She resembles a human lobster pot.

Girl Who Reads Fifty Shades is noticeably keen to move the conversation forward from this revelation, declaring: "Oh my god there's, like, booze!" spotting a table bedecked with wine bottles and glasses. "Ya, but it's like not allowed until afterwards." "What?!" says an outraged Lobster Pot. "Apparently you have to stick it out to the end to get a drink," says the other one in the trio, presumably forfeiting something for failing to employ the word "like" in her response. The others concur. "I just went to get some wine, and this girl was like 'it's for afterwards', and I was like 'Okay, but can I have some like now as well as like afterwards?' and she's like 'no' and I'm like 'that's so rude'."

The three react like an infringement of their basic human rights has just occurred. One starts scrolling her iPhone – presumably to find the contact details for Amnesty International.

"You should report her," says Lobster Pot. "She like so totally has," says an Oxford University student, mangling the English language beyond comprehension. One refers to studying English. Somewhat ironically, given they appear to be on a mission to reduce the English language from an estimated 200,000 words down to just ten – with "like" assuming the role of the previous 199,990 words in our national vocabulary.

Then Fi Glover is introduced by the college's Master. He quotes some magnificent praise of her illustrious broadcasting career, balanced by a quote from Jeffrey Archer describing her as "a jumped up little prat". This last quote prompts an affectionate gush of audience warmth towards her.

"Telling stories is the vertebrae of our lives," she begins. "Storytelling enables us to understand past and future generations. It is the best link we have to our ancestors." We all nod and make agreeing noises. One of the three behind me concurs, "That's like so true." Stories are our message in a bottle to future generations.

Fi instructs us to don eye masks and asks if we have any questions. Thankfully Girl Who Reads Fifty Shades doesn't ask, "What's the safe word?" In the recording, two anorexics, Amber and Sophia, are discussing their future. Thankfully it is a conversation and future both tinted with hope as they discuss the insidious and illogical appeal of the disease. Determinedly optimistic, both are expectant of overcoming their food phobia. And the two have applied to Oxford University. "They're much better now," Fi informs us. "Both girls have become campaigners on the issue and hosted a mental health awareness conference at their school chaired by Emma Thompson."

Fi Glover describes it as a gem of a deposit in that bank of wisdom that constitutes the *Listening Project* that she has presented since 2011 – a collaboration between Radio 4 and the British Library. Each week two members of the public are recorded discussing a true life event. Stripped of all distracting visuals, we hear the purity of their spoken words. In common with the three undergrads behind me, the girls on the recording litter their sentences with the word "like" deployed as an aural comma.

Somehow the three undergrads, in spite of being on the opposite side of the room, manage to occupy the first three places in the wine queue when the talk ends. They each hoover up a glass with one breathless glug and then collect an immediate refill.

With social embarrassment disintegrating with the prospect of free alcohol, Lobster Pot grabs two more glasses. Now perfectly balanced with a glass of wine in each hand, she retreats towards her friends. But she never makes those ten yards. After only five paces she is ambushed by a tutor. "Ah, Miss Changedhername, I see you're thoughtfully taking a wine to Fi Glover." "Hm? Er, that's like so totally what I'm doing," she fimble-fambles. Now denuded of any other option, she meekly approaches Fi and dolorously hands over her surplus glass of wine to the former *Saturday Live* presenter. New mothers giving away their first born would exhibit less emotional trauma.

"Hopefully I've inspired you to listen to some of the fascinating conversations of our fellow humans," concludes Fi. She like so totally has.

THE ONE WITH THE FRIENDS EPISODE

I am attempting to walk along the High Street. This is proving frustratingly difficult. Distracted phone checkers zigzag like drunks failing the straight-line test. As both have their heads down, the inevitable then occurs and a phone checker rams into a texter like dodgems.

How I envy anywhere with wide Parisian boulevards – like er ... I can't think of any city with Parisian boulevards. Oh yeah, of course ... Southport. One of my favourite facts coming up: Paris' spacious boulevards design was specially based on Southport in Lancashire. Really, it was. No, I didn't get that fact from Wikipedia. Napoleon had been to Southport and thought, "Yip, we're having this for Paris. Not so much the amusement arcades, whelk stalls and semi-dilapidated pier covered with one-arm bandits, but definitely the wide pavements. It would make a fantastic luxurious dog toilet."

Then a bus draws up and releases a swarm of terminated passengers onto the pavement. Whoever coined the phrase "it's as easy as putting one foot in front of another" clearly wasn't walking along Oxford's High Street when they invented it.

Then I see a further blockage ahead. The cause is a tall blonde. Five excited people are forming a protective circle around her, rotating strict turns to have their photos taken. As I millimetre closer, tutting like the second hand of a loud clock, I hear their foreign accents. The huddle breaks up and the photographers and the photographed disperse in deliberately different directions. They look at the pictures on their phones – instead of where they are going – necessitating me to tut even louder.

They all repeat an Eastern European name of the woman they have just captured on their cameras, like a hunter proclaiming the big game he's just tied to the safari jeep roof-rack. Then someone says the distinctly more prosaic name: "Lisa".

The awareness that I have seen someone famous – without any idea who – becomes inexplicably annoying. "Hmm," concludes my friend, when I eventually reach my destination, "it must be someone famous in an Eastern European country. You've probably just seen Poland's equivalent of somebody from *Eastenders*." Yet I felt a piercing recognition – she is somehow familiar.

Walking back along the High Street later I receive a phone call. This causes me to stop suddenly. An audible tut originates from behind me - how rude! The caller is a fellow scriptwriter. She is asking me for advice on whether to include a ten percenter in a script. Since "a ten percenter" is a joke that only 10% of the audience are expected to comprehend, I steadfastly caution against it: "Never include a ten percenter."

That night I search "Polish soap actress Lisa" in Google. Caution: Do not do this if not alone. Turns out there is a Polish soap actress called Lisa and Google immediately locates countless pictures of her enduring what is euphemistically captioned throughout as "a bikini malfunction". But when I eventually look up at her face, I notice she has dark hair. I am not particularly skilled at facial recognition, but even I know this is not the woman I had seen earlier in Oxford – with or without her top on.

Several weeks elapse and my acceptance that the conundrum is destined to remain unsolved hardens. But my frustration is also fanned by the seductive allure of a mystery. Long after the Polish actress's unsolved identity has been consigned to the cold case file, fate contributes an unpredicted breakthrough. Channel-hopping through TV stations in a dispiritingly futile attempt to avoid exploitative low grade TV ("...and coming up next on ITV2, *When Minor Celebs Get Attacked By Bees*...") provides a lead.

They say you are never more than ten metres away from rat. That may or may not be true. But you are definitely never more than ten minutes away from a *Friends* repeat. And I inadvertently find one – a *Friends* episode not a rat. "You're not going to believe this," I remark to my wife, "but I think I saw this woman off *Friends* a few weeks ago."

My wife does not consider this remark worthy of raising her gaze above a magazine. "I mean in Oxford – not on TV," I clarify. "Which one?" she asks, her tone spiked with ambivalence, though considering the new information still unworthy of raising her eyeline. "The tall blonde one." My wife doesn't say any words in her reply. But she does emit a noise: "Pah!" The translation for those who don't speak sound language is concisely this: "There are things more unlikely than that expressed eventuality, but given several days and a limitless supply of LSD I would be unable to imagine anything more mind-bendingly unlikely and implausible. Now shut up."

Granted, the chance of me encountering the blonde one from *Friends* blocking my pavement approach to Carfax is unlikely. Besides the last episode of *Friends* was transmitted over eleven years ago. And like us all, she will have physically altered. That's how time and human appearance works. And no, I don't like it either.

Googling *Friends* I discover the tall blonde one's character is called Phoebe Buffay. Oh well, she does look similar, but perhaps younger, I conclude. Then I check the name of the actress who portrays her: Lisa. Hmm. Well, a lot of people are called Lisa. There's a Lisa in *The Simpsons* and I haven't seen her near Carfax – although a bright yellow person in a red dress playing a saxophone would be more memorably conducive to recognition.

Then I discover her surname is of Polish origin: Kudrow. Her family were Polish Jews who escaped to the US from Germany. Although my certainty never reaches totality, I'm now at least eighty per cent sure I saw her.

That evening my wife, used to wearing her incredulity proudly, asks me: "Seen Lisa Kudrow again today? Or spotted Jennifer Aniston at the Cowley Centre?" "No," I report honestly, "but just now a black cat crossed my path." "Was it a smelly cat?" she asks. Never include a ten percenter.

The Celebrity Interview Attempt

I am standing in front of 160 people. 159 of them currently have an arm raised. Purely because I told them to. This is the sort of authority you can obtain once you are given a lectern and a working microphone. I have just asked the audience at a Literary Festival to "raise your hand if you can name a celebrity associated with balloons". One hundred and fifty-nine hands shot up. Then I add, "apart from Richard Branson." 158 hands come down immediately – my notes wafting in the ensuing breeze. Only a single lone hand remains upright, as noticeable as a lighthouse on a moonless night.

Hence I point to the arm's owner to elaborate. "Nena," he says. I suggest he elaborates further. "You know, with her 99 red balloons." Even allowing a dilution of "celebrities" to "slightly famous people" fails to prompt any further responses. After several minutes we have only Nena of *99 Luftballons* fame. Like Dr Samuel Johnson, the Germans spell "balloon" with only one "o". Dr Johnson should have used a dictionary – if he had one.

Richard Branson is a rather diminutive individual – in height if not stature. Not quite you-have-to-pick-him-up-to-say-hello tiny, but still a rather vertically challenged person. Which is a knowingly ironic observation, given that he has attained great heights himself – reached in both business and balloon. And he remains seemingly the only celebrity associated with aerostation. Strangely, it appears that there are not many well-known people associated with the 250-year-old tradition of ballooning.

Since Nena is voted by my impromptu focus group as the second most famous living person associated with balloons after Richard Branson, and I've been commissioned to write a magazine feature on famous balloonists, I decide to track down Nena instead. After all, we are surely intolerant by now of Branson doing everything in an attention-seeking, self-publicising way. I can imagine Branson popping out to buy milk would involve him skydiving into the corner shop or arriving at Tesco on top of a motorcycle pyramid. Do us all a favour, Branson, and spend more time at your pickling factory.

Nena's *99 Luftballons* remains the most successful German song in both UK and US chart history. The song succeeded where the Luftwaffe failed and conquered Britain. (That's enough war references.) Blitzing, storming and occupying the UK (Okay, that's definitely the last one) charts in 1984.

In fact, *99 Red Balloons* was primarily re-written for its English-language version. Nonetheless the English- and German-language original convey similar sentiments, both poetic and polemical: the ability to float away with a balloon serving as a functioning metaphor disrespectful of man-made borders. The song's germination occurred at a Rolling Stones concert in 1982 when the eponymous red coloured balloons were released – wondering whether they would reach East Germany and spark a military incident. In essence the song is about the innocence of balloons prompting fears of military intervention. Far from Europap it is actually a protest song. Which shows the unfortunate effect of the *Eurovision Song Contest* in polluting our assumptions that continental Europeans are incapable of producing any lyrically worthwhile tunes. "Boom-Bang-a-Bang" it ain't. Although, as an aside, it is worth pointing out that after fully sixty years, hasn't anyone else in our affected continent noticed by now that the *European Song Contest* isn't very good?

Eventually I acquire a contact from someone who knows someone who knows someone (there are two more "knows someone" in the chain) and I ask if they can broker me an interview with Nena. But the trail soon goes cold.

Anyone attempting to trace Nena may need to establish earlier than me that Nena is the name of the band, not the proudly 1980s and defiantly youthful-looking hair-gelled lead-singer adorning the band's album covers. That is a lady called Gabriele Kerner. Whereas the band split up in 1987, and the guitarist tragically died soon afterwards, Gabriele still records under the Nena moniker. One observation on the now 57-year-old is that she is still fitter than a butcher's dog's fiddle. Hearing Nena's superb song *Wir sind wahr* – recorded over 25 years after *99 Luftballons* – offsets a life's worth of prejudicial belief that the German language is unfitted to soulful expression.

Then an Oxfordshire musician reveals a German contact who provides me with an email address for Nena … er, I mean Gabriele. She is an uber celebrity in German but thankfully, I'm assured, speaks perfect English. Danke Gott. My first question to Nena will be, "So, have you ever been up in a balloon?" followed by: "Was it red?"

My plan is to arrive at the interview and present her with a fully inflated red balloon. Then remark: "There – now you've finally got a hundred." Hopefully it will transpire that Germans do have a sense of humour. Actually, there is a fairly vibrant comedy scene in Germany but the last thing comedy needs is a dismantling of convenient stereotypes. So I hope to track down Nena and discover her arriving punctually, eating a huge sausage in a bold, over-confident manner while sitting on her efficiently engineered, towel-draped sun lounger.

Determined to broker an interview, I send her a joke thoughtfully translated into German that I once wrote for Teutonic comedian Henning Wehn: A German, an Irishman, a Spaniard, a Greek and a Cypriot go into a pub and the German says, "Looks like this round is on me then."

One of Nena's people pings me an email and apologises in a rather formal Germanic way that Nena is currently busy working extremely hard (spot the stereotype) engineering her new CD. He quotes the title of her latest CD seven times in a short email – top PR work. I'd mention it here, but I've forgotten. If only he had mentioned it eight times – or granted me an interview – I might have remembered. Because I never did obtain an interview with Nena. It was a "nein".

But the Nena nein is offset by British singer Martha Tilston agreeing to grant me an interview about her ballooning experiences. A balloon adorns the cover of her *Machines of Love and Grace* album. See, I remember the name of her new CD, Nena!

SUGAR SNAPS

Celebrity sightings are like buses (and recessions): none for ages, then two come along at once. These two encountered celebrity anecdotes genuinely happened to me recently.

When I arrive early for a job interview, a receptionist instructs me, without lifting her gaze from a keyboard, to go to the second floor and help myself to coffee. But there's no milk. Or coffee. Then the door opens and two people enter, one explaining the layout of the building to a shorter man with a beard. It is Lord Sugar. Off. The. Telly. And I begin wondering if I've had this dream before.

The grumpy Lord departs shortly before my interview inquisitors arrive. Anxious to appear employable, I decide against announcing my celebrity sighting. Then I snap and unwisely declare: "I've just seen Lord Sugar in this room!" Yeah, course you did.

The interview limps to a conclusion, and I depart into the stairwell where Lord Sugar is being asked for an autograph. "Haven't you got a pen?" he gruffs like a bear with a hangover and thorns in all four paws. "Er … no," replies the woman behind this clearly under-planned operation. Offering an unnecessary "sorry" as I go past – there was plenty of room to pass him untroubled, but he has that effect on you – I receive a withering "you're fired!" look. On the way out, the receptionist informs me that "he's considering buying the building," still without raising her gaze above a monitor. Then Lord Sugar walks past me and leaves. My interviewers vanish, but significantly a few seconds too late to see Lord Sugar. I don't get the job.

The next day at an Oxford college I enter a room in search of milk. Perhaps compensating for not having any milk in it, the room does contain Stephanie Flanders.

Immediately a small group of people migrate towards her, forming an imperfect protective circle as if orbiting the brightest star in the room. And I can report that she is an immensely bright star, dazzling her entourage and chatting with impressive natural erudition. She is clearly now confused as to whether she is having a conversation or engaged in public speaking. She's also naturally prettier than allowed by uncharitably harsh TV lights; in natural luminosity her features are softer and more feminine. Basically, I'm reporting that Stephanie Flanders is HOT (well, now the *News of the World* has gone, someone has to report this sort of news, and *Oxfordshire Limited Edition* might as well muscle in on that vacant market). Luscious, pouting economist Stephanie takes care of her own figures … (OK, that's enough *News of the World* nostalgia).

People make conversation easily and visibly think, "Wow, my life doesn't suck 'cos I'm in a room talking to someone famous!" This is the basic motivation that prompts people to see celebrities. It's an odd calibration of meaning; an unusual place to go looking for purpose – or milk.

Then the piercing realisation strikes me that I haven't been talking to her – I've been listening. This is actually a better plan, as learning usually starts with Lesson One: Now Shut Up. And her naturally pedagogic tendencies ensure it's an autodidactic gift. Mindful about boasting later that I spoke with her, I commission my brain to come up with something to say – if not actively insightful, then at least a remark that avoids exposing stupidity: "Ms Flanders, does one of your relatives live next door to Homer Simpson?"

Meanwhile, Stephanie is effortlessly expounding clever theories about austerity budgets and expects us to know the difference between micro and macro economics. Clearly panicking, my brain keeps returning to the one fact I know about Stephanie Flanders: she is the daughter of the Flanders in the famous musical duo Flanders and Swann – you know, they sang *The Hippopotamus*. Asininely, I consider telling her this fact. Thankfully, though, one part of my brain calls another part an idiot, pointing out that she may already be in possession of this information.

Then she says something about Eurozone bailout projections. Surprisingly, I have a ready-polished conversational diamond in my pocket which I can pull out to dazzle the room: I once wrote a gag for the *Now Show* on a similar theme, and it killed in the Radio Theatre – though I could really use Hugh Dennis in my other pocket (or, more practically, Jon Holmes) to deliver it. Tried and tested material – it's morally acceptable to test jokes on live human beings – is exactly what I now require. So I await an opportunity to spring my comment.

When Stephanie indicates she's ending her sentence, I draw breath and clench my joke trigger – but then her brain sparks a follow-up point which leads to someone else returning a point, and Stephanie is now back to the net smashing, lobbing and volleying insights all around the court she's currently holding and winning every point. By the time I can speak, my remark is already five subjects out of date.

I consider checking Wikipedia on my phone for another Stephanie fact, then remember that this is unlikely to be a fruitful plan – and not purely because my phone is a Nokia – but because Wikipedia once informed me that musician Van Morrison was born in a van while Jim Morrison was born in a gym.

Stephanie talks about doing "the ten"; I realise that this is how the cool people refer to the news. I decide instantly from now on I'm going to call it "the ten" too. Hence that night I announce to my wife: "The ten's on soon." "The what?" "Thought we'd watch the ten?" "Watch ten what?" "News." "Oh, the 10 o'clock news? Why didn't you say so?" "I was saving time by abbreviation." "Really? Like when you asked for the TOBOA and it took ages to discover you meant The Oxford Book of Abbreviations?" She shoots me the same look I recognised yesterday from Lord Sugar.

Then I recall that Stephanie Flanders writes a superb blog and decide I should inform her that I appreciate it – but someone important has now ushered her out of the room and it's too late.

I never did find any milk in the room, though I did find Sugar in one the previous day.

THE KATE MIDDLETON VISIT

It's the sort of event that prompts strangers into volunteering information: "I was just standing at the bus stop on our council estate and I saw Kate Middleton – you know, the Duchess of Cambridge. She's lovely!" enthused a star-struck local. It's surely one of the highest impact lines ever uttered on the backseat of the no. 3 as the bus dutifully chugs through thickening traffic towards Rose Hill.

Having lived on the estate for over twenty years, I want to be in attendance on the only day the world is going to be interested in us. A sizeable crowd, later wilfully exaggerated by all the national news bulletins, gathers outside Rose Hill Primary School's newly painted rails.

A royal car appears – just like royal cars on the TV, only without the number plates pixelated - and The Duchess materialises wearing what is described to the press as "a black personalised apron"; typical, I think, she's coming to Rose Hill and they force her to wear a bulletproof vest. However, it transpires to be a genuine apron, with the words "Miss Catherine" affectionately embroidered especially for her visit to The Art Room charity taking place in the school. The children responsible for making the apron are probably still residing in detention and writing 10,000 lines of "The Duchess of Cambridge is Katherine with a 'K'".

Rose Hill becomes the third item on the national TV news. Furthermore, it's a positive story: take that snooty North Oxford with your distinctive lack of royal future-Queen blood.

Even so, part of me is attending her visit with detached aloofness, wishing that if I was a ten-year-old pupil at the school, then I would hold up my homemade artwork: a banner proclaiming "Power is not a birthright!" before being marched off to the detention room by Special Branch.

Yet it is hugely important that Kate regally blesses our area of Oxford ahead of the more pampered inhabitants beneath their Dreaming Spires; there are no spires within two miles of Rose Hill, but she has chosen to visit Town not Gown. When you observe her republicanism-melting smile energetically provided afresh for countless children, I can confirm that the woman on the bus was right: Kate is indeed lovely – though I'm concerned about metamorphosing into one of those toadying, sycophantic royal reporters terrified of filing any negative copy in case they forfeit their seat on the press bus. One journalist once obsequiously grilled HRH the Queen Mother on TV with his unrelenting Paxmanesque interruptions: "It is such an honour, ma'am, to hear you speak – is there anything at all, ma'am, you would like to say to the nation?" Rude.

Back at work, the women want to know what Kate was wearing when I reveal seeing her earlier; my reply, "A brown coat and some shoes" is greeted as being woefully insufficient. Fortunately there are numerous websites and blogs with names like WhatKateWears.com dedicated to revealing her daily wardrobe choices. This must be a persistent source of annoying pressure for Kate, though not as big an annoyance as WhatPippaWears.com obtaining more hits!

I ask my wife, who is not the speediest of getting-readyers, how long it would take her if numerous websites were reporting her daily clothing decisions. "Probably four to six days," she replies honestly.

For those who consider "brown coat and some shoes" insatiately inadequate, I'll elaborate: Kate wore a walnut coloured long sleeve wool dress coat with dove patterning from Irish designer Orla Kiely. Once papped and reported, this designer creation instantly disappeared as copykates everywhere required only a few minutes of frantic mouse-clicking to eradicate Kiely's entire online stock. Copykates (I would love that word to be included in the OED – anyone know Susie Dent's email address?) then rushed to identify her ankle boots, and even her earrings, before swooping to clear any remaining stock from the High Street. "She is good for the struggling High Street," remarked my wife; true, but so is Starbucks, and they are not due to receive quite as much from the Civil List. Nevertheless, Kate's mother Carole spent her formative years living in a North London council estate flat in Southall, so perhaps the blue blood is turning redder?

Remaining in recently rejuvenated Rose Hill (over 200 properties have been stylishly rebuilt) for fully two hours, Kate mingled with many locals – which concerned me, as I expected several people would have to put fags down first if she did a handshaking walkabout, but her security seemed relaxed. "Can her bodyguard woman do Kung Fu?" asked a child.

Another child presented her with some treats for her dog, and then Kate Middleton, The Duchess of Cambridge, gave the world's press an exclusive to knock the Euro debt crisis off the front pages by choosing Rose Hill, yes our Rose Hill, to confirm that the gathering rumours were true: the happy royal couple had already chosen a name. Kate stepped purposefully forward towards a reporter's microphone to announce that they are having … (going to pause here to build effect … just a bit longer) … a cocker spaniel puppy called Lupo (the Italian word for "wolf"). The kids seemed delighted, the adults less so. The *Hollywood Reporter* leads with the puppy story that evening, name-checking both Lupo and Rose Hill.

Then more waves and smiles, and Kate is photographed inspecting a red dot on her dress coat – the Special Branch team becoming noticeably relaxed after making sure it is a speck of children's paint, not a sniper's tracer dot. Eventually she departs along Ashurst Way, the no. 3 bus courteously allowing her right of way.

Later I casually mention seeing Kate Middleton at the Rose Hill bus stop too; they ask me if she had the correct change for the fare. Clearly they don't believe me.

HOME LIFE

THE SOCIAL FAUX PAS

I am wrong. Remarkably this is the 3,468th consecutive occasion that I've been wrong – according to my wife. I thought that on the 2,317th occasion I was actually right, so lodged an appeal – but the appeal was unanimously rejected and I was still wrong. My wife handles all the appeals.

Last weekend we visited a friend's house. I say "friend", but unfortunately my wife insists that her title must now wear an uncomfortable "ex" prefix. Disinclined as regular readers may be to consider other possibilities, this newly awarded ex-friend prefix is entirely my fault. It is because I am apparently afflicted by a form of comedy Tourette's.

When we arrive at our friend Michelle's home she ushers us into her tidy garden where she finishes watering her courgettes. Yes, she is quite middle-class. If you are middle-class you say "courgettes", while the upper classes prefer "zucchini". If classless like me, then you say "your tiny marrows aren't very big this year."

Irrigating her veg patch necessitates Michelle filling her watering can. A manoeuvre accomplished by bending down with her derrière protruding in order to control the tap on a plastic tank that neatly harvests rainwater from her roof.

"Nice butt," I casually observe to my wife and friend (sorry, ex-friend). No one laughs. Tough garden.

"What??!!!" declares my horrified wife.

"I meant that it's a nice water butt she's got," I quickly clarify.

"No you didn't," says my wife with some justification. We had not been to this lady's house before and my wife is keen we make a good impression. If we visit her again, I will basically have to be tied up in front of the house like a dog outside a supermarket, whilst my wife goes inside alone.

"Oh it's a clever *double entendre*," comments Michelle with gracious emollience.

Classily Michelle sprays occasional French phrases into her conservation like puffs from a scent bottle. "*Jeu d'esprit*," she declares. "With me it's always *esprit de l'escalier*." The latter literally means "wit of the stairs" – a scrumptiously descriptive phrase for formulating a witty comeback too late when already departing.

Ordinarily my absolute *bête noire* is people pretentiously importing French phrases *de rigueur* into English; it's so *passé* to show off being *au fait* with *bons mots*. But Michelle is sufficiently likeable to be forgiven such behaviour.

You may be concluding that my inability to resist inappropriate jokes accounted for the friendship-costing social *faux pas* here. I certainly did at the time.

Having written for several comedians, I can report that some comics are permanently "on". Shakespeare was correct and the world really is a constant stage to some – while others erect a tall fence along the demarcation line that separates work from personal life. This has always struck me as odd; there's nothing worse than a glorious open gag opportunity missed, the ball left neglected on the comedy goal-line with the goalkeeper stranded. Hence if there's a gag tap-in opportunity available, my foot will be twitching.

Sometimes people take surprising offence at comedic intention, regardless of an obvious motive to amuse not abuse. Recently one of Europe's foremost geologists kindly consented to help check some journalistic copy I had written. He branded me flippant for authoring a sentence that included a gentle gag about the processes involved in the earth's formation exactly 4.54 billion years ago – give or take a fortnight. How can a joke about something that happened 4.54 billion years ago be offensive? What – too soon?!

With courgettes suitably watered and husband suitably chastised, we retreat inside Michelle's house for promised tea and cake. Michelle is a good host and carries a chinking tea tray into the lounge, augmented with the exciting addition of individually wrapped Rocky Road marshmallow biscuits. She makes a joke, pointing out, "I'm sure there aren't any rocks in them. Or bits of road." We laugh and I add, "In the same way there's no toad in toad-in-the-hole, no dog in a hot dog, and cock-a-leekie soup doesn't contain any…"

My wife sits with her mouth wide open, paralysed by social embarrassment.

… leekie," I conclude.

To her credit Michelle laughs profusely, although she attempts to repress it for the sake of my wife's somewhat puritanical stance on the tone of proceedings.

Michelle excuses herself to fetch some more biscuits. "Behave!" orders my wife, "Michelle is a classy lady, she doesn't want to hear filth from the likes of you."

Glancing around the front room reveals that this appraisal of her classiness is correct. Ornaments – or *objets d'art* as Michelle refers to them - rest on doilies; figurines of ballerinas are positioned on dustless window sills.

En route to her mouth – still wide open from gasping at my earlier felicitousness – my wife drops her miniature Rocky Road resulting in crumbs cascading down the expensive-looking sofa. Michelle rushes to the kitchen and returns with a dust pan and brush. "Don't worry, there's no stain at all," Michelle announces calmly. "Help yourself to another one." My wife, glowing with embarrassment, tears the foil wrapper off her replacement marshmallow biscuit.

Then she lifts up the settee cushion to ensure all the crumbs have been recovered from her previously jettisoned teatime snack. Retrieving what she concludes is the wrapper from her earlier Rocky Road, she places it onto a dainty bone china saucer before positioning it on the low coffee table. All of us stare at it for some time, while our six eyes and three brains process the information.

"So, I think we should be going soon," says my wife. Michelle is suddenly silent, glowing sufficiently red to match her tasteful burgundy curtains. One of her cats enters the room and we all seize on the provided conversational topic this represents with transparent relief.

"Well," says my wife in a tone that conveys the sentiment is spiked with sarcasm, "that went well," as we depart after spending the last thirty minutes determinedly undeviating from the sole conversational subject of Michelle's cat. I nod, afraid to speak. "Obviously we'll never be seeing her socially again," she adds. I suspect this is a temporary overreaction, and unwisely proffer the opinion that my wife should forgive herself.

"I mean," continues my wife, "what an insensitive and embarrassing thing to do. And poor Michelle's so nice. What an egregious social *faux pas*." I nod sagely, my expression a mix of ruefulness and regret.

"What were you thinking of," announces my wife, "making such an insensitive remark about the water butt?"

She doesn't mention the empty condom wrapper she had retrieved from the sofa. *C'est la vie.*

THE GAME OF PASS THE PARCEL

It was just an unassumingly small white card. As it lay on my doormat it didn't look important enough to ruin my entire week. But it did.

Left by a parcel company, the card was written in an accusatory style of "How dare you be out?" with an accompanying tone of 'Have you considered getting agoraphobia? – it makes our job a lot easier."

The card implored me to ring a number. You are greeted by a pre-recorded woman who, clearly recorded in the same way they make hostage videos, has been forced to say with exaggerated cheerfulness, "Thank you for calling We Despise Our Customers (name changed for legal and comedy reasons). You now have 173 options. Press 1 to hear about exciting new business solutions." By about Option 9 "To learn more about our exciting business products, press…" there is a distinctly audible wavering in her voice, and it is at this point that her captors probably showed her a photo of her family to ensure she carries on with restored perkiness.

The option I want – the one everyone who would ever call this infernal number only ever wants – is the very last option. I am then required to read the card's number into voice recognition software. For the machine to recognise me this necessitates having enunciation like a 1940s BBC announcer reading the news from Alexandra Palace. This prompts the prissy hostage woman to infer with pitying aloofness, "Please pronounce that letter or number again," whereas it's obvious what she's really saying is: "Are you Northern? If so, goodbye."

They tell me to go to a specific post office. Hence I go there but am greeted with "Why did you come here?" as we push my card to and fro between each other in the dipped counter tray. "They told me to go to this post office." "Why did they do that?" We are going around in circles so quickly the centrifugal force is starting to make me feel faint.

"Could you please have a look," I implore. "Well," he harrumphs as if I've just informed him he's a rare blood group match and asked him to donate a kidney, not look through a pile of packages immediately to his left, "It won't be here." He moves at the pace of an arthritic sloth. "Not there," he declares with detectable triumphalism. This is evidently a man who has pruned all unnecessary activity from his working life; he likely won't take sugar in his tea, to remove the need to do all that energetic stirring.

Sensing an impasse and that I am customarily out of my depth, my wife steps in and attempts to ensure the man searches for our parcel. She decides upon a tactical activation of feminine charm. "Okay, anything for a pretty lady," he says. An audible squeak emits from my wife struggling to repress her default feminist settings. Even after a proper look – or, more accurately, a proper glance – the parcel remains unfound.

I go home and arrange delivery online. This requires creating an account password so long that my computer risks insufficient memory to store it. The computer tells me the parcel is at a different post office. So I go the next day. Different post office, different man, same encountered recalcitrance and outcome. "Why did they ask you to come here?" he enquires.

Then the company call me. The woman sounds so distracted she must be overtaking on a busy motorway while simultaneously attempting to talk down a Boeing 747 with only one engine not on fire. "It's already at the post office," she says. "No it isn't," I counter. "Yes it is." "Oh no it isn't." It's too early in the year for pantomime dialogue. She remains insistent that if I go to another post office the parcel will be there.

I go there. It's not there. Obviously. I knew that. You knew that. "Well," says the man, "if we had it there would have been a £1 pick-up surcharge. So you've saved that." Which is similar to telling someone who has just lost a hand in a freak accident that at least he now won't have to fork out for two gloves.

I ring the company again. After pressing more keys than a copy-typist could feasibly manage in an especially productive day, I am connected to what they term "a customer care professional" – formerly known as "a person". They ask a series of prepared questions, vanished hope audible in the poor call-centre operative's voice. His workplace environment must routinely confiscate staff's shoe laces and belts before each shift.

He asks, "How do you actually know your parcel is not at any of the post offices?" This is surely unanswerable. "Is that a question from the All Souls entrance exam?" I enquire. He arranges a guaranteed re-delivery for the next day. "Guaranteed," he repeats.

They don't deliver the next day. The day afterwards I ring them. "We'll get it delivered to your house as 'priority'," they announce, "in four days' time. If you want it sooner, have you considered collecting it from a post office?"

I now appear to be trapped in a Kafkaesque plot of inescapable self-repeating loops. Had Kafka written *The Trial* today he would have retitled it "The Week I Spent Trying to Collect My Parcel".

Four days later a van squeals to an abrupt halt outside my house. With the engine left running impatiently, a man thrusts a package into my hand and apologetically confirms it was at the designed Post Office all along. It could probably have fitted through my letter box.

"This had better be worth it," announces my wife. The parcel has American postage, and is a (by now considerably belated) birthday present from my elderly Godmother. It contains packets of peanuts from her home State – the postal charge overwhelmingly greater than the value of the contents.

"Oh, it's only peanuts," confirms my wife. Something she's akin to saying when opening the mail – though usually my pay slips. "Peanut?" asks my wife opening the box. "I can't," I reply. Not because they are now probably well past their sell-by date, but because I have become severely allergic to them. Parcels. Not nuts.

THE NICE AU PAIR

Our neighbours have recently taken delivery of a French au pair. You really can get anything off the Internet these days.

Bernadette is from Nice and uncompromisingly French. "We do not mind if our prime minister has a mistress. You English are much more concerned about this than us French," she tells me during our first meeting. I enquire as to how the numbers compute in France with gender demographics, given that every Frenchman appears to have both (1) a wife or girlfriend, and (2) a mistress. "It is because a wife receives her lover when her husband is visiting his mistress." Clever. Though I genuinely do not know if she is joking.

I ask her what the French stereotypical view is of Englishmen. "You all eat roast beef, carry an umbrella because it always rains, and you all have ginger hair." Right. "That's a relief," I reply, "as I thought you'd say we were terrible lovers." "Oh yes, I forgot – you are all terrible lovers." *Merci* for that.

We meet her for the second time when she is sent round to borrow chairs for her employers' house party. Being French she immediately sits down without being asked, and makes it clear she intends to take a coffee break. French coffee breaks tend to last … well, from 9am to 5pm in my experience, so I wonder how long she intends to stay. Probably until after we have served a nine course lunch. The French spurn fast food and appreciate slow food – especially snails.

I decide to impress her with my sophisticated fluent French. "Bonjour," she says, batting my offered word straight back to emphasise my incorrect pronunciation. "My employing family cannot speak any words of French," she says. "What about the words 'au pair'"? I ask. "Non," she replies. Before repeating the words "au pair" correctly.

The next day she returns the chairs. And immediately sits down, like a dog in front of an empty bowl awaiting food. Basically, it dawns on me, she is here to laugh at my pathetic comedy French; clearly to her I am like that Englishman in *'Allo 'Allo* constantly mispronouncing French: "Good moaning, Bernadette."

A week later we see her again. Her employer rings and asks if she can send Bernadette to borrow a lemon. "Nous avez une citron!" I say opening the door, glowing with pride at my bilingualism. She answers me in English. Dismissive of my pathetic attempt at French, she repeats my sentence, correcting every word I have just embarrassingly uttered. Then she asks if I have a map of Oxford. In my *'Allo 'Allo* French I probably say, "I have a mop if you want to take a leak."

My wife enters the kitchen and remarks, "Oh, I see for Bernadette you've opened the expensive special coffee you got me for my birthday." "Well," I justify, "the French are very discerning about their coffee." My wife responds by asking: "Can I have quick rendezvous in the hallway?" Bernadette correctly re-pronounces "rendezvous" for my wife's benefit. "Hmm. Bernadette's very attractive, isn't she?" announces my wife. "Err, is she?" I respond cautiously. "You mean to say you didn't notice?" my wife checks. "Err … no, not really," I reply unconvincingly. "Just nice to have someone with whom I can practise my French, er, what's the word … you know … vocab," I say. "Your French what?" asks my wife. "Vocab," I clarify. "You haven't got any French vocab." I do my best to look offended.

A few days later I am making cupcakes for my birthday. Well, no one else has offered. Then I discover I have no baking trays. Hands covered with chocolatey dough is not the best time to make this discovery, so I ring up my neighbours. Bernadette answers. "Oui, we have them. I will pop them round in a jiffy." Already she is *au fait* with English idioms. For which I compliment her when she arrives a few seconds later. She corrects my pronunciation of *au fait*.

She teaches me the French word for baking tray. I repeat it twelve times like a parrot with learning difficulties. After thirteen failed attempts we both give up. However, I inform my wife that evening, "I've learnt another French word today." "Was it the word for midlife crisis?" she asks. "Er, no," I reply surprised, "do you know the French word for midlife crisis?" "Yes," replies my wife, "Bernadette".

We visit our neighbours for a coffee and a catch-up. Initially Bernadette is not around. After ten minutes she enters the kitchen where we are assembled and washes paint brushes in the sink. Even for painting she is elegantly attired. Presumably French women can order a range of designer dresses from Versace's "For Decorating" range. There is, however, a blobby smudge of azure paint in her hair. "It is nearly done," she announces. "*Fait accompli*," I say.

Predictably she corrects both words. She starts to make a coffee but doesn't ask anyone else if they want one. Clearly ten minutes is the longest time any French worker has gone without a lengthy café break. It transpires that she has been painting the tiny downstairs toilet for four days now – it is no larger than the average cardboard box.

She helps herself to another coffee and beats me to the last *pain au chocolat* – pronouncing the word as a pre-emptive correction of any mispronunciation I may be planning. Unusually for a French person she curtails her coffee break after only fifty minutes and goes back to put in another lengthy ten-minute shift. This short absence is used to discuss her merits as an au pair. "She's fantastic," declares our host. It turns out that decent au pairs are difficult to find, harder to keep and expensive to run – just to keep them in superior coffee, designer dresses for decorating and hair paint remover.

"No," says my wife when we return home from next door with a detectable this-is-the-final-word-on-the-subject, "You'll have to choose something else for your birthday as we're not getting a French au pair".

EPILOGUE

Shortly after I had filed this column Bernadette (not her real name, obviously) returned permanently to France. My near neighbour informed me of the memorable news: "Bernadette has an STD." My instant reaction to this news was to declare, "I've got an STD too: 01865 for Oxford". Then it clicked. Oh.

"You mean Sexually Transmitted Dis…." "Yes, of course." Only later it transpired – Bernadette's English not being as good as our French is woeful – that her boyfriend, who lived in southern France and never visited Bernadette in the four months she had been residing in the UK, was the one – not Bernadette – who had recently caught the STD. And I don't mean (01765) for Clermont-Ferrand. This awards him a 10/10 for maximum stereotypical Frenchness. What's that Blackadder line? He's "as likely to move as a Frenchman who lives next door to a brothel!"

Unassailable evidence had accrued that he had been caught dipping his baguette into someone else's saucy French dish du jour, greedily helping himself to the à la carte when he should have stuck strictly to the available set house menu.

It was remarkably understanding of Bernadette to go home and "look after him, as my poor *chéri* needs nursing." My wife assumed that the form this bedside palliative care would take included several hefty kicks to his *boules*.

Incidentally, I once read this column to a class I was asked to lecture on comedy writing techniques and asked them to identify who was cast in the 'straightman' role. Nearly everyone declared it was my wife. Wrong, I'm afraid. My wife gets the best line in the piece. In fact the straight(wo)man is Bernadette – she may be responsible for causing most of the laughs as comedic chaos circles around her like angry bees next to spilt honey – but she remains crucially aloof to the comedy throughout.

NIECE TO SEE YOU

This month a relative visited. We had a niece time, you could say, if you have a proclivity for low grade puns. Both parties have agreed not to inform her parents about illegal activities she undertook on our watch. She would like to say hello to her mates Sasha and Sarah.

At 17 her maturity is clearly of the late flowering variety. Her parents believe she passed her driving test – without seeing her have lessons – but I'm not so sure. Suspicion was aroused when she arrived on the driveway and shunted our recycling bin. Her parents decided they required a break – a necessity I cannot overestimate given our 48-hour exposure.

Last time she was left unsupervised for a weekend, all three emergency services were called. Chastised but worryingly unrepentant, such nefarious behaviour ensures home alone is no longer an option. She has agreed to pay for the damage out of her pocket money. Estimates conclude that she will be eligible to start receiving pocket money again when she turns 53. She's starting her A levels; I think she's doing English, History and Delinquency.

Her parents bring her over. "Why couldn't I drive?" she whines when getting out of the car. I make a point of stroking the huge crack in our wheelie bin. "We are so grateful," gushes her mother. This amount of gratitude does not bode well.

Missy (a name agreed for this article) doesn't want to greet us, saying, "show me to my cell," and scurrying upstairs in a teenage huff that can only culminate in one sound: the traditional door slam.

We worried about what to feed a teenager. Her mother advised us: "Serve whatever she wants. Walk to Waitrose and get it. Believe me it's easier in the end." "Weren't you hoping she'd grow out of this when she turned three?" "Yes. We're really hoping 18 will be the year when it happens."

We select conversational openers but they all bounce off teenage recalcitrance and truculence. Then she suddenly becomes communicative, buzzing like she has received a change of batteries. "He's like so cool, so I'm like 'get serious' like..." She's speaking into her phone while I say to my wife, "Like this tea is like good, like." "Excuse me," she says into the phone before addressing us, "Are you attempting to mock me?" "Err. No. Yes. Sorry." "I don't think that's appropriate." "I'm very sorry." My wife, who laughed earlier, chastises me.

Missy then makes a change more pronounced than a chameleon with a drag act. "That was superb ham, Mrs Smith. Did you make it yourself?"

"Er, no, I didn't make my own ham. But thank you." She's clearly up to something. I flash her a strong "I know what you're up to" look. (I have no idea what she's up to.)

"Mummy and daddy" (oh, please – you're 17) "allow me a likkle drinkie to help me sleep. May I have a drink?" "Of course, sweetie. What would you like?" asks my wife, disappearing into a carefully laid trap. "Just a tiny vodka".

"WHAT?! NO! You can't have vodka!" "I shouldn't have asked," Missy moves. "Not all generations are progressively modern enough to teach responsible drinking." She then clicks an imaginary chess clock.

Surely such transparent manipulation would never work on an adult. "We're modern – we could get her a tiny vodka," suggests my wife. "We don't have any," I retort. "We could walk to Waitrose."

"There's somewhere I should go tonight, to help my future employment development," says Missy. What an actress. "Where should you go?" asks my wife. I suggest RADA. They ignore me. "I know not everyone will be supportive of my endeavours," Missy continues, shooting a look at me and neatly dividing us into nice wife and nasty husband. Clever. She's decided my wife holds the power here; she probably picked that up in the driveway upon arrival.

"Two requests please: can I have a glass of milk and see a band tonight in Birmingham?"

"OK," I say.

"Thanks for being cool, guys."

I leave a cruel gap just sufficient to believe she's got away with it. "Can I just ask about one of those things? The glass of milk one, obviously." "Cold milk is fine," she replies trying to make her bedroom – but there are just too many stairs. "How are you getting to Birmingham?"

She wants to drive. This will involve a death toll equivalent to major earthquakes on the news, so we persuade her to go by train. We pick them up from Banbury station afterwards. Ignoring her directive

not to speak with her friends, I converse with a lik
me that because she is overweight, when joining
kids snubbed her, except Missy. Suddenly prou
Missy in the mirror.

At 2am the Oxford ring road lights diffract across tin
now sleeping faces, projecting kaleidoscopic patterns. The lioness sleeps
tonight. Who knows what fresh chaos and destructive mayhem she
will bring to the watering holes and savannas of her teenage landscape
tomorrow, but for now there is a calmness possessing her, as I catch a boy
looking at her with honest affection. Maybe if she discovers redemptive
romance, love will be the artist in the sculpture garden of her future,
shaping her ambitions and ideals, crafting hopes and accomplishments,
exhibiting her successes and failures ahead. She lazily opens one eye and
says to the boy, "What are you looking at, perv?"

The next morning her parents pick her up. "Can I drive?" "Not
really. We just got the insurance claim for that wall, sweetie," counsels
her mother. Missy says she won't tell her parents we granted permission
to attend an over-18s gig (she never told us it was over-18s) or that
we allowed her access to vodka. As soon as she departs I check the
securely locked drinks cabinet. The vodka has been expertly removed
without any sign of a break-in; I have no idea how she did that. Later
we find in her vacated room, amongst multiple nail vanish stains and
an inexplicable dent in the skirting board, a bottle of vodka with a
post-it note declaring: "Thx for stay." My wife is overcome. "Ah, she's
lovely," an opinion she refuses to be diluted by me announcing that it
is our vodka bottle. "I feel deceived," says my wife. "You said we didn't
have any vodka."

Later Missy sends a text: "You can write about me if you say hello
to my mates. And you MUST do it in the first paragraph." There is no
way I am agreeing to that.

THE SEQUEL

Previously I wrote a column about my niece coming to stay for a
weekend. This seemingly mundane domestic occurrence resulted in
an appearance on Radio 4's *Woman's Hour* describing how I looked
after a relative's teenage offspring for 48 hours with ensuing defused

...ageddon (an actress read out some of my despatches from the ...ont line of childcare).

Shortly afterwards a correspondent demanded via the *Oxford Times* letters page that my niece Missy [an agreed alias] stayed again because of the entertainment value her visit will no doubt reprise. Hence, like an applause-drunk clown sliding himself down the greased barrel of a human cannonball gun barrel one more time, I invite Missy to stay again for a weekend.

To say her parents are grateful of their 48-hour leave pass is an understatement – people handed water after being discovered lost roaming the desert have displayed blasé insouciance compared to the gratitude they express. My wife makes arrangements to move all breakables into storage while I consider sticking brown-tape on our windows with World War Two chic. Missy's delinquent antics have ensured her reputation. She is banned from being home alone even though she has reached 17 – a sensible policy that has already significantly reduced the workload on the already overstretched 999 operatives. It would genuinely be unsurprising if we had to dial 999 and request all three emergency services – and not because we had an ill burglar on fire.

Needless to say, Missy's sudden spike in fame has not been lost on her and this time she is a willing visitor, hoping that another column about her will generate further Radio 4 mentions, raising her fame stock so highly that she considers herself a shoe-in for a *Celebrity Big Brother* appearance next year. Already she is work-shopping product names for her own brand of perfume. When did celebrity become a valid job aspiration for school leavers?

It's only a few months since I last saw her, but there's an identifiable maturity stating to break out of the teenage egg – cracks appearing in her truculent shell announcing an overdue hatching of adulthood.

A few hours into her visit Missy enquires, "Have you got anything for your column about me yet?" "No, not yet." Watching TV, reading magazines and early to bed hasn't given us a lot to report. On Saturday we pick up a neighbour's greyhound. The dog's owner is elderly and unable to walk him, so we volunteer. This is appreciated by all parties concerned, except the dog. He is remarkably reluctant to be taken for a walk and it is clear that we are dealing with probably Britain's only agoraphobic greyhound. I drag, rather than walk, the dog along the path. At one stage I pick him up and carry him, so that we can reach the nearby park in less than thirty minutes. As Missy points out, this probably does not constitute dog walking – dog carrying being a separate entity which may provide him with less beneficial exercise. Although it remains socially acceptable to carry dogs on escalators, apparent this does not extend to parks.

Once at the park, I drag him along the turf like a reluctant water skier. Two trace lines of stubbornness appear on the turf marking our route. Missy has already complained about the walk and asks, "has anyone walked this far before, like ever? We should get charity sponsorship for walking this distance," after we have gently strolled 500 yards.

"Have a go with the dog," I say handing her the lead. The dog is motionless. I can see how this might not help raise Missy's boredom threshold. "I'm bored," they both say (OK, only Missy communicated this in English.) Then something happens to transform both their moods.

A middle-aged man and a teenage boy who is likely his son appear together, walking their dog. Our greyhound and Missy immediately prick up their ears, and head straight over to them. Both canines form an instant attraction to each other, as do the two lead holders. Yapping and pawing, Missy and her new teenage friend communicate while the dogs sniff each other. I've never seen Missy or the greyhound behave like this before, their demeanours utterly altered. Missy starts laughing like a hyena at a comedy club during a nitrous oxide leak.

After several theatrical watch checks the other teenager's father announces it is time to go, but his son remains steadfastly rooted, flirting back with matching alacrity. The father starts to pull his dog away. The dog reacts by digging his paws into the ground so he can continue sniffing our greyhound. Missy and her new friend replicate almost exactly the same reaction. I reclaim the lead and pull our greyhound away like I'm participating in a tug of war contest as the other dog owner pulls his dog. He groans with the expressed energy. Placing an arm on his son's shoulder he tries to drag him away too, eventually managing to slowly slide both dog and son backwards while they carry on yapping. Both leave a trail in the cut-up turf. I consider clasping the strap on Missy's shoulder bag to drag her away.

Eventually unstuck, the uncoupled duos are fully separated. Both Missy and the greyhound give me a teeth-displaying snarl. Missy pants, "he ... was ... like ... so ... fit." The greyhound's tongues hangs out dribbling saliva onto the already slippery turf as we head towards a café. Neither of them show any signs of curtailing their whimpering. "Can't we stay for longer?" they whine.

Rejecting the momentarily tempting idea of tying them both up outside the café to treat myself to a ten-minute peace break, I obtain a water bowl for the greyhound. At the café Missy is concerned we have yet to experience adventures worthy of column inclusion. When two teas are dismissively plonked in front of us by a visibly bored waitress who has forgotten our accompanying muffin order, old-style, unreformed delinquent Missy makes a brief comeback. Family reporting restrictions forbid me from recounting what she did next. Needless to say, I am forced to chastise her.

"You're boring," she says and punishes me by inserting two white headphones playing music so loud on her "personal" music device that people at other tables can no longer hear their conversations. "Why did you do that?" I ask. "To try and get material for your column. It might help me to become famous." Yeah, that's me – comedy writer, occasional stand-up, low selling author, local paper columnist and star maker. Still, if it impresses Missy, and she's delusional that I can help her become famous, it's a manipulation technique I'll shamelessly deploy to ensure she behaves. Few things impress Missy, I've noticed, other than "well fit" teenage boys.

I ask her where she intends to be in five years. "Still here, probably. Service is slow, isn't it?" she replies. "I dunno. People say I should do law as I can be quite the lawyer." Then we have a proper adult conversation. It's like speaking to an actress backstage, as if Missy has stepped out of her deleterious teenage miscreant character and we are discussing unswervingly grown-up themes, expressing a shared apprehension about our futures. Then she snaps back into her familiar obstreperous character, like a silent interval bell has rung backstage at a theatre announcing the performance is about to recommence.

Walking home, Missy whines that her feet hurt walking in heels, matched by the dog acting like he has a thorn in his paw; I can only carry one of them.

We go to a shop where Missy announces she has "walked for, like, ever. Can we get a taxi?" I plead that I am very lowly paid, thus cannot justify spending money on taxis. She consents to get the bus as a gesture of self-sacrifice normally reserved for someone denoting a kidney.

But Missy has far more spectacular plans.

THE SEQUEL TO THE SEQUEL

"Did you take the dog for a carry again?" asks my wife when we eventually return home. Missy immediately announces her intention to tackle homework, thereby triggering the suspicion alarm; "I really should get on with my homework" being a completely original phrase unuttered in her previous sixteen years on this planet. She bounds upstairs with visibly too much enthusiasm.

It has been dark for several hours when she reappears downstairs. "How was homework?" asks my wife, the word "homework" emphasised like a winking code word. "I'm off out now," Missy announces. "Can we ask where you're going, sweetie? We're supposed to be looking after you," my wife asks. "I'm going to the library." "Okay, you do realise it is 8pm on a Saturday evening?" "Yes," she replies. I deliberately leave a gap in the conversation to allow her to fill it with detail. She ignores the hole. "Be back by Twelve," says my wife, adding, "It's quite cold out, sweetie. Do you want to consider wearing a coat? Or [under her breath] a skirt?" "I'm fine, thanks." My wife scribbles down her name and phone number and begs Missy to put it in her pocket. "It's in my phone," Missy reasons. "Please, in case you lose your phone, then you can still contact us." She takes the note and puts it her tiny pocket in her tiny jacket. Covering her tiny dress. "Don't wait up," says Missy. "Twelve!" retaliates my wife.

We both pretend to each other that we had not fallen asleep when a turning door key awakes us in the no-man's land between night and morning. The red light on the cooker displays 3.14am.

It is late. Some of us have been drinking. So I count the number of people in the kitchen. There are four of us. My wife, Missy, myself and the boy from the park this morning with the dog.

"This is… [I've been asked to remove his name]," announces Missy unembarrassed. "I'm slightly late because we walked here – which was at least six miles." "It's one mile," the boy specifies. "It would have felt like six miles in those heels," remarks my wife. "Yeah, well some people are too tight for a taxi," Missy says. "I've got a lowly paid job so I can't justify money on taxis," says the boy from the park. If it wasn't for the circumstances, I think we would get on.

"So why did you come here?" asks my wife, relishing Missy being in the witness box. "So we could … er … in order to … er …" They are now required to provide this sentence with a verb. "To … see your dog," interjects the boy, massively unconvincingly.

"Not here, as she doesn't live with us. That's right," says my wife, "she not actually ours, but we are charged with looking after her. And we take our responsibilities of care seriously. So you won't be seeing her for a while as she's going to be tethered on a short lead." He does not appear to understand this hardly opaque extended metaphor. "Okay, just thought I'd see the dog. Anyway, it's late," he yawns. No one does a yawn to illustrate their tiredness, unless you are in a mime class. We willingly let him out. My wife opens the front door, hurls him outside and quickly slams the door behind her in one unbroken movement – a manoeuvre I've witnessed her do countless times before with spiders but never with a human.

Sensibly aware she has just peaked in personal liberty taking, Missy scuttles up the stairs and reaches the sanctuary of her bedroom without further interrogation. Cleverly she turns the light off immediately. Outside we hear a fox scratching a wheelie bin – or it could be the teenage boy banging his head in frustration.

The next morning Missy keeps teenage hours and descends for breakfast and routine questioning at 11am. "Well, at least I've given you some material for your column about me." "There is no way on God's earth you are making what happened in this house last night public," fulminates my wife. What I really need now is a first class negotiator and manipulator.

Enter Missy the lawyer. She clicks her metaphorical briefcase open and takes on the case. She proffers that there are reasonable grounds for including this incident in an article – clearly hoping her continuing infamy will helps her become famous. "No. You were massively out of order again, Missy – we respect you're maturing, and it's not easy being

17; I can actually remember," says my wife. "Really?" says Missy ill-advisedly, before attempting to save herself with the mollifying remark, "you always seem so wise, I can't imagine you being as immature as me." "You can't smuggle boys back to other people's houses, you just can't – and you lied about the library," I point out.

"No, I didn't."

"Oh please, Missy, are you honestly telling us you went to a library dressed to the nines at, er, nine on a Saturday night?" snaps my wife.

"Yes. I arranged to meet him *outside* The Library pub on the Cowley Road. He lives near there and I ate with his parents – the man from the park. They were going to drive me home, but were worried they had some wine, so their son walked me home."

"There is a pub called The Library. It has bookshelves. Er, that's true," I concede.

Missy arrows me an "I don't need to call a witness yet" look and returns to advocacy. "I don't go to pubs anymore as I'm nearly 18 and don't want to get in any more trouble with the authorities. I'm trying to turn my life around. I realise I've been a struggle for my parents and everyone. If only I can be given a chance to make amends." The last protestation is overplayed, with an am-dram flourish when executing the line, but it is more than sufficient to win the point convincingly. Awarding the benefit of the doubt to Missy and believing this version of events enables my wife to banish any unpleasant alternatives from her mind.

A deal is cut. Missy will spend the rest of the day completing her actual homework rather than getting ready for a night out. The negotiated terms include not informing Missy's parents about her nocturnal social sojourns when they pick her up. Instead we tell them how good she's been by not frequenting pubs again before her 18th birthday.

As a reward for good behaviour her parents allow her to drive, "since she's behaved so well." My wife wobbles at this point, but recovers to preserve the pretence. Pulling out of the drive she flattens our lone hydrangea that had just started to bloom. My wife says Missy is finally maturing and we should now trust her.

Later that day, a pub in Reading phones my wife to say that they have found a jacket with this name and phone number contained in the pocket – should we know the owner who would like to claim it.

HOME TO ROOST

It is already late when the call comes in. Perhaps too late. Five lives are at stake. And I am the only one who can save them.

The caller's tone immediately signals concern as she audibly struggles with calmness retention. "Can you scramble?" the voice on the phone asks anxiously. Nervous insecurity that I may not be up to the task competes for space in my brain's reaction alongside flowering pride that I have been selected as the go-to-guy for such an important life or death mission.

"We've rung everyone else we could think of," says my friend Helen, "and then we thought of you." Oh. It's okay; luckily I don't have any feelings. "It's just that you don't live close to us and...well I wouldn't ask but lives might be at stake." She is not exaggerating.

Helen says she understands if I cannot help. But this would render me an accessory to murder. Forever destined to imagine passers-by whispering, "That's him – the chicken murderer!"

Helen keeps five ex-battery hens in her Risinghurst garden. A fox had been sighted the night before viewing the chickens like he was studying a menu. "It's disgusting how foxes want to kill the chickens," says my wife, taking keys out of her purse – the same purse that contains a much stamped Nando's loyalty card. "Yeah, disgusting," I agree.

Apparently the chickens voluntarily go into their hen house each evening as darkness approaches. It's then the job of a human to shut and bolt two doors thereby fox-proofing the coop against nocturnal predators. Foxes may be forever associated with the word "cunning", but their foxy ingenuity is insufficient to pick padlocks or disable latches with a credit card.

Unfortunately Helen's appointed coop locker, permitting her to have a rare weekend away, has been forced to cancel his intended duties due to a sudden family emergency. Hence a fox-proofer is required at exceptionally short notice – and if one cannot be found in the only remaining hour before daylight disappears, it looks like Mr Fox will be singing the nauseating *I Feel Like Chicken Tonight* song.

"I'll do it," I announce.

"Thank you!" says Helen, before repeating the phrase at least four more times. "You can have the half dozen eggs I collected this morning before we left."

"That's egg-traordinary generous of you," I say.

"I'm quite prepared to deduct an egg for every egg-based pun you make," she warns.

"Egg-xactly," I reply.

"Your five eggs will be waiting."

She pauses to help usher the tone back to serious from light-hearted. After all this is a critical mission I've been handed – five potential deaths have to be averted. Already I am tingling with the anxiety this responsibility carries.

Anyone who has witnessed the aftermath of a fox attack on a chicken coup would realise the seriousness of my duties. Foxes routinely massacre every chicken present once they access a hen house. Although many purport that foxes kill the entire flock merely for demented sport, this remains a misconception. Foxes do indeed frenziedly slaughter all the chickens, but they intend to return for the carcasses later, using the carnage as their meat larder.

Returning to see your beloved hens beheaded by a fox does rather risk permanently ruining Basil Brush for you.

Chickens are the largest predator of hens in the UK – except in the Isle of Man where none live (presumably as foxes don't have to avoid income tax).

Hence we need to depart for Risinghurst. Quickly. Sensing the urgency my wife and I both decide to go. Being a struggling freelance writer precludes me from car ownership, but my wife has a 24-hour Oxford bus pass not due to expire for another hour. Demonstrating the maturity of our collective 90 years, we decide to race each other. I am going to pedal the 3 miles; my wife will ride the buses. Splitting up will ensure we double our chances of getting there on time.

Hurtling along the cycle track, head bowed aerodynamically forward over the handlebars, I imagine myself as Bradley Wiggins casually ticking off yet another world record. Only he never pedalled to save lives – just for some lousy medals he can one day post to Cash4Gold.

Darkness is already beginning to cloak the garden when I arrive. Then I spot it. Hiding behind a bush, two menacing eyes reflect the moonlight. Silent, stationary and hopefully clandestine behind a gooseberry bush, the full moon silhouettes the unmistakable shape of a large mammal with a furry tail.

It appears I have averted the vulpine threat by seconds not minutes. My wife arrives. I gesture silence and point to the furry shape. "That's Helen's cat," says my wife. "Oh yeah," I conclude feebly.

"Did you think that was a fox?" Asks my wife. "Seems like..." I know something is coming next that my wife is proud of as her voice starts to wobble with laugher as if speaking while rattling over a cattle grid, "...you've been outfoxed!" She then points to Helen's snoozing dog. "He'd give the fox a shock if it jumped out of the bushes now," says my wife. But the fox doesn't. The quick brown fox jumps over the lazy dog -- remains a sentence still unused in a real context.

All five hens are safely put to bed, with keys turned and bolts slid. Even in the dying light the birds still look magnificent. One possesses princely black plumes. "That's an australorp," I announce, "so named because the species originated from Australia. They became popular in Europe in the 1920s after press reports that the breed won an egg laying contest." My words decay into the thickening darkness. Rather than being impressed at this dispensed information, my wife simply remarks, "So you've had time to google before engaging in this life or death race against time."

At dawn the next day Helen calls to ask if we can open the coop and feed them. This necessitates buying specialist food for the hens. My wife asks me how expensive it is when I return from the pet shop. "Let's say it's hardly chicken feed," I reply. "Are you proud of that one?" asks my wife in an accompanying tone that suggests I had better not be.

For breakfast we eat the eggs. They are far tastier than supermarket sweat shop eggs. And it turns out that I can scramble.

EVENTS

THE BY-ELECTION

Tension is filling the room like an escaping gas. We are awaiting the announcement of a result. The omens could not be worse if a black cat had walked under a ladder, stepped out in front of us and been promptly run over by a number 13 bus.

We're squeezed into the Long Room of the Town Hall to observe the count of an Oxford City Council by-election. Moreover, my friend Richard is one of the candidates seeking political glory. In his selfless quest for public service and social duty (and claiming free stuff on expenses) he has put himself through the democratic process as an election candidate. Former Home Secretary and Oxford alumna Jacqui Smith once famously claimed 88p on expenses for a bath plug – presumably to try and stop her career disappearing down the plughole.

Richard was certainly contesting issues right at the heart of Oxford because he stood in the Carfax ward located in the dead centre of the city. Although the location was central, some of the politics were not so centralist. One contestant lambasted Europe's open borders policy leading to overburdened public services – seemingly unaware that the level of world-changing authority councillors wield is capped at deciding which day the bins are collected.

Disappointingly the count is not open to the public. It is very exclusive. To gain access you have to be invited, proposed, seconded, checked and approved. Or just say, "I'm with him."

The 18th-century voting technology (pencil crosses on paper counted by hand) is laid out for all to see. Two black boxes containing ballot papers are tipped onto a long table. This causes a surge from forty people, like livestock at feeding time, who move towards the emptied boxes. Some have clipboards and furiously start crossing out numbers like they're participating in a world record attempt for the fastest ever bingo game. I ask Richard's agent what they are doing. He explains in detail twice. I still have no idea what they are doing.

Oxford East MP Andrew Smith then arrives at the count and also begins purposefully jotting things down.

After thirty minutes the Returning Officer craves our attention. He informs us that the Verification Process has now been completed. Apparently this ensures that the number of votes in the boxes tallies with those cast in the polling stations. A sensible safeguard for democracy. I ask a veteran party campaigner, his demeanour salted with political experience, if the verification process ever throws up any anomalies. "Yes," he answers with enthusiasm, "once in 1997 there was one extra vote."

The Returning Officer returns. Hence his name. He announces: "These are the postal votes and so not from any specific region." An agent translates for me: "He's telling the party workers they're wasting their time looking at the postal votes as they're not from one area. So there's no point whatsoever looking at them." All the party workers then go and look at them anyway. I detect a slight eye-rolling from one of the counters.

Being a counter is not easy. Three pairs sit behind a long table, silent and focusing diligently on their counting job. All the politicos stand on the other side of the table pressing their unattractive faces intimidatingly close. As if this was not enough of a distraction, they speak thunderously loud, often reciting numbers. While the poor counters are attempting to count.

"The count will now begin," announces the returning Returning Officer. At least he's dressed for the role, wearing a suit and tie. One of the Labour Party team is donning a blue T-shirt, traffic-light red shorts and blue plimsolls accessorised with a huge red rosette. With this combination his rosette just looks odd and completely out of place, like spotting a grizzly bear holding an umbrella.

The UKIP candidate is the best dressed, complementing his suit with a purple tie. Richard complains that he doesn't have a rosette as this is a rare opportunity to wear one. There are only three environments where it remains socially acceptable to don a rosette: elections, football matches (but only if it's an FA Cup tie) and pet shows.

Normally the outcome of the Carfax election is always academic. Literally. The constituency is overwhelmingly populated by students. Therefore holding an election outside of term time during the late summer recess is a brand of democracy usually favoured by despots, tyrants and anyone else who doesn't like the pesky inconvenience of voters affecting the outcome of elections. Consequently the turnout is 8.6%. This is hardly a mandate to govern. The people have spoken. And they've mainly said: "There was an election? When? Oh you deliberately held it when everyone was away."

Once again the Returning Officer returns. Then it's the part of the job that appeals to anyone seeing a vacancy for "Returning Officer". The sole reason why anyone applies. This is the glamorous bit. It's the results announcement.

How often do you get the opportunity to say "I hereby declare" in public without everyone immediately concluding you're an award-winning prat? Yet when the Returning Officer declaims the line, pulsing with pomposity, it's exactly what we want to hear. He should consider saying it more often: "I hereby declare that I want a tea with one sugar."

Richard representing the Green Party receives a mammoth 63 votes, beating UKIP/Monster Raving Independence Party and the Tories (24 votes each) but behind Labour (168) and Lib Dems (101). Quite possibly the lowest election figures I've ever seen.

He sportingly congratulates the winning candidate. Understandably he's anxious to head straight to the pub. However, I suggest waiting for five minutes in case the newly elected Labour councillor resigns. After all, three Oxford Labour councillors have resigned recently – one sparked this by-election.

Whatever the agent did with his numbers board was impressively accurate. He predicted the votes cast for Labour and Lib Dems correctly, although he estimated Richard would only get 57 not 63 votes. Typical agents – they do nothing apart from take 10% from you!

THE STAMPEDE

"HELLO?! 999?! I need to report an emergency!"

The mundane weather perfectly matches the mundane morning. Grey. Unassuming and uninspiring. Another ordinary day awaits as I commute on my bike through a familiar landscape towards a mundane meeting on a mundane subject. After only a few hundred yards of my regular journey I apply the brakes so desperately they emit a piercing squeal.

Suddenly all my presupposed mundanity for the day dissipates. Its replacements are shock and fear. I suddenly realise that mundanity is underrated. Mundanity – even in its most tedious incarnation – would be royally welcome right now. I promise never to be rude about humdrumness again.

I know what I am witnessing warrants an immediate 999 call. My shaking fingers jab 9 … 9 … 9. It's ringing.

The 999 operative asks my name. I tell them as quickly as possible, concluding that my name is rather inconsequential. Surely they're not going to ask next how I am, then not move forward with the conversation until I've reciprocated the question. Perhaps we'll progress to discussing the weather.

Then they hit you with a hard question. Really hard for someone who has never dialled 999 before, seeks direction and could easily be coaxed into panicking.

"Which emergency service do you require?"

"Err … I don't know." Then they go multiple choice. Fire, Police or Ambulance? That makes it easier – but it's still puzzling. Hmm. I mull over the choices. "Police, I think."

They transfer me. I expect to be placed on hold listening to an instrumentalised Simply Red song before a computerised female voice calmly offers me the following options: Press 1 to add to our burden of under-resourced, under-budgeted workloads. Press 2 to report whatever Jeremy Clarkson has done now. Press 3 to purchase an exciting range of branded 999 goods available from our exclusive 999 shop (probably an inevitable innovation since privatisation).

"Where are you calling from?" They ask me. This is another deceptively difficult question. Turns out you need to be more specific than "a road" or even "a road with some houses." It's an incontestably difficult job to be a 999 operative – just the sarcasm restraint requirements alone would undo me. "Okay, I'll send a fire engine to a road with some houses in it." "Really?" "No, of course not, you moron." Is how the conversation would probably proceed if I were on the other end of the line.

"And what incident are you reporting?" they ask.

This is my moment. My chance to narrate something of coffee-spluttering drama. Something a city centre 999-call centre operative who has heard humanity at their worst, been exposed to the most dramatic misfortunes, will consider anecdote-worthy down the pub this coming weekend. A call that a 999 worker will reference in their leaving speech. From this moment they will perennially be known as "Oh, you were the guy who fielded that 999 call about …?" I am about to make *that* call.

I am standing in a densely populated area within Oxford in a residential street that leads directly to Iffley Road. From here I report the incident I am currently witnessing.

"Stampede!"

"Okay. And where is the location of this, er, stampede?"

"The main street in Iffley."

"Alright. What sort of stampede?"

"Horse stampede."

Given this is Oxford in 2015, and I am not a frontiersman in the Wild West circa 1870, my call understandably requires some factual verification.

"Where are the horses now?"

"Sprinting along the middle of a busy residential street. Traffic could come round the blind bend near the Prince of Wales pub."

Some people – or more accurately, some idiots – abuse the 999 service. This is rightly a criminal offence. Idiots need to be sifted out from genuine callers – but surely not at the expense of delaying the response. They ask me to confirm my name again. But surely even an idiot can remember their name?

"I'm ... er … um … hm…" I stutter abstrusely.

Avoiding the misuse of vital emergency services would seem screamingly obvious. And yet such misuse is disturbingly commonplace. A woman from the West Midlands recently dialled 999 to complain that a fast food store had added sprinkles to her ice-cream without first seeking permission. But even that idiocy can be topped (with or without sprinkles). A 999 caller in Cardiff contacted the emergency services to inform them that a prostitute whose services he had just procured "was not attractive enough to be working as a prostitute". Really. That happened. As did the incident when a Lancashire woman's fingers stabbed 999 to seek assistance in finding a film on her TV.

Meanwhile a South Yorkshire woman felt compelled to notify the emergency services that McDonalds had been unable to fulfil her order for chicken nuggets. Elsewhere a parent wanted a police officer despatched to reprimand her son for not eating his breakfast cereal. Another mother requested Nottinghamshire constabulary helped get her son's toy helicopter airborne – presumably she wanted the Flying Squad.

Other 999 timewasters included a schoolgirl wanting her teacher arrested for telling her off, a literal lunatic in South Wales who required the authorities to turn down the brightness on the moon (and no doubt help him discover what planet he is from in the process) and a disgruntled drugs customer who had purchased £60 of crack cocaine. He reported being ripped off to police as his purchase "was barely worth £20". You can probably guess where the last caller is currently residing.

Elsewhere in Wales a Pontypool diner rang 999 to report that he just eaten a scotch bonnet chilli and "now my face is burning". Greater Manchester police had to deal with an outraged woman traumatised after she reported having something valuable stolen. "What have you had stolen?" inquired the 999 operative. "A parking space," replied the crime "victim".

A 15-year-old girl dialled 999 and requested the fire brigade after becoming stuck in a cat flap. No, she was not a cat burglar, but had forgotten her door key and decided to squeeze into her kitchen via the cat's entrance. Adding to the cat-egorical cat-alogue of 999 cat-astrophes. An ambulance took her to hospital – no, she didn't have a CAT scan. But she has 999 lives.

Each one of the above represents another burning log of regret tossed onto the raging fire of stupidity that will one day engulf us all.

In Iffley I pursue the horses on my bike like a 21st-century urban cowboy, executing an insufficiently strategised plan to get ahead of the sprinting animals and warn oncoming traffic. Thankfully the horses spot an inviting patch of lush grass on the junction with Meadow Lane and stop for an al fresco roadside lunch. Soon afterwards a man arrives on a bike to tend to the animals. He thanks me for staying with the horses and alerting the authorities.

Returning later I spot all four perpetrators of the equine breakout back in their field, munching contentedly. The lady in the local shop informs me someone left a gate open. And the horses are the ones currently locked up!

THE GHOST OF CHRISTMAS PAST

Well, that's the whole Christmas and New Year thing over for another fifty weeks then. As you're packing away the last of your unbroken decorations this Twelfth Night, wondering how it's still possible to get Christmas tree needles on a carpet from an artificial tree, you may wish to ruminate on the brief respite offered before the next Festival of Commerce comes bullying for your lunch money and threatening you with self-perceived social exclusion if you refuse to comply (Valentine's Day, Mother's Day, Easter, Father's Day, Halloween, Something Else Blatantly Made Up and Probably Imported From America Day).

Currently much of our festival tat is returning on a slow boat to China from whence it arrived, only this time destined to go into landfill. Disposing of, as well as originally manufacturing, are booming Chinese industries. Santa's relocation from the North Pole has been somewhat under-reported, since a persuasive combination of global warming and cheap Chinese labour markets provided more competitive tendering than Lapland's elves.

Plotting the trajectory of my Christmas and New Year mood on an age timeline reveals that my enthusiasm has decreased exponentially the further I ascend out of childhood, peaking in my formative years, troughing in approaching middle age, prior to an expected rise in old age isolation. Personally, I'm relieved it's all over.

Everything at Christmas and New Year is exaggerated. At any other time of the year it's acceptable not to have a brilliant time, not to consume a perfectly prepared meal accompanied by thirteen different types of homemade sauce. Between 2 January and 24 December it's tolerable to eat a turkey flavoured pot noodle while breaking a deal with yourself that you were only going to watch Matthew Wright until the first advert break and then realise your entire morning has vanished and no, you can't see anyone about getting it back.

Advertisers understand this festive pressure and groom us by inflating our expectations towards unattainable perfection – rebranding customers as "revellers" and meals as "celebrations". (What's the difference between a regular pub goer and a New Year's Eve pub reveller? About £8 per person entrance fee). Unless you're sharing private jokes with resplendently attired attractive guests next to glistening buffet spreads lit by glowing candles bathing beautiful faces in soft incandescent light before the inviting orange warmth of a restorative winter fire (as depicted in all seasonal adverts), then your pointless life officially sucks. The message here, delivered as subtly as Ian Paisley with a megaphone, is that you can't be a beautiful person in a beautiful house with beautiful friends completed by an adoring spouse (who's beautiful, obviously) unless you've purchased an Iceland all-in-one frozen finger buffet. Really?

Anxiety levels at Christmas and New Year regularly see the needle pressing against the extreme edge of the red zone. Because Everything Must Be Perfect. I genuinely saw a magazine cover last month proclaiming "351 ways to ensure a simple Xmas/New Year". Since no. 246 was devoted to making your own glacé cherries for decorating homemade loganberry infused mince pies (no. 137), it's little wonder this time of year sees a spike in suicide rates.

Place a group of relatives in a room, causing the assembled guests to recall exactly why they only see these people once a year. Cancel all transport, close all shops and restaurants, cease all theatre and sports: basically close down the outside world on 25 December, thus rendering escape impossible. Then introduce alcohol: the only day of the year when it's socially acceptable – nay mandatory – to consume potent cocktails at breakfast (well, outside of Charles Kennedy's house). Add to this pressure cooker environment a literal pressure cooker where sprouts are cooked for two hours (and then given another twenty minutes just to be on the safe side); the uniquely British word "veg" is an accurate, almost visually onomatopoeic reductive abbreviation for what is left of the original nutritious word "vegetable" prior to being boiled for several hours. It is unsurprising families report fractious behaviour over the Christmas/New Year period that can blight the year ahead.

Then there's the food we don't eat (like those sprouts). Scary statistics estimate we waste between thirty and forty per cent of purchased festive food. The fault lies with those who buy enough food to have rendered the German tactics at the Siege of Stalingrad ineffective, just because the shops are shut for 36 hours.

Turkey is basically a chicken who's hired a decent spin doctor. It's not necessarily better because it's bigger, in the same way that Birmingham isn't better than Oxford. Fashionable people increasingly reject the immigrant turkey (goose is indigenous, turkey from the

Americas). The word "turkey" is a semantic monument to British ignorance: we thought it originated from Turkey, hence the name. Even posher people reject goose: "Ya, this year we sourced an organic snow owl from Waitrose."

This festive season I witnessed numerous adults complaining about the crippling stress associated with the annual rigmarole, deploying the line "We only do it for the kids" – usually spoken when queuing in off-licences. But for some the festive season can mean a fast-flowing stream of acute despair and colourless depression (and that's just the Christmas Day edition of *EastEnders*).

Yet perhaps more than Xmas, New Year celebrations enforce an orthodox conformity of fun. Edited revisionist memory, bordering upon amnesia, appears significant in respective evaluation: "I fell in a fountain, broke two ribs and lost my door key – best New Year's ever!" Yeah, right. Mind if I stay in and read? Regardless of how many people attended your New Year party, no one will have known all the words to *Auld Lang Syne*, though everyone still sang it.

You've probably earmarked this weekend for Xmas present redistribution i.e. charity shop donating while contemplating how we've fallen for the same old tricks persuading us to buy pointless tat yet again for a festival long since uncoupled from any higher meaning. Anyway, must go – there are only 353 shopping days until Christmas.

THE MANAGEMENT CONSULTANTS

After staying up to witness the general election results as they were announced by an increasingly sleep-deprived and irascible David Dimbleby, I walked home through Oxford in the dark pre-dawn hours — a murky, amorphous twilight time when you are genuinely unsure whether it is really late or really early.

Given the paucity of buses in Oxford at 4am, coupled with my natural frugality disqualifying the taxi option, I endured a lengthy walk home on a route that took me past three of our city's public libraries. All three were closed: "Wow," I thought. "These Tories work fast: they have only been in power for a few hours and yet every library in Oxford is already closed." Although that could have been because it was 4am.

Just over one year later, and I realise that observation was ominously prophetic. Indeed, I was working in an Oxford library when it was announced that management consultants had been sighted on the premises. This is akin to discovering leeches in a public swimming pool, or an infestation of bed bugs in your bedroom. They are very difficult to get rid of, even harder to kill (even with a licence) and they will almost certainly suck your blood.

Being respectful of library protocol, it was evidently difficult for the librarian to tell these "people" what they needed to hear, especially at the required volume. Everyone should respect silence in a library, although a Sheffield library recently generated press attention after permitting the Sugarbabes in their library. Sadly, the Sugarbabes were not sitting in the periodicals room asking some homeless bloke if he had finished with today's *Times* – instead their music was being piped over the PA. In a library! I know.

Whereas it costs £2 million a day to fund an unpopular Middle Eastern war, governments appear considerably less enthusiastic to support libraries. Well, if it is a case of bombs or books, then clearly bombs are what we should be spending our money on.

Midsomer Murders, filmed in Oxfordshire, was recently criticised for not depicting accurately the true components of a typical modern English village – criticism that was quite fair, in my opinion, given that Midsomer still has a post office and a library.

I overheard the following conversation while working in an Oxfordshire library recently – though a functioning sense of social justice and natural propensity for happy endings may have partially distorted my recollection of the exact dialogue.

CONSULTANT 1: Are you paid to work here?

LIBRARIAN: Yes. Welcome to our library. Can I help you?

CONSULTANT 2: Here, have a helpful Big Society leaflet.

LIBRARIAN: "Making the Most of Redundancy". Are you closing our library?

CONSULTANT 1: No, no, no. This is a just an initial consultation job risk evaluation, with absolutely no finalised figures

LIBRARIAN: Apart from Fahrenheit 451?

CONSULTANT 2: No closure decision has yet been taken, but could you just hold the end of this tape measure.

CONSULTANT 1: Do these rectangular papery things . . .

LIBRARIAN: Books.

CONSULTANT 2: Yeah, books, generate an increasing year-on-year profit?

LIBRARIAN: They benefit society of all wages and ages. Like Ethel here who is 86.

ETHEL: I'm 86 you know.

LIBRARIAN: There Ethel, this book's due back in three weeks.

ETHEL: Oh, I will be finished with it before then, dear.

COSULTANTS: [In hushed voices] ... reduce spending ... efficiency drive ... natural waste ... make a note of Fahrenheit 451.

LIBRARIAN: [loudly] Stop whispering and speak up! Yes, I am a librarian, and yes that was a professional first. But I cannot understand a word you are saying.

CONSULTANT 1: We are initiating a helicopter view of business critical perceived silos for customer facing best practice organisational spans control.

LIBRARIAN: No. Audibility was obviously not the problem. I still can't understand a word you are saying.

CONSULTANT 2: Business change depth testing models charged with revenue generation strategic cross aim risk deliverables to ensure broad-brush blue sky functionality business causality.

LIBRARIAN: We have a good grammar section over there in Reference.

CONSULTANT 1: In layman's terms – books, libraries, they should have gone with the ark.

LIBRARIAN: Libraries are an ark for saving learning from the rising floodwaters of corporate greed. And you are corporate henchmen hired by some slash and burn consultancy spouting [*date stamp sound*] ... bull [*date stamp sound*] ... you total [*date stamp sound* x3] ... and utter [*date stamp sound*].

CONSULTANT 2: Yeah, that's right. We are henchmen – with jobs!

LIBRARIAN: The good thing about henchmen is they always die before the end of the film.

CONSULTANT 1: Well, you are overdue for closure.

CONSULTANT 2: Overdue! Good one. Bet she's got a stamp for that ... [date stamp sound]

CONSULTANT 1: Oh she has. On my Armani suit too.

CONSULTANT 2: Right, we are leaving – we have seen enough to recommend closure.

LIBRARIAN: You have only been here for ten minutes.

CONSULTANT 1: That is where you are completely wrong.

CONSULTANT 2: Yeah, it was five minutes.

CONSULTANT 1:Shut up. Right, back in the Porsche. We have got to close another two old people's homes and a job club today, or we won't get our bonus. [*car departs, then crashes*]

LIBRARIAN: My God! The business consultants have crashed and probably died.

ETHEL: I will return that book now, dear.

LIBRARIAN: That was quick, Ethel. Did you enjoy … err … B*rake Cable Cutting For Beginners*?

ETHEL: Very much, dear. And two management consultants dead. Proves libraries really do benefit society as a whole.

BEWARE GREEKS BEARING GIFTS

Beware Greeks bearing gifts – they've almost certainly bought them on dodgy credit anyway. Yet Greeks have benevolently gifted our country multiple items from which we make grateful daily practical use – no, not the Elgin Marbles which really don't do much apart from sit on a shelf harming international relations – but gifts that enable us to communicate: words. Whereas the conquering advance of mobile phones and *The Apprentice* wannabes have ensured we now occupy an age where never before have people said so little, so loudly, for so long, the English language pings and fizzes with wonderful communicative nouns imparted by, and imported from, the Greeks. You're looking at me like you require an example? Okay, here's a few: comedy, ovation, agoraphobia, halitosis, democracy, bacteria, idiot and phrases such as "you retire at what age?!"

I recently conducted a walking tour for some Greek visitors to Oxford. The party were all in their mid-forties –– or as that age is routinely known in Greece: "retired" – and I marched them towards Radcliffe Square anticipating they would become architecturally star-struck by Oxford's buildings.

As they were Greek nationals, I considered it expedient to commence the tour with the following Health & Safety briefing:

"During today's route we will be passing several parked cars – please refrain from setting these alight."

Not as they were unruly at all – but they did witness several Oxford public sector protests; public sector workers going on strike risks private sector workers tendering for the same strikes, claiming to deliver an identical strike more efficiently with only half the strikers.

We then discovered that Radcliffe Square was entirely in lockdown. This was because our tour had coincided with another word the Greeks kindly gave us: Encaenia. It means "dedication festival".

Encaenia, where Oxford University annually bestows honorary degrees, formerly represented a shared amalgamation of Town & Gown – hundreds of townspeople would pack into Radcliffe Square, Catte Street and outside the Sheldonian to witness the procession with the University joyously showing off its pomp and heraldry.

Not anymore, as all routes including Brasenose Lane (a Freedom of Information request reveals no application for closure was received, nor granted, by Oxford City Council), were blocked by barricades manned by men in black suits and bowler hats looking like a psychotic Mr Benn or the paramilitary wing of the Homepride Flour men.

This year Encaenia became inclusively populist with the Christ Church choir singing the Beatles tune *Yesterday*. George Martin was simultaneously honoured and humiliated: the rather rare doctorates of music (I fear Handel may have been one of the more contemporary ones) are forced to wear pink gowns.

Then there are the vexatious protesters obscuring everyone else's view, spitting viperously under-rehearsed chants. I've always loved animals, wouldn't hurt an ant me (well, unless it was called Adam – never could stand *Stand and Deliver*) but a tiny minority are akin to an animal-loving Taliban. If you're going to chant in public – rehearse. This is a big audience: you've got George Martin present; if he liked you it could lead to Militant Protestors' Choir Competition: next year's surprising Channel 5 reality show hit.

An ironic reminder of mankind's animal status was now being provided by displayed animalist behavioural instincts – divided by tribal loyalties and defending newly won territories.

Protesters hand out leaflets depicting abhorrent cruelty; if the end of *Reservoir Dogs* was portrayed by animals instead of actors, these would be the resultant stills from the final scene. The message here is that Oxford University contains kitten-stampers: Top Trumps winners in the Most Evil category (way ahead of Bin Laden, Stalin, Mini Me and Piers Morgan). The University releases countering information showing that animals are humanely treated, kept in 5-star accommodation with full minibar privileges and all the Sky Sports packages. Furthermore, advances in genetic research have ensured they only select animals who share their genes with Max Mosley.

The truth, I suspect, lies ignored somewhere between the two campaigns.

Then the police arrive and attempt to close Turl Street. A convoy of black windowed 4x4s, which Michelle Obama would have considered indulgent (note to Oxford City Council: if Michelle Obama visits Christ Church again, ensure she uses Redbridge Park & Ride), rumbled noisily through narrow streets causing cyclists to ride into walls to avoid them.

Typically, the police are visibly keen to be on the side of this invading climate calamity cavalry. Noticeably the convoy's lead driver bought his SatNav from some guy called Dave in a pub who wouldn't provide a surname, as he immediately turned into Turl Street like a failed Pied Piper interviewee. The rest of the convoy dutifully follow him, necessitating an attempt to turn around in Market Street.

Hired security and the police clear pedestrians and tourists. Why does the presence of much loved fifth Beatle George Martin require a huge police presence? Why would anyone want to attack George Martin (well, apart from for sanctioning parts of the over-indulgent *White Album*)? Policemen move from "hello, hello, hello – would you like directions?" to the Custody Sergeant explaining matter-of-factly how another 37 detainees carelessly fell down the stairs again. It's a jolting reminder as to the thin fragility of our democratic freedoms.

Meanwhile the walking tour concludes, leaving the Greek visitors to speculate that, in comparison to Oxford, Athens is a peaceful place with relatively little civil unrest. A Greek lady stays behind after the tour disperses, and kindly offers me a sweet. Beware Greeks bearing gifts is just bad advice. And Greece can have its Elgin Marbles back, as long as Oxford can have its Encaenia back – since Oxford's clearly already lost its marbles.

OXFORD TAKES A BEATING

I adore Oxford's twin charms of eccentricity and stubborn immutability. Sometimes they are magnificently combined, which is why I am sitting expectantly in the pews of the High Street's University church.

I am attending St Mary's annual Beating of the Bounds ceremony, which commences with a Eucharist service. Since the University church is currently clad in scaffolding, tensions are raised when four helmeted builders appear in high-vis jackets seconds before the service is due to commence and stand where the altar would ordinarily be located, purposefully holding hammers, nails and planks of wood. Friendly priest Rachel sensitively suggests they vacate the altar spot behind her until after the service – perhaps temporarily forgetting that the person who usually stands behind her at the altar throughout church services is also a carpenter. Christ was an actual carpenter, unlike every member of pop group The Carpenters, none of whom were – deceptively in my view – actual carpenters.

Before the service, conversation is dominated by speculation about who will be appointed the next Archbishop of Canterbury following Wadhamite Rowan Williams' shock resignation earlier in the year. Anxious to contribute to the discussion and prove myself capable of conversing on the subject matter, I announce that there has been considerable press speculation that the job may go to Harry Redknapp. I receive odd looks.

After the service, pupils and chaperoning parents from New College School arrive, with one teacher delegated the uncomfortable role of carrying twenty canes in the procession. Passer-by reactions range from horrified liberals to the endorsement of presumed *Daily Telegraph* readers, nodding approval for this visible return to corporal punishment. Schoolboys in gowns and teachers holding multiple canes do ensure a scene more reminiscent of the *Beano* than Oxford city centre in the 21st century. However, the canes are not for striking mischievous boys, but ancient stones that mark parish boundaries. Each year the church reasserts its boundaries by marking them with chalk and cane in this endearingly eccentric ceremony.

The parish boundary of St Mary's and St Michael's runs directly through Brasenose College, where our ensemble enthusiastically thrashes boundary stones at our first three stops whilst roaring, "Mark! Mark! Mark!" Really. Apparently it's an ancient thing. And surprisingly good fun. At no stage does someone called Mark turn around and impatiently demand, "What?!"

Graeme the college chaplain – the best sort of priest in my opinion: someone whose short talk demonstrates he considers a decent sermon and a "tight ten" at the Comedy Store to be indistinguishable – entertainingly explains Brasenose's history. He expresses a noble concern that lofty intellectual pursuits risk isolating Gown personnel from Town concerns – a worthy view, if only partially undermined by his decision to end a sentence with the word "solipsistic". Even Susie Dent had to look that one up.

Here's my tip: if you wish to obtain some serious respect when out and about, get yourself an accompanying choir. People appear automatically impressed when you've got your own choir in tow. Everyone except for the Bodleian Library. Here some Old School Quad old school jobsworth needlessly points out that our accompanying choir and "Mark"-ing activities can be heard in three libraries. The schoolboys briefly consider beating him instead of the boundary stone.

Brian the vicar makes an excellent master of ceremonies. Disappointingly, though, he doesn't use his I'm-on-speaking-terms-with-God position to come over all Old Testament and smite the jobsworth with a curse for his crops to fail for a thousand years. Modern vicars just don't do enough retributive smiting in my view. But exposure to a mild jobsworth is nothing compared to the animosity encountered at the next boundary stone.

Determined to do its bit to uphold Town & Gown divisions is Hertford College. And, given that St Mary's is the official University church, it is upholding Gown & Gown divisions too. Hertford allegedly declines access to mark its boundary stone and a large locked gate blocks our progress, casting a shadow across the Radcliffe Square cobbles. One nine-year-old schoolboy proclaims, "The church with psalms must shout, no door can keep them out!" Only in Oxford would a nine-year-old be quoting lines from the 19th-century composer and writer Basil Harwood, though some would cite the fact that he opted to do this in English rather than Latin as further proof of Britain's irreversible descent into dumbing down.

Sensibly, an 18th-century Act of Parliament enshrines the right of our Beating of the Bounds posse to have annual entrance to our next stop, All Souls, where thankfully a perpendicular opposite to the welcome provided by neighbouring Hertford is offered. The college's informative librarian mischievously invites us to make some serious noise in the Codrington Library. Within full glare of "Silence" signs, the schoolboys birch the floor-set stone in front of a surely disapproving statue of judge Sir William Blackstone who already displays a missing finger resulting from previous unruly behaviour when Fellows routinely played cricket inside the library in the 1920s.

Having been star-struck by the college's buildings, and the college's buildings in turn being struck by the stars of New College School choir, once inside All Souls splendid hall we are served traditional cherry cake – commemorating that the college was built on a cherry orchard formerly belonging to St Mary's. It is exceedingly good cake – probably because it has not been manufactured by a mass corporate cake company with clever advertising slogans. If there's one thing the Church of England does undisputedly better than all other brands of religion, it is cake.

The ceremony now cranks up the eccentricity to a Lewis-Carroll-on-acid setting. Once inside University College, an upstairs window opens and reveals the Master's wife generously showering coins and sweets onto the schoolboys below, culminating in scrimmaging for goodies. Meanwhile, adults in cassocks trample carefully through flowerbeds while singing hymns and beating stones with bamboo sticks. This is all reassuringly normal for Oxford.

Fittingly, Oriel is the final stop, rebinding the link between St Mary's and the college, which goes back a rather impressive 700 years. Tradition decreed that from 1326 to the 20th century, the vicar of St Mary's would be a college Fellow. Included among the post holders was ecumenical dissenter John Henry Newman. A founder of the Oxford Movement, he famously switched to Catholicism – a defection akin in controversy to moving from marmite hater to marmite lover. Yet this move proved expedient as he was beatified in 2010. Aspirants harbouring ambition towards sainthood are statistically better off becoming Catholic. Scope to become a Church of England saint appears more limited, even if you are really, really good at baking Victoria sponge cakes and flower arranging.

Later I see what looks like a vicar marking a cross on Hertford's wall, presumably imploring a subsequent visitation of boils, plague and locusts upon the college. Don't mess with the C of E. They've got the best cake. And canes.

HISTORY

THE MAMMOTH TASK: EXPLAINING EXTINCTION

This month Oxford University made the news for stating as an incontestable fact that 99.9% of all species on earth have already been eradicated. Yet extinction would have been incomprehensible until incredibly recently in human history. Mainly because we thought the earth just wasn't old enough, plus God's going to get pretty angry when he discovers that after all the hard work He put in to designing woolly mammoths, sabre toothed tigers and dodos – especially those really intricate bits around their beaks that took ages – they are now all as dead as a ... er ... dodo. Subsequently humans have spent 99.9% of their own existence wholly ignorant about extinction. We didn't know about dinosaurs until the mid-19th century – which means that for the first 100,000 years of human existence the free toy in cereal boxes was rubbish ("Includes free pebble!").

For centuries, the bible's account of creation, and thus our planet's age, was uncontested. Irishman James Usher calculated in 1654 from biblical lineage that the earth was created on Sunday 26 October 4004 BC. Which was surely unlikely, as wasn't Sunday supposed to be God's day off? Yet Usher even provided the time: 9am. Hence the world was 5658 years old. This was deemed a sufficiently impressive scholarly feat for Oliver Cromwell to permit him burial in Westminster Abbey. However, this calculation turned out to be the very slightest, tiniest bit out – but only by four and a half billion years.

Scholar Bernard Palissy had earlier observed that landscapes were surely shaped by rain, wind and waves – concluding accurately that it must take longer than 5,000 years to produce the effects already visible on earth. Clearly he was right – mature valley formation by rainfall deposits would take millions of years of rain – apart from in Wales, where that's possible over a Bank Holiday weekend. For his correct hypothesis, he was burnt at the stake (by the French in 1589, not the Welsh Tourist Board).

Understandably, this somewhat immense over-reaction discouraged future delving into the planet's age. The earth became like a much loved lady of a certain age: everyone suspected she may be a lot older than was said, but nobody would ever dare ask her age, while generally agreeing how great she looked for her age. This is known as The Joanna Lumley Principle. Anyone who did question the earth's age could expect a visit from the Catholic Church, who would send round some of their heavies to intimidate scientists: "So, you ain't seen no fossils, right!"

Yet a Catholic bishop was among the first to correctly recognise fossils. Nicolas Steno observed in 1667 that living sharks' teeth were identical in shape and proportion to some rock specimens.

Until the earth was suspected of being a few million years old, rather than a few thousand, no one had connected fossils to extinction. Then in the early 19th century Georges Cuvier first worked out that animals must have become extinct. Observing nature, he considered continued survival as simply a case of horses for courses – which was probably also true of his lunch, given he was French.

But there was an elephant in the room – particularly when Georges Cuvier presented his 1796 paper on fossilised elephants with a mammoth fossil in the lecture hall. He announced by demonstrating anatomical differences that some species must have become extinct. Although fossils were now being correctly identified, scientists postulated that these animals must have migrated to the tropics when Europe became cooler where they could still be found today – to the presumable annoyance of the indigenous tropical animals: "Bloody Northern European woolly mammoths coming over here, eating our leaves…"

Cuvier reasoned that massive woolly mammoths roaming around may have been noticed by now if they were still about. Which is logical: it would certainly be difficult for woolly mammoths to blend in unnoticed in a post office queue.

Finally, with the advent of radiometric dating measuring radioactive decay in rocks, the earth was revealed as being 4.54 billion years old, by Clair Patterson. Clair was a guy by the way – anyone else think his parents may have wanted a girl? We had invented colour TV and launched the first satellite into orbit before working out the age of our planet.

A great mass extinction occurred 250 million years ago. Possibly caused by volcanic eruptions in Siberia – although it's difficult to locate just one smoking gun – the Permian Extinction eradicated the overwhelming majority of all life forms, destroying 95% of every species. One day 250 million years ago ought to put into context anyone's subsequent bad morning: "What a morning! The world exploded with the force of a billion nuclear bombs, sulphuric acid rained down indefinitely, temperatures hit 9000 degrees, the seas boiled AND there was no semi-skimmed milk in the fridge – absolutely bloody typical!"

Within the last 500 million years there have been five mass extinctions: Ordovician Silurian 450 million years ago, Permian 250 million, Triassic Jurassic 210 million, Late Devonian 360 million (when the sea became almost devoid of oxygen and eradicated most aquatic life) and the Cretaceous Tertiary (known as KT – yes, CT would make more sense) 65 million years ago which did for the dinosaurs but not, annoyingly, ants, wasps or house flies.

The symbiosis between interacting mutually dependent organisms can be torn by mankind in just a few years. The browsing kangaroo was rendered extinct by humans – probably shot by shopkeepers after perennially replying to their "Can I help you?" with "No, just browsing."

Although humans didn't discover the Stellers' sea cow until 1741, we managed to hunt it to eradication in under thirty years. The last remaining flock of Great Auk were traced to an island off Iceland, where they were killed in 1844 by natural history collectors for museums exhibits! Hashtag irony.

The thylacine, commonly but inaccurately known as both the Tasmanian tiger (it's not a tiger) and Tasmanian wolf (it's not a wolf) lived in similar environments to koala bears (it's not a bear), before being hunted to extinction. Concentrate on the next two dates: in 1937 the thylacine was awarded protected status. The thylacine had become extinct in 1935. Good job, humans.

Oh, and it's a statistical certainty that humans will become extinct too. So stop looking so smug right now!

SAVING THE WESTGATE'S BACON

Safely reaching February means I have lived in Oxford for exactly 21 years. Dwelling here has enabled me to see many beautiful things [*start imagining an Elgar symphony playing*]: The cluttered colours of Eights Week, spires piercing through dawn mist hovering over the city's roofscape, scholars' bicycles rattling timelessly across ancient Merton Street cobbles and the Westgate Centre [*imagine sound of needle scratching and Elgar suddenly halting*].

Hardly anyone, it seems, loves the Westgate Centre. It is even probable that the word "carbuncle" did not exist in the Oxford English Dictionary until 1972 when the Westgate was erected, and the city's foremost lexicographers hastily sanctioned a meeting upon realisation that existing derisory architectural nouns were too inconsequentially tepid to describe Oxford's latest dreaming spire — yes, it does have a complying spire. Hence inventive neology was their only available option.

The name Westgate evokes a promise of something historical — a promise that remains harshly undelivered. The medieval name Westgate was resurrected in 1972 with the new shopping centre, although by 1973 several people evidently believed there remained unreached potential to make it uglier. Planners clearly briefed: "come on, we've now got one of Britain's ugliest buildings. But with more effort and harnessed imagination, we could have THE ugliest building. Let's turn up the ugly-o-meter past ten, past imagining Ann Widdecombe stepping out of the bath and carelessly dropping a towel (11), right up to 12 (John Prescott, same bathroom scene)." So in 1974 they added the car park. Forty-one years later, they saw sense and literally blew it up in 2015.

All of which is harsh on the Westgate. After all, it is a functional building, housing a scrumptious public library and local studies section crammed with nutritious reading. Oh, and some shops. And the Westgate certainly appears popular — if popularity is measured by numbers passing through the door, it would be difficult to prove empirically the existence of a more popular building in Oxford.

It's just that … well, it is consistent with the 1970s fashion for allowing architectural beauty to become irreversibly moribund. Of course, it does not help being located in Oxford and thus surrounded by some of England's finest buildings. If the Westgate had been built in Hull, it would probably feature on the postcards. Instead, it is forced to compete with Oxford's extraordinary surrounding buildings – and if you are not considered attractive, then it is probably not a good idea to go out surrounded by your super-model friends.

Oxford's finest buildings are not the Westgate's friends — the Rad Cam, Clarendon, Sheldonian are all redolent of Town's perceived subjugation to Gown.

However, the Westgate does possess a pleasing secret. A plaque commemorates Roger Bacon, the man who first predicted (centuries ahead of Copernicus and Galileo) that the planets revolve around the sun. Unfortunately, I have seen more attractive plaque on teeth. This one is cemented to the car park wall, behind a tree, in an area regularly carpeted with dog mess.

Bacon was nicknamed Doctor Mirabilis — meaning "wonderful teacher" — and published *Opus Majus* a 13th-century bookshelf-buckling 900-page tome. The title translates, fittingly, as "Major Work". Whereas most books ultimately fail to live up to their titles: the *Little Book of Calm* is not little (it has more than 100 pages), is not a book (it is a list) and is not calming. It made me livid and bilious with its noxiously dispensed twee aphorisms ... sorry, I need a moment.

Opus Majus deserved, and lived up to, its immodest title. Mixing philosophy, astronomy, anatomy and religious criticism, the work foresaw the future would include powered flight, space travel and steam power. Strangely, it failed to predict that the i-Pod Shuffle would come with white headphones as standard by 2007.

Bacon had taken holy orders after the Franciscans arrived in Oxford in 1224 and established Greyfriars. As a practising monk, contradicting the Bible by declaring that the earth had not been created as the centre of the universe must have come up at his annual workplace appraisal. Historians have not discovered any documentation covering the Franciscans' response, so we will have to surmise...

ABBOT: Ah, come in Eggy. Why are you standing in the doorway?

BACON: You know perfectly well I do not answer to "Eggy". Just because my name is Bacon doesn't render it hilarious to nickname me Eggy.

ABBOTT: You must admit it's a bit funny. The lads in the belfry this morning thought it was hilarious.

BACON: Maybe I should have joined a silent order.

ABBOT: Well, Eggy is better than that ridiculous nickname you want everyone to call you – Doctor Miserable.

BACON: Doctor Mirabilis

ABBOT: Yeah, whatever. Look, I've got your 12-month appraisal form here and on the whole it has been a good year. Lots of overtime in the chancery chanting for the souls of our paymasters the rich to get into heaven – a good prayer outsourcing contract to get. Brilliant work on copying out the Bible with an impressive amount of fruit illustrations prettifying the capital letters.

BACON: Thank you – pleased you've noticed.

ABBOT: Yeah, it's just that the Brother Superior is making a big fuss about some peccadillo you did last month. Ah, here we are – published book rendering the entire concept of God's existence obsolete.

BACON: Oh, you mean that whole Bible is massively wrong thing?

ABBOT: Yeah. I have checked, and as a Franciscan monk you may have gone slightly off message there.

BACON: Will this affect my pay rise this year?

ABBOT: Not really. I think everyone upstairs has been more than reasonable about this, and after careful and fair discussion they have decided upon either death by being burned alive or ... do you what me to list the alternative?

BACON: Hmmm. Okay, go on then.

ABBOT: ... or placed under house arrest in St Aldate's.

BACON: That's a bit of a shock. I was expecting the punishment to be picking up litter in the cloisters after morning prayers.

ABBOT: There is some good news too. 'Cos the lads thought it was a bit harsh, they have consented to call you Doctor Miserable.

BACON: Doctor Mirabilis.

ABBOT: And we're getting a plaque put up for you.

BACON: Where?

ABBOT: The Westgate cart park

BACON: Actually, do call me Doctor Miserable.

THE ROMANS: WHEN IN OXFORD

Although we've been married for several years, my wife still refuses to experiment in the bedroom. Needless to say, I find this highly frustrating. "There's nothing wrong with our current colour scheme; the wallpaper and curtains are fine," she insists.

I go downstairs and do something no writer or homeworker should ever do: turn on the television during the day. Scriptwriters have a rule: never watch anything in the daytime unless you wrote it. Even more uncharacteristically, I am watching *Loose Women*. [Depress sarcasm key.] I've heard it is very good. [Release sarcasm key.]

My explanation is that a friend is appearing as a guest. When I join the show, a panel of brash extroverts are discussing, er, *cough*, pubic hair topography. At 1.30 in the afternoon. "Unfortunately we can't show you pictures," cackles one of the shouty, over-confident presenters who abandoned subtlety twenty years ago and has floored the accelerator pedal ever since to get as far away as possible. Her fellow panellists collapse in giggles like schoolgirls claiming the backseat of a bus.

My friend is introduced and has around 18 seconds to provide some semblance of intellectual insight. My fear is that they have booked one of Oxford's most eminent historians and authors, and their opening question will be about whether she waxes or trims. Perhaps anticipating this, she mocks their bawdiness, and cleverly links to how people at Henry VIII's court behaved – grabbing the conversational subject's steering wheel and re-routing the discussion from Smut Street to Academic Avenue. She hints that Tudors could be magnificently rude, rendering the contemporary *Loose Women*, veneered in their 21st-century smugness, comparative puritans.

Whenever she mentions the second Tudor monarch I expect her to qualify it with: "Henry VIII – you know, fat bloke with a commitment problem?" Later, an ambitious deployment of the word "interregnum" prompts looks of bewildered perplexity from the panel. The owners of these flummoxed faces appear unable to express their bemusement – like zoo animals discovering they've been mistakenly given the wrong food by a distracted keeper.

Yet history can be popularised without lowbrow inevitability, as I discover that evening when I go out.

Probably sensing that I am about to arrive at an entrance and go inside to escape the weather, the rain makes an extra effort to lash down just before I reach a door and evade the furious elements. I am in Beaumont Street and a Roman centurion from 74AD gives me an "alright?" nod as I enter. Nothing odd about that. Not if you are entering the Ashmolean Museum for their monthly Live Friday openings.

Luckily, both the ancient outer doors, and the uncompromisingly modern inner ones, are twenty feet tall. This is presumably to ensure that any visiting giraffes won't feel excluded. Once inside, I notice two things: 1) It's dry. 2) There is a shirtless Roman soldier demonstrating something to a group of enthralled woman. Mainly his uncovered muscles. My wife instantly heads to his table – disappearing as quickly as an unleashed dog arriving at the park.

Boastfully shirtless guy introduces himself with a statement that begins: "My name is Bigedus (*or something*). I am a Roman centurion, commander of an army." This reminds me of that movie starring A-list git and silly accent specialist Russell Crowe. I can remember the quote exactly: "My name is Maximus Decimus Meridius, commander of the TV remote, General Knowledge quiz specialist and loyal servant to Arsenal, the TRUE champions. Father to a lazy son, husband to a permanently disappointed wife. And I will have pizza, in this life or the next." I think that's spot-on.

Greek ghouls are also loose in the museum. In the darkened recess of "Hades' Underworld" (or "Basement Café", as it's usually called) a barefooted girl in a black leotard, face covered with grey theatrical make-up, spooks children and one adult: me. She's actually a drama student but her forte is competitive staring. With an ambitious actress, staring roles evidently come before starring roles. She stares at a group – they all lose. Then she stares at me. I don't blink. So she moves her face to within a millimetre of mine – sufficiently close for our noses to briefly touch. "For a woman who never washes her face, you're very nice," I remark. She stubbornly stays in character and refuses to smile. Then I blink. She wins.

My wife announces she wants to visit the Toga Station. Since I have no intention of visiting the Toga Station whatsoever, I put my foot down. And then my other foot. As I meekly follow my wife to the Toga Station.

It turns out to be (wo)manned by a group of gorgeous girls from the Oxford University Classics Society. "Oh, you're keen now, aren't you?" remarks my wife. "Err … no. I just like the vibrant colour of the materials." My dressers are all wearing white. "What, the extensive range of whites?" my wife queries.

My dresser relays some fascinating Roman information. Apparently Romans were literally uniformed by class, wealth and status. Nevertheless my knowledgeable toga-tier demonstrates effortlessly how a long rectangle of cloth can be transformed into a garment ideal for either casual daytime or formal evening Roman-wear. Challenged to a race with my wife to see who can tie a toga the quickest, I narrowly lose. But brazenly suggest: "surely we can call that a tie!"

Elsewhere a girl wearing a sackcloth tunic introduces herself. "My name is Servilia and I am a Roman slave." She then flashes me an unmistakable message with her eyes that I interpret as, "Don't say anything as I've almost certainly already heard it tonight."

"So Servilia," I begin, noticing my wife raising her hand in readiness to deliver a backhand should I say anything deemed inappropriate, "are you available for purchase in the museum shop?" Luckily everyone laughs, so my wife opts to descend her arm peacefully.

Servilia enlightens us about the lives of Roman slaves, noting how forty per cent of Rome's population was composed of slaves. Hence Romans lived in permanent fear of slave rebellions. Paradoxically, she elaborates that some slaves could reach comfortable status, even owning their own slaves. My opinion of the Romans is dropping by the minute.

So, apart from the slavery, genocides, invasions, war crimes, sexism, enforced death matches for entertainment and general barbarism, what have the Romans ever done for us? Well, there's the feeding people to the lions. Personally, I don't think producing the occasional nice mosaic and aqueduct are going to re-balance the injustice scales.

My wife buys something from the museum shop to help decorate our bedroom. It's not Servilia.

THE PUNCH & JUDY SHOW: PC WORLD

Here's something that has often puzzled me: how can a reader of the *Sunday Sport* spot the mock April Fool story in the newspaper's 1 April edition? Paradoxically, the *Sunday Sport* announced its own discontinuance on 1 April … and since previous genuine headlines have included "B52 Bomber Found on Moon", "The Virgin Mary Built Our Shed" and "Tony Blair to be Appointed Middle East Peace Envoy", I counsel keeping a large pinch of salt handy.

Earlier this year newspapers and broadcast media ran their traditional April Fool stories with competing alacrity. BBC Radio 4 stuck with a prolonged routine about 3D radio that was painfully unfunny (if you've got access to some of the best comedy writers in the world, here's a tip: use them!), yet heroically persevered with the "joke" in the *Today* programme for fully three hours – a bit like an uncle who considers himself "eccentric" while everyone else thinks "annoying", as he constantly squirts people in the face with his joke flower, believing that eventually someone WILL find it funny.

The Independent ran a piece covering Spain's intention to buy Ronaldo's nationality from Portugal. Yet the best April Fool story I saw was closer to home ... in this newspaper: proclaiming that politically correct Health & Safety execs would ban Oxfordshire's own Pooh Sticks event from using wooden sticks. Even quotes from a Terri Fied and Ivor Chestikov didn't enable everyone to spot the joke! The Best April Fool story is a long overdue category for inclusion at the National Press Awards.

Any area involving children is particularly vulnerable to the invading march of Health & Safety executives and Political Correctness – that nemesis of Middle England, sanitising everything by spraying it with PC disinfectant – potentially explaining why many believed the story. Suggs was recently rumoured to have revised some early non-PC song lyrics: a case of Madness gone politically correct. And surely the days of Punch & Judy are limited...

PUPPETEER: I've got a Council letter asking me to come in for an audit on my show.

OFFICIAL: What's your act?

PUPPETEER: I do Punch & Judy for the kiddies – been a family business for years.

OFFICIAL: Who's Punch?

PUPPETEER: Punch is Judy's husband.

OFFICIAL: Co-habiting partner.

PUPPETEER: Oh, yes, I'll make that change.

OFFICIAL: Besides, why would the audience assume they're married?

PUPPETEER: Well, they spend all their time bickering, throwing stuff at each other and never have sex.

OFFICIAL: Okay, you can say they're married. What happens in the show?

PUPPETEER: Well, Punch argues with Judy.

OFFICIAL: You're happy with Punch subjugating Judy?

PUPPETEER: OK. They conduct a constructive dialogue identifying positive outcomes of shared matrimonial challenges.

OFFICIAL: Better. What action takes place?

PUPPETEER: Well, Punch and Judy hit each other with rolling pins – the kids love that bit.

OFFICIAL: What?!! Does Act Two take place in a Women's Refuge for victims of domestic abuse?

PUPPETEER: No … Act Two is when Punch steals a string of sausages.

OFFICIAL: What sort of role model is that for impressionable watching children?

PUPPETEER: You're right. He probably shouldn't steal.

OFFICIAL: No, I mean eating sausages – meat is murder. Couldn't he have tofu instead?

PUPPETEER: OK, I'll make that change too.

OFFICIAL: What happens next?

PUPPETEER: A crocodile arrives and tries to eat the sausages.

OFFICIAL: Crocodile! Glorifying the illicit trade in endangered animals!

PUPPETEER: … but I need a crocodile for my "get me some sausages waiter, and make it snappy" gag.

OFFICIAL: Here's my marker pen – you can draw a line through that bit of the script yourself. Then what happens?

PUPPETEER: Punch gets so angry he beats the crocodile with a stick.

OFFICIAL: Animal cruelty – do you want animal rights activists picketing your show?

PUPPETEER: Okay, change made.

OFFICIAL: What happens next?

PUPPETEER: Punch and Judy bash each other with rolling pins for another five minutes until a policeman arrives.

OFFICIAL: No! Can't they just cuddle instead? And what's the policeman's role?

PUPPETEER: The policeman beats Punch and Judy repeatedly in a sadistic and unprovoked attack, clubbing them mercilessly with a terrifying sickening brutality.

OFFICIAL: That seems okay, realistic enough – you can keep that bit in.

PUPPETEER: Then he arrests Punch.

OFFICIAL: Hmm … can we acknowledge violence as a negative expressional outlet? Could Punch and Judy maybe promote a knife amnesty?

PUPPETEER: [*sarcastically*] How about a rolling pin amnesty?!

OFFICIAL: Yes, good idea.

PUPPETEER: What!? This is PC nonsense.

OFFICIAL: Is that the name of the policeman character: PC Nonsense?

PUPPETEER: No, I mean political correctness nonsense.

OFFICIAL: Anything else in the act I should know about?

PUPPETEER: Maybe … Punch has a big nose.

OFFICIAL: Poking fun at a physical disability, that's practically a bully's charter.

PUPPETEER: Okay, he's now got an ordinary sized nose. I'll buy some sandpaper.

OFFICIAL: Good. What happens next?

PUPPETEER: The hangman appears.

OFFICIAL: You're putting capital punishment – punitive state-endorsed murder – in the showroom as a viable option for today's kids?

PUPPETEER: Punch could be sentenced to do community service instead, meeting his victims in an empathy establishment exercise.

OFFICIAL: Better. How does it end?

PUPPETEER: Traditionally, Punch smacks Judy over the head saying "I love clubbing at the seaside". That's my best Punch line – literally in this case. No? Okay, I'll end with a group hug instead.

OFFICIAL: Licence granted. That's the way to do it!!

WOMEN

THE CLUCKING HEN PARTY

I appear to have become the go-to-guy for hen parties in Oxford. No, I am not a stripper. Instead, hens (as participants prefer to call themselves) organise a weekend for their hen (the bride) and book me to provide them with a comedy tour of the city. As the lone male within a group of hens, this apparently means I am called "a cock". Great. One tour involved an unembarrassed hen brazenly wearing a T-shirt proclaiming "World's Biggest Slapper" in bold fuchsia lettering. I asked if that statement had been independently verified, as otherwise she would encounter ineligibility for inclusion in the *Guinness Book of Records*.

Recently I received a booking for a group of hens from Essex. There should have been an early geography-based warning there. On making the booking, they insist that I should be "funny and risqué but also provide some quirky QI-type facts about Oxford". Clinging to the last detail, I accept the booking.

Conscientiously, I email the organising hen Sue to provide details of the bride so I can incorporate material specific to her into my set. Just before the tour she pings me an email that sighs, "I can't think of much." I ask her to try again as it will benefit the experience for Charlotte [name changed] if I can interweave observations about her life. "Okay," she consents and then sends an email prefixed with, "Don't think there's much of interest here, but…" It is probably the best email in the history of the Internet. What follows is a mere sample of the two page email:

"Charlotte was once in an orgy. A couple of the other hens were involved. It's gone down in folklore in our Essex town as 'The Orgy', although it was just taking turns snogging different boys. Sadly I wasn't invited. Charlotte's favourite thing to do is drink a lot of wine. She has been sick on lots of famous people. Charlotte has been sick on two members of Take That. One of them signed something for her, saying 'Stop being sick on me!' She recently accepted a police caution for being drunk and disorderly, and her parents had to pick her up from the police station even though she's 34! She once wrote a message on the wall of her boyfriend's house telling him 'consider yourself dumped you two-timing scumbag'. She later accepted a police caution for graffiti and again had to be picked up from the police cells by her parents. She once went to Madagascar where a monkey removed her bra."

The next morning I am waiting, shivering with regret, for the hens to arrive. Unpredictably, the bride turns outs to be surprisingly demure, bordering upon taciturn. Though I suspect she's currently in her dry Gremlin mode, not yet fed wine after midnight. Quietly spoken, she regularly sips water to offset dehydration incurred by the previous evening's drinking, and is not the booze-addled party monster I feared. "Wait until she's been at the wine," confirms one of her fellow hens. "Do you know where we're going tonight?" the organising hen asks me excitedly. "Err … is it an AA meeting?" I ask.

I enquire about the Madagascan monkey: "Was it the most inexpert attempt you've experienced at removing your bra?" "No, not by a long way!" she replies, against a backdrop of chuckling hens. She is nervously awaiting "The Orgy" being mentioned. I decide to make them wait.

Standing in St John's I try infusing the comedy with some nutritious historical facts, when Essex hairdresser Tracy asks an impossibly hard question. As a tour guide you should always admit to not knowing an answer: "I don't know. I'm not Google – I pay taxes." "That's Okay, 'cos I'm really thick," says Tracy, pronouncing "thick" in that Essex way as if it's spelt "fick". She's not fick – thick people don't tend to ask hard questions. But she is enormous fun and happy to put her (impractically-heeled for a walking tour) foot in it again and again. Being blissfully unaware of the concept of rhetorical questioning ensures I have considerable audience banter.

Outside New College an opportunity presents itself via spoonerisms to do material rude enough to make a docker blush. The hens love it and demand more. After four decreasingly patient attempts at explaining the concept of spoonerisms to Tracy she replies, "I still don't get it." "You should see her sick duck," I say. The girls collapse into giggles. "Why, can't she take it to the vet?" enquires Tracy. "No, remember you have to interchange the letters…" counsels her friend.

Fully twenty minutes later, the tranquillity of Radcliffe Square is shattered. Standing next to a formally attired elderly tour guide and his dignified party of pensioners, Tracy blurts out at equivalent volume to most emergency vehicles' sirens: "Oh, I get it! The girl with her sick duck. You should see her s…" Prior to decoding some even ruder ones. Very much out loud.

Soon it is time to raise the subject that at least three hens have been dreading. "Okay, hands up who attended the notorious orgy. Come on Charlotte, we know you did." Following Charlotte's lead, two more hands are reluctantly half-raised. Tracy raises hers apologetically. I arrow her a mock "I'm so disappointed" look. "It was only snogging," she protests.

Raising my voice to an abrasive tone previously unfamiliar to the tour group, I admonish them like a disapproving parent: "You three should be thoroughly ashamed of yourselves for such disgraceful behaviour." And I pause, while they half-nod their bowed heads, as timing is important in comedy. "Appalling conduct! Really! Organising an orgy with lots of fit boys and not inviting your close friend Sue to share in the fun." Comedy is also about creating tension then releasing it.

Before we part Charlotte kindly remarks, "That was the best tour ever!" and insists on a hug. Meanwhile, Tracy loudly declares: "Oh, I get the one about Jeremy Hunt being careless. You mean he's a hairless…"

THE CHANCE AFFAIR

Loitering around the produce section of Tesco just got interesting – and not because Antony Worrall Thompson started the year with a cunning plan to ensure his bag of ingredients came in at under £5 for *Ready Steady Crook* (no, not a typo).

Repressed British people don't tend to interact with each other, as everyone on a packed Tube train or bus expertly peering into neutral nowhere can testify. So I was initially surprised when an Oxford student spoke to me while I was engaged in the traditional supermarket practice of squeezing an avocado. "Are they ripe?" she enquired, accompanied by a world-improving smile. Initially I did what most British people do in such circumstances: assume she was (a) talking to someone else or (b) mentally ill. Then, realising she was speaking to me, I replied in stunned staccato fragments of partial words: "giv ... err ... squee ... yeah." Think I handled that well.

Her warm personality contrasted with being a cold person (in a literal sense), as her clothing choices were a thick coat buttoned chokingly high, a huge scarf accessorised with ear muffs and a pair of mittens so vast it must have produced the equivalent kinetic effect to walking around with both hands permanently embedded in two buckets of steaming hot porridge. "I'm tempted by your ripe tomatoes" (depressingly not a euphemism), she said looking into my basket, "I can eat a whole packet in one go." And off she fluttered, leaving the world a tiny bit friendlier behind her. Indeed, she was a diminutive bundle of cheery loveliness, someone who had clearly decided to behave out of kilter from an otherwise thoroughly unfriendly and unresponsive society, and adopt a cheerful disposition interacting with strangers. I prefer her world and want to join.

She's no doubt representative of most parents' imagined futures when the consultant announces at the twenty-week scan that they're having a girl. They project someone like her, glimpsing a future where she's purposefully striding through Oxford with gown flowing importantly behind her, determined to improve the lives of everyone she meets and somehow managing to look effortlessly pulchritudinous in unflatteringly thick woolly tights and two buckets of porridge on the end of her hands. Her dress sense is surely consistent with most parents' dream involving their daughter. Leaving the house with sensible coat and a scarf longer than some B-roads may win parental admiration, though she might have overdone it a tad, forcing some parents to demand: "You are NOT going out dressed like that, young lady. Back to your room and change. You're not leaving this house until you take something off!"

Then I go to Jams & Preserves and try to decide if I should buy the one that is 98% sugar or the alternative aggressively marketed as the healthy option that contains only 97% sugar. Sweet Disposition Girl then stands next to me with an undergraduate friend I hadn't noticed thirty seconds ago, but then again she's clearly the type that makes friends quickly. I concentrate on the marmalade labels in case she asks me any follow-up questions about other purchases in my basket.

This time I'll try and use whole words in my reply. Her friend speaks: "Gosh, Abigail, I can't believe you're involved with a married man. And he's so much older."

Wow. Like a nun with a past, there's salacious sauciness in the world of sweet cheery loveliness, no matter how many layers you wear. And, somewhere, a bloody lucky married man. Though I doubt if this sequence features in parents' dreams of their future daughter.

They move to Milk, Butter & Yogurt – and I decide to covertly follow. Abigail (name changed to protect the guilty) chides her friend. "Keep your voice down – we don't want it in the papers." Er, that's what I'm kinda doing now. Sorry, Abigail. But I still think you're lovely and I did change your name. Though you may want to take your moral compass back to the shop to get the needle fixed.

Leaving Tesco I see them ahead, disappearing into Debenhams – presumably to buy a bigger coat. Convincing myself that I'm an investigative reporter, more Bernstein & Woodward than Glen Muldare, and intent on proving my idiocy, I follow at a distance, immediately concluding that I'll never follow anyone again, as my face glows with shaming concern that this won't look good on my charge sheet if my wife spots me following two girls onto an escalator, and I commence my explanation with "But she has affairs with much older married men", even without the risk of prompting a potential appearance before the Leveson inquiry.

Stepping off the escalator, they become distracted by the perfume sniper, and my cover will be blown if I enter any deeper into territory that is so obviously behind enemy lines. Her friend gets sprayed, but the grassy knoll dweller of the cosmetics industry is bemused, and freezes her trigger finger when she spots that Abigail doesn't possess a square millimetre of exposed flesh to spray.

The last line I hear Abigail impart is "I didn't mean this to happen." No, of course you didn't. Presumably "I didn't mean to keep accepting drinks invitations, I didn't mean to text him 47 times one weekend, I didn't mean to furtively arrange to 'accidentally' meet him wearing my best outfit: a flattering pink chiffon dress (though I was very cold), I didn't mean to deliberately wear the same perfume as his wife so as not to arouse her suspicion." I'd fear for her diminutive being should the angry Other Woman ever ring her doorbell – although with ear muffs that large, she'd undoubtedly never hear the bell. But I can understand: I'd met Abigail for twenty seconds, and all she'd done was offer to feel my avocados (no … stop it), and I was besmitten, while she was behatted, bemittened and bemuffed.

A week later I'm on an Oxford bus. A woman with a harsh, unforgiving demeanour impatiently answers a phone and begins a jeremiad: "Okay, I guess. Solicitor phoned and said he wants to collect some stuff. I told him not to bother – 'cos I chucked it all out. He wants his big coat back. I told him to get his new tart to buy him one!" I think I've found The Other Woman.

THE WOMEN WHO STAND UP FOR THEMSELVES

This month I've been scripting and mentoring two stand-up comedians. They have never previously done stand-up. But they have been comedians before (with friends, family, releasing workplace tension) and they've definitely stood up loads of times (every time they've left a chair in fact) so they should be able to do stand-up comedy, right? Perhaps that is a leap of Greg Rutherford proportions.

My comedy prodigies Gill Oliver and Rebecca Moore are stand-up virgins. Indeed, both were happily enrolled in the abstinence programme when it came to the difficult and dependably humiliating ordeal of stand-up. Then a commissioning editor suggested they illustrate a newspaper feature bemoaning the lack of females in stand-up by … er … doing a stand-up gig.

This meant a comedy professional needed to be recruited. Quickly. I agreed to take the job, but only after playing some tough hardball negotiations. "Is there a fee?" "No." "Expenses?" "No." "Will there be biscuits?" "Yes." "OK, I'll do it."

Gill is ginger and "out", not living a closeted "strawberry blonde" lie. Talking to her establishes how far Her People have suffered decades of comedic prejudice. This helps formulate a strong established character for her act.

Rebecca is unlike anyone I have previously met. In a good way. Luckily for the purposes of undertaking something as off-the-scale terrifying as stand-up, Rebecca is up for anything. Ask Rebecca, "Do you fancy swimming the English Channel tomorrow?" her default response would be, "Pick me up at 3am." An endearing, unembarrassable extrovert constantly sticking her fingers into the plug socket of life means she is a gift to write for. We chat through her past to discover if anything may be "routine worthy". It transpires that most of her time on this planet is routine worthy.

Some males appear to believe that God created Eve so that men had someone to laugh at their jokes. And with this comes an evolved spurious distrust of a woman's capacity to be funny. Our collective mission is to dismantle the ludicrous prejudice that not possessing a Y chromosome somehow renders you incapable of being funny. Professional contrarian Christopher Hitchens opined that women don't need to be funny because they already hold such strong appeal to men. Hmmm. So the argument goes that women presumably therefore don't aspire to literacy, personal hygiene or fulfilling employment, as men will always be attracted to them regardless. It's impossible to finish an article by any Hitchens brother, as there's a point reached at about the third or fourth paragraph where you just fling it across the room.

And yet this view is oddly prevalent among an unenlightened minority. To paraphrase Dr Samuel Johnson's – formerly of Pembroke College, Oxford – comment on female preachers: "Sir, a woman doing stand-up is like a dog walking on its hind legs. It is not done well; but you are surprised to find it done at all."

I have statistics! Trawling through the shelf-buckling 398-page Edinburgh Festival brochure, I calculated that out of the hundreds of stand-ups doing a turn at the latest comedy trade fair that the Edinburgh Fringe represents, only 18% were female.

That stat may not necessarily be as sexist as it looks. If 82% of the applicants who applied to work in garden centres were male there would be a resultant gender discrepancy in their staffing levels. But would that be the fault of garden centres? Horticulture in general? Or just reflective of women's choices?

So why are there not more stand-up comedians in dresses (Eddie Izzard notwithstanding)? Current fashion dictates that men, not women, are portrayed as the traditional victims of jokes, i.e. man sees attractive girl and walks into a lamppost. This joke was probably around in the Neolithic period – that's when Bruce Forsyth would still have only been a teenager. That joke is freighted with gender politics. He's the stupid one, supinely distracted.

That said, analysing humour is said to be a lot like dissecting a frog – no-one laughs, and the frog dies. Whenever a famous frog is laid bare for examination and public inspection, it dies – as proved by François Hollande's presidency. Notice how that joke has suddenly now become satire. Satire is perceived as a higher art form than jokes. But here's a trade secret: satire is ordinarily more about confirming existing stereotypes (i.e. endorsing our existing shorthand vision of bankers, the French, Bruce Forsyth, bankers again).

Yet in every sitcom you've ever watched there are likely to be funny female characters. Women are funny in films and in print. And there are capable acidic humourists like Dorothy Parker.

Yet Lee Mack expressed the view on *Desert Islands Discs* recently that there are fewer female stand-ups because women aren't such pathological show-offs. Nice attempt there to justify the gender discrepancy with a positive re-frame. In fact, this viewpoint is easily dismantled. If women are incapable of being egotistically extrovert stand-ups, then how do you explain Ruby Wax's and Jenny Éclair's 30 + year careers? And Joan Rivers' 60-year one. I'd do a joke here about Joan Rivers' repeated facelifts, but don't consider it appropriate to initiate bitchy humour about someone with a kindly, genteel and empathetic act like hers.

When Jo Brand appeared on the same show – although on second thoughts she might have been on *Dessert Island Discs* [get in!] – she did funny fat jokes. You can only do fat jokes if you're fat, only crack gags about being Muslim if you're Muslim, but you can do gags about being a massive git without necessarily being Piers Morgan.

Another theory as to why stand-up traditionally draws males to the recruiting office is the compensation argument, i.e. "I've never been good looking, so I get status, validation and affection from being funny." Some male stand-ups indubitably peacock to potential peahens. One customarily controversial US comedian once told an American chat show: "Stand-up is the easiest way to attract pussy". I disagree – opening a tin of Whiskas is much easier.

I've also heard the judgement: "To appear physically funny isn't sexy." Expressed by a woman! Miranda Hart doesn't need to be sexy, in the same way that your dentist doesn't need to be sexy. But there are jobs where there is a compulsory requirement to be funny: stand-up comedian/talk show host/Ben Elton until 1989. And for some reason there are jobs where you do need to be sexy: presenting the weather on Sky.

So how did Gill and Rebecca's debut gig go? Everybody started laughing at them in public. So it went brilliantly.

THE UPSET ACTRESS

My wife is angry. Proper angry. This has been signalled by detonating the hostilities-escalating phrase: "I suppose you're too insensitive to even know what you've done." Part of me reaches to point out the split infinitive usage, fortunately restrained by a more persuasive other brain part which muzzles the urge just in time. That comment would not constitute water off a duck's back, but water on a chip pan fire.

Didactic enlightenment through cruel experience has taught me to stay silent in these situations. There is nothing I can possibly say that won't make the situation deteriorate. It's like spotting a tiny fire in the kitchen and then attempting to decide which bucket to throw on it: the buckets are marked: "petrol", "paraffin" and "wood shavings". Pretty soon you've lost the house. As can happen with divorces.

"You've honestly no idea what you've done, have you?" she yells, stretching the world "unbelievable" to five lengthy syllables. "Un-be-liev-ab-le!" Told you.

This does seem to be quite serious. At this stage I am unable to calibrate the magnitude of my injudiciousness. My indiscretion potentially ranges from the epic (caught sleeping with the Lithuanian au pair – again) to the slight (depositing a dark sock into the whites wash laundry basket – again.) Fortunately we can't afford an au pair – so it's unlikely to be the former. Unfortunately we cannot afford a laundry basket either, so it's equally unlikely to be the latter.

"Still no idea, have you?" mutters my wife, arms folded, gaze stubbornly locked to the side, clearly wishing there was an accompanying female in the room who could catch her eye and sagely nod agreement. Once I was in a shop when I did something (obviously

I still have no idea what) that caused my wife to interact with a passing stranger. "Look at this insensitive idiot I have to live with," said my wife, prompting the other woman to reply with a confirming, "I know, I do sympathise – mine is equally pathetic", "but surely not as bad as mine – it's like living in *Project Nim*!" The fact that my wife and stranger lady were able to conduct this entire conversation with just two fleeting facial expressions demonstrates the incontestable superiority of women.

Recently, in a series of jobs that the struggling Ed Reardon-esque writer cannot afford to refuse, I covered the Wife Carrying World Championships. Discovering that this was staged early on Sunday morning, and a long train journey from Oxford necessitating travel and accommodation, it felt like a body blow to discover expenses were not provided. But not as much as the body blow encountered by one of the participants. While carrying his wife over one of the course's regulation straw bale obstacles he dropped her with a shuddering thud to the ground – like a coalman emptying a sack. Luckily, the fastest running in the race was demonstrated by the St John's Ambulance crew who dashed to treat the spilt wife at the scene. I can envisage the couple at the breakfast table the next morning, her tilting in a neck brace while cautiously drinking through a straw, with her husband sitting opposite experiencing the silent treatment, asking, "Okay, I know I must have done something to upset you, but if you're not going to tell me what…"

"No idea?" continues my wife. I commission my brain to research what transgression I've committed recently while Radio 4 chatters to itself in the background. I retune and hear an actress on Radio 4 Extra.

This immediately sends me back to a bedsit in South London where I first met the actress years earlier. She required a writer to gag-up a script, while the Guinness World Record people were also presumably due to pop by at any moment to adjudicate the World's Untidiest Flat. Had the RSPCA visited they would have declared it unfit accommodation for pigs. Upon arrival she instructed me to make a coffee. Moving more discarded clothes from the kitchen than a professional jumble sale organiser would consider reasonable for a week's work (I'm sure there was an explanation for the bra in the microwave), I eventually revealed a fridge. Opening it I discovered she had obtained breakfast from Starbucks (two astringently priced croissants in a brown bag) and lunch, tea, dinner and supper from Threshers.

Suddenly I deduced that the earlier showbiz peck-peck-peck greeting had revealed an alarming smell of alcohol on her breadth (never a good sign at 10am on a workday). My wife would have spotted earlier the eyes blurred red from crying.

"We'll obviously need a strong opener for your stand-up routine. So what do you want to tell the audience about yourself that'll deliver a really big laugh?" I ask.

"My life is crap and I hate myself," she replies. Tears suddenly gush around the kitchen like an activated sprinkler system.

"Yeah, golden rule of stand-up comedy: always open with a guaranteed big laugh," I remark. After an hour's work all we had down on paper was multiple tear stains. Sensing she could use the company of a friend, I scrolled through her phone contacts. "How about ringing Abigail?" "She's a bitch." "Okay, how about Adel?" "Bitch." "Alison?" "Bitch." Basically we were having the conversation that the people responsible at Battersea Dogs' Home for naming and sexing new arrivals must have. "Amanda?" "Bitch." "Ann?" "Bitch."

Anyway, it all worked out. After patiently scrolling down alphabetically I eventually found a friend she tolerated – if memory serves her name was Zoe. And we wrote the script. Some jokes even survived the edit for an unbroadcast panel show pilot. When I left her flat I distinctly remember her hugging me and not letting go for a long time, while thanking me for being a good listener.

When I snap back to the here and now, and focus on the present kitchen scene, my wife is ending a sentence: "… which is why you're in so much trouble. OH MY GOD! You're doing it again now, aren't you?! What are you thinking now?"

I hypothesise that replying, "I was thinking about the time I held a beautiful actress in my arms," even with mitigating chivalrous circumstances, would be an incendiary response. Whoever said telling the truth was the best policy was clearly an idiot. And probably divorced.

"You never listen to me, do you?"

Oh, that's what I've done! Why didn't she mention it earlier?

THE PANEL DISCUSSION – PART ONE

A Cambridge University society has asked me to join a panel discussion as they "want someone who can introduce a bit of humour". Fine, I say, flattered to be asked and I try to disguise my obvious gratitude to be invited to anything. Now I can enjoy infuriating everyone I encounter in the months beforehand by casually announcing, "By the way, I've been asked to speak at Cambridge University."

"So, will you be available?" they enquire. "I'll just check my schedules. Hmmm … I suppose I can fit in Cambridge University." My diary is emptier than that of someone who works for a lookalikes agency impersonating Jimmy Savile. Hence I say an instant "yes". "When is the panel discussion?" I enquire, wondering if I need to open my 2016 or 2017 calendar. "The day after tomorrow," they confirm. Not much time for pre-event infuriation creation, then. "And what is it about?" I ask. "Feminism," they reply. Oh (is one of the two words I use in my reply).

Less than 48 hours later I am in a distinctly under-filled and over-lit lecture room affiliated to – but significantly nowhere near – a famous Cambridge college. I have opted to get to Cambridge by spending four hours on a Megabus. Believe me, there is nothing "mega" about Megabus.

There is no speaker's fee, but there will be promised biscuits and expenses. Not for the first time in my career of hanging around in green rooms, I anticipate explaining "I'm one of the writers" as my justification for surreptitiously tipping a plate to an optimum 40-degree angle to ensure all the biscuits slide into my bag. Surviving on food stolen from green rooms is a staple diet of many comedy writers. I once lived off Alan Davies' abandoned birthday cake for five days.

Arriving aggressively early, I am met by the event organiser. She greets me with, "It's great to have you here – we made a list of the people we wanted when setting up the event, and everyone thought you'd be an ideal first choice. Bring as much humour as you can – that'll be great." Another organiser, who turns out to be chairing the event, shows me where I'll be sitting, before letting slip, "Thanks for stepping in at such short notice and helping us out." I knew it! An eleventh hour (and 59 minutes) cancellation. First choice my ... (are three of the four words I thought).

I optimistically ask if there's a green room. "Sorry, we don't have anywhere for you to wait like that, or refreshments, but there's a water cooler and chairs over there." There are no biscuits.

Glancing at my watch at 7.55pm, with the event due to start at 8pm, only three of the rows have anyone sitting in them. Small audiences are difficult for comedy. "There'll be lots of people along soon – they're just finishing dinner in hall," I am reassured by the lady who said I was their First Choice. Within two minutes, the chairwoman – who presumably had a truth serum slipped into her afternoon tea – admits, "We never get many people at these events."

An additional sprinkling of arrivals ensures there is a light dusting of attendees on seats. Fully ten minutes after we are due to start, the chairman stands up to begin – at which point the door flings open like dramatic new evidence arriving to change the course of a TV courtroom drama. A group of undergraduate girls noisily appears, looking like they have been sheep-dogged into the room by a stern looking lecturer. They reluctantly make their way to chairs as slowly and disruptively as possible. One of the new arrivals glances towards an obviously tempting Fire Exit door located immediately on her left, prompting her tutor to tap her handbag as if communicating "don't make me use the Taser again". I spot that several of the latecomers are wearing lacrosse sweatshirts. A small audience – including forty per cent who are clearly being held here against their will – is not conducive to comedy.

As I sit down my fellow panellists greet me warmly and shake hands, which helps to calm my nerves and provide an upswing in my confidence – they all appear to be pleasant human beings. Apart from one. She refuses to shake my hand, which stuns me. I have always been impractically over-sensitive for this world, and this act of unkindness from a total stranger bruises me. "Don't take it personally, she's like that," counsels one of the kind majority.

Then the chairman stands up, holds aloft purposefully a piece of paper and immediately declares, "Feminism today, and why men still want to claim power. Why it is our duty as women to wrestle control back from the patriarchy. I thought we'd start by asking our distinguished panel to say a word, or very short sentence, to define what they think 21st-century feminism should be about." Thanks for that – you could have warned us beforehand in the green room/five chairs near the water cooler.

The frankly scary academic on the panel – who turns out not to be from Cambridge University - interprets "one word or very short sentence" as an opportunity to deliver a five minute uninterrupted diatribe against penis-wielding oppressors of the sisterhood. Or "men", as she viperously calls them. Or, more specifically, me – as it feels. Apparently I am part of a governing male conspiracy to retain the patriarchy – or did she say "phallicarchy"?

The other three participants thankfully display more humanity towards me, and conform to the chairman's (better start calling her chairperson) instruction, and define feminism as "control of our own bodies", "equality" and "choice". For my word, as the booked clown, I momentarily consider saying "ironing", but can't risk losing the audience with literally my first word. "Err … I agree with what they all said. Though my wife usually decides my opinions for me. Oppressive bloody matriarchy." I receive a supportive laugh, grateful that I had sensibly ensured the ironing joke was a line that never made the short journey from brain to mouth. What would the reaction have been? Has anyone lost an audience so quickly since the abrupt ending to the Pied Piper of Hamelin's tour guiding career?

Scary Academic then remarks: "Richard is here because he doesn't believe woman are capable of being funny, so they need him – a man." I am shocked by the sheer wrongness of this remark, as much as I'm stung by it. A weal of painful injustice appears on me blushing red. My anger escapes: "That's just not true. I have worked with numerous female comics. There are countless brilliant female comedians, comedy writers, actresses, humourists, columnists, stand-ups, authors, etc. Saying women are not as capable comedians as men is akin to saying men are better singers or writers than women, i.e. you'd have to be very, very stupid." The audience like my remark. So do my fellow panellists. With one obvious exception. She drones on another minute until the chairperson successfully interrupts her to the relief of the entire room.

Scary Academic appears to be adopting a Maoist stance on the discussion, i.e. she's not only right about everything, but no-one else should be allowed to speak. At one stage she bellows like a banshee war cry, "I have a vagina!" as if a significant number of people in the room were somehow disputing that and were about to ponder aloud, "Oh, we assumed you were a drag act."

Her continued attempts to monopolise the discussion are thwarted by the chairperson with a succinct and timely: "I think we've heard a lot from you already, and I'm keen to involve more people who haven't yet had a chance to contribute." This garners a round of applause. Wow, I'm contemplating doing gags about women ironing at a feminist conference and I'm not the unpopular one in the room.

Then I make a joke about the girls wearing lacrosse shirts, saying I worry that if I come into contact with them I might have an allergic reaction – in case I'm lacrosse intolerant. And also clearly mildly dyslexic. Someone explains the joke ("lacrosse, not lactose, intolerant") which is never a good sign in a comedy performance. There are some playful boos, but mainly laughter – significantly from the students being held against their will under what are clearly becoming siege conditions.

However, much worse is to come.

The Panel Discussion – Part Two

My co-panellists make erudite and sensible points, thereby emphasising my clown status. Someone from the audience shouts out a statistic that 85 per cent of all televised sport features only men. "Yes," I concur, "but 85 per cent of all internet porn features only women – so it's swings and roundabouts." This gets a reasonably decent laugh from just about everyone in the room – you can guess the exception. Proving ironic intention in comedy can be exceptionally difficult, and delivering it akin to treading on eggshells lining thin ice in a minefield. Integral to making that last joke work is the audience's understanding that I am being ironic. I must convince them I am the revealed idiot, and hence the joke is entirely on me for being such a massive idiot – rather than on feminism and the abhorrent gender injustice that the quoted statistic reveals. Luckily, I am a convincing idiot – in fact, people often report, a true natural. Significantly they have already had thirty minutes of my company to reach that conclusion. This is why the ironing joke would have ended in a deserved lynching if cracked right at the beginning.

Then the conversation moves into themes I deem a comedy no-go area. This is why I was secretly reluctant to take the booking, as I am now an uninformed comic who can offer only empathy rather than insight into the appalling sexism still prevalent in the 21st century. For example, the Spanish for "spouses" (esposas) is also the same word meaning "handcuffs".

But I try and add some light to the darkness when the subject of odious internet trolls is raised. Trolls can usually be tracked down easily by the police. "By using computer ISP numbers?" asks the chairperson. "Yes, and by looking under bridges," I interject.

In my opinion, everyone should be a feminist. And that includes men. Especially men. However, there is a small sub-section of feminists who have become so radicalised with quasi-religious zealotry that dogmatic ideology contributes to sectarianism, entrenching the genders into polarised opposition. You know ... the sort who probably wants to ban Waitrose from selling grapes because the fruit contains the word "rapes" in its name.

There is undeniably likewise a miniscule minority of male morons who consider themselves somehow superior to women and believe our problems as a society really started when women got the vote. This unenlightened type believes women incapable of working in certain jobs and instead that they should stay at home cleaning and cooking. Unless there's a war on of course – and wars to this day are generally started by men – in which case it is fine for women to demonstrate their ability to work capably doing every imaginable job. But as soon as the war is over, then it's back to dreamless drudgery for you, missy. Just when you hope this anachronistic brand of male chauvinism has exhibited signs of extinction, you can still spot the occasional breeding pair on public transport. Once I overheard an elderly man fulminating to a nodding wife that "it's time women were put back in their place." I have no idea where that place is, but I am sure it is very nice and has lots of cushions. Then there is also a rash of younger male buffoons who treat women as if they are basically deluxe willy warmers. Console yourself that their numbers are in irreversible decline.

Other than the flotilla of nutters that constitutes misogynists and ultra-extremist all-men-are-potential-rapists feminists bobbing together in a cold sea of animosity, the overwhelming majority of the population revels in displaying remarkable gender similarities – proselytising the view that up to a point gender is merely a social construct. Seeking parity, equality and not remotely preoccupied with how many X or Y chromosomes belong to whom.

However, this startlingly obvious reality is ignored by large swathes of the press. Some elements of the media – from the *Daily Mail* to the *Guardian* – are responsible for billowing out sexist pollution, then cattle prod men and women into pens of behavioural conformity. But oversensitivity occurs on both sides of the debate. On average men receive sentences 63 per cent longer than women when convicted of the same offence in a UK court.

As a comic it is possible to crack jokes about a subject without belittling it. I once wrote a joke for a famous female comic. It went like this. (You have to image her delivering it in her trademark cheery voice.) "I was on a train the other day and a girl shouted 'Rape!!' And we all looked out of the window and saw a lovely field of yellow flowers."

That gag works – like a lot of jokes – because it turns out to be about something other than initially expected. But what really adds an extra cylinder to the gag is how it classically raises tension before dramatically releasing all that same inflated tension. Not bad in the range of just a few short words.

We are asked by the chairman to offer a concluding message about the future of feminism. I flounder, like a new born foal on a frozen lake. Meanwhile my fellow panellists make succinct and brilliantly articulated points of sagacious perspicacity. I reprise the Voltaire line about men always being destined to be inferior to women because "possessing a penis is akin to walking around permanently chained to a mad man". Scary Academic helpfully adds that this problem could be solved by castration. It is her first attempt at humour – yet fails to receive the laugh it deserves because no one is quite sure if she is being serious or not. Including me. I check my body language and discover both my hands guarding my groin.

There is arguably a reoccurring problem with the militant feminist fundamentalists: they have one destructive weak spot. Humour is their kryptonite. This, I believe, is nonsense – as contrived as the belief feminists burn bras (if you knew how expensive bras are at M&S, you would not believe anybody burns them either). Anyone, regardless of their X and Y chromosome count, can reflect differing personal levels of humour tolerance.

We take questions. "Are you frightened of women having power?" asks an audience member. "No," I reply genuinely hurt that I am believed capable of holding such a stance. I commence my answer with the line, "As a responsible penis owner..." which the audience enjoys, "I think women should be in power. In fact, every member of a nation's government should be compulsorily female. Starting with all countries in the Middle East." I also point out that another way to mediate the ongoing Middle East situation is to announce, "Right! No one will get any telly for a week until you've sorted it all out!"

More controversially I risk a rare salvo into seriousness and suggest that young girls should be allowed to choose Barbie dolls and princess dresses. Likewise women are fully entitled to wear short skirts and heels wherever they wish – if that's what they genuinely want. In the noble dash towards equality isn't there a risk we may be branding girls' preferences somehow inferior to boys? "Leave Barbie alone," I say. "She's had a hard time of late – what with her weight problems. At least role model Barbie has several jobs." In fact, at the last count Barbie has 86 jobs including astronaut, architect, sea life trainer, palaeontologist, vet, dentist and McDonald's cashier. So Ken will certainly be cooking the dinner each night in that household.

I finish by announcing that I was grateful for my appearance fee which was 22 per cent higher than my fellow female panellists. The 22 per cent is an oft quoted figure for gender wage disparity. This is a Cambridge University audience so I can allude to that reference without an explanation. As proven by the audience laughing generously. Obviously I received nothing for attending, but am happy to participate. Even a small laugh escapes from Scary Academic. I think I may be warming her up. A few minutes earlier I would have expected her to brandish a remark like: "Your laughter is the nectar that feeds him and his fellow oppressors!"

The chairperson announces we have overrun and closes the discussion. The lacrosse girls appear reluctant to leave. I did alright, but there is an unavoidable truth that I was out of my intellectual depth compared to my fellow panellists.

Back in the biscuitless "green room" later, I generously help myself to another free water. "I enjoyed that. You don't do this sort of thing for the fee?" says Scary Academic. "Fee?" I ask. "Yeah, £50 plus expenses," she confirms, adding, "I thought you were someone else – an anti-feminist blogger. But apparently he got uninvited at the last minute." And then she offers to shake my hand. I accept.

JOBS

THE EXAM INVIGILATOR

For reasons that I cannot have adequately examined at the time, I have agreed to oversee some examinations. I am going to be an "invigilator". This sounds important until I arrive and am greeted by a "proctor". He confirms that "proctor" is more important than "invigilator". The supervisor agrees, her job title self-evidently trumping mine. Then an "Exams Officer" arrives and busily points out that her status surpasses mine and everyone else's present by several rungs on the greased career ladder. Though the ladder she has climbed career-wise is smaller than the one she currently has in her tights. The last time I saw a ladder that big, it was on the side of a fire engine.

The Exams Officer explains my principal duties. On no account, she states firmly, should I leave the exam room. "On no account," she double stresses. I begin to hope even harder than usual that there isn't a fire.

"I am not allowed to leave the exam room either," she adds, anxious to demonstrate parity with her workforce. Pausing respectfully for fully three seconds to allow her words to decay before adding, "Actually, I have to pop out and buy some tights." She moves towards the door then swivels to announce as an afterthought: "Sean here will be in charge of the exam until I get back." Sean the supervisor relishes her role. "It's a customer facing role," he announces boastfully, his torso visibly inflated with pride. It would be difficult to invigilate an exam without being customer facing – unless he conducted it with his back permanently turned.

The Exams Officer returns and apologises for popping out, reiterating it's not permitted in the rules. She immediately examines her bag bearing the name of a popular chain of chemists. "Oh crap, I've bought the wrong size," she announces inelegantly. "Just need to pop out for the tiniest little mo. You won't notice I'm gone." I will notice she's gone – there'll be no-one telling us we can't pop out. Sean will also notice, relishing his opportunity to be in charge again.

I can already sense him fermenting changes he plans to implement in his latest five-minute reign.

True to her word, the Exams Officer returns instantly. An insufferably obsequious Sean keenly reports that no-one has left the room in the brief time she has been gone. "Good," she says, thereby stressing again that no-one is allowed to leave while the exam is in progress. Allowing a respectful fifteen seconds to pass before announcing, "Right, I'm popping out to change my tights." She has changed her tights but not her attitude.

We are conducting several cosmetology exams over four days. On the second day I am given a list of new tasks. One is to make announcements. "Have you done any public speaking before?" asks a person who was not present on the first day. Her job title is something like "Part-time temporary junior deputy under-assistant apprentice work experience kid". Yes, she willingly points out, her status is above mine. "I've spoken in public before as I'm a stand-up comedian," I inform her. "Oh my God," she exclaims. "Yes, that is quite impressive," I think to myself. "That doesn't mean," she continues without displaying any sense of being even feebly impressed, "you're going to say anything funny are you?" she checks. "No," I reassure her, "I haven't the slightest intention of saying anything remotely funny," thereby resolutely fitting the booking criteria for working as an examination invigilator or on any ITV2 panel show.

For several hours on Day Three nothing happens. Then a petite girl with purplish hair tied up so tightly she has lost the ability to blink, raises her arm. This is the first exciting thing to happen.

I rush over importantly, feeling the adrenaline surge surely only a first responder in the emergency services can truly match. I reach her desk in three seconds, thus surely hitting my callout response target. "Can I go to the toilet, please?" she asks. "Er ... you're like 27 years old," I think to myself. "Yes, of course," I say, revealing my shock that she feels the compunction to ask me. Wow, I get to decide the power of whether candidates can relieve themselves or not. I do have authority after all.

Promenading purposefully down the tastelessly patterned carpet, the Exams Officer constantly scans the candidates. One candidate sips from a mug proclaiming, "I'm a beautician not a magician!"

Another candidate has a bright fuchsia pencil case. The Exams Officer is suspicious of this, and adopts an air of authoritarian fastidiousness that an East German border guard would have considered unduly officious. She insists that the girl empties her pencil case. It contains her main pen plus her second, third and fourth best pen, her fifth and sixth reserve back-up pen and her just-to-make-sure seventh, eighth and ninth biro. Plus her you-never-know tenth, eleventh and twelfth pens.

"Have you ever caught anyone cheating?" I ask her. "Not yet," she replies, as if this situation has only been caused by her own laxness. She asks me if I have inspected the purple-haired girl's mug. "No," I reply, "what for?" "In case she has concealed information on it that she can use in the exam," she replies, before adding, "of course." Unless two of the answers to exam questions are: "Made in China" and "dishwasher proof", it will be of little use as a crib sheet.

Following orders I walk along the aisle, peer strangely into the mug owner's Ribena – drinking unprecedentedly huge quantities of Ribena may explain her purple hair colour – and then walk back to report, "It's an all clear." I feel the inspected candidate's eyes following me for several seconds as I walk away while a massive invisible question mark forms above her head.

On our final day the Exams Officer casually announces, "Right, I'm nipping out to the shop – anyone want anything?" "Yeah," I reply boldly given it's my last day, "I'd like another rule book as you appear to have thrown the current one out of the window."

THE SILLY COW

Sitting in an Oxford café I notice that one of the waitresses is dressed as a cow for an ice cream promotion. We are the day's first customers and if she dared to hope no-one would recognise her throughout the shift, her cover is already blown by 8.02am. "Hello, Emma? Nice outfit," I remark. "If you say anything about the udders," replies Emma, "I will get the kitchen rolling pin and smash you so hard they'll need dental records to identify you." "Hello" or even "Good morning" would have been a more traditional response to my greeting.

"Pull the udder one," I say. She gives me the look – her eyes scanning me like the red dots of a sniper's tracer light. Unwisely, I continue: "Could you turn the heating up, it's Friesian in here!"

"Right, that's it!" she proclaims, swivelling purposefully away from our table and disappearing into the kitchen.

A flurry of customers arrive and she is set to work scooping ice cream. Throughout the ten years I've known her, Emma has always been cleverer than me so I wonder what retaliatory gesture she is planning.

I am here with a male friend whom I have not seen for a guilt-inducing amount of years we soon set about calculating. Men are rubbish at conversation. If you're a woman reading this, and have allowed your impression of men's conversations to be formulated from Radio 4 exposure, then you have been deceived. Usually men's conversations mainly proceed like this: "Alright?" "Yeah, alright?" We're often not alright, but fear no-one would be the slightest bit supportive or interested if we elaborate. It is easier to nod confirmation. "So, Spurs are struggling then…"

If men were unable to discuss football, then pubs would just be the sound of men crunching crisps while women talk. For generations men made puerile jokes about women which came with Freudian subtitles so large they covered the entire screen of our perception. "Wouldn't mind a lock-in with the new barmaid, eh!" managing to be both painfully unfunny and ridiculous. In olden days this type of comment would receive a cheeky conspiratorial laugh. Latterly, the conditioned responses would include, "I'm uncomfortable with your objectification of the bar person." And nowadays: "What barmaid? This pub became a Tesco Extra three weeks ago."

So when I meet my friend after ten years our conversation opens predictably: "Alright?" "Yeah." "You alright?" "Yeah." "Arsenal are…" "I've become an adulterer."

"Cheesy Chive Toasty?!!!!" shouts Emma from behind the counter. No-one responds. It cannot possibly be because she was not shouting loudly enough.

"Good," I reply.

"Good?" he checks. "Yeah, it's about time," I say smiling. "My wife and I were hoping you'd get round to it."

His facial expression is concerning me.

"I always knew you'd become an adult," I confirm.

"I said 'an adulterer' not 'an adult'."

Believe me, it sounds a lot funnier now than it did at the time.

"Oh," is the best my brilliant brain can initially offer. Thanks for that, brain. "It was an impulse thing at a conference. We both had too much to drink."

I should probably ask him about the wife and kids. My wife will check if I've asked about them. I decide now is probably not the best time.

"Is the other woman pursuing you for a relationship?"

"Not quite. She's getting a new phone to stop me contacting her."

"That's good," I say.

This time "good" is the correct response. "Perhaps she doesn't want to risk a marriage for a bit of frantic drunken fumbling," I conclude.

It dawns on me we're having one of the most emotionally intense conversations of our grown-up male lives. "CHEESY CHIVE TOASTIE!!!!!!!" booms Emma, so loudly that the entire top deck of a no. 5 bus outside all turn their heads to look our way. Elsewhere in Northern Europe, seismologists excitedly check jumped needles. Still, no-one claims the neglected snack.

"You need to wean yourself off her before you mess up peoples' lives including your own," I counsel. He nods comprehension and remarks, "So, Manchester United are having a shocker..." I deliberately don't respond.

"I've learnt my lesson," he sighs. "Learnt what lesson?" asks Emma, choosing a spectacularly inappropriate time to clear up our mugs and somehow arrive stealthily whilst dressed as a seven-foot ruminant. "Just men's stuff," my friend lies. "That'll be tedious then. And no doubt involves football and willies," she predicts. Told you she was clever.

An enervated woman enters the café chaperoning young children, looking like she is already well past her bedtime at 8.30am. They immediately spot Emma. Two giggling children pull Emma's tail. It's the first time I've heard a farmyard animal swear. Even through her elongated bovine snout it's possible to read her facial expression clearly: "I'm a 41-year- old woman with an Oxford degree currently dressed as a cow. Please send me to the abattoir now!"

My friend thinks about pulling her tail too, but that would end in months of traction – plus he's vowed not to pull any more women ever again, regardless of circumstances. Emma then returns to a table of four undergraduates lost in self-obsession and slams down the unclaimed Cheesy Chive Toastie with such a force it is remarkable the plate doesn't break. Or the solid mahogany table. The four remain oblivious to its cold, late arrival.

We decide to vacate the café and go to the Covered Market. "We're going to the market, Em. Would you like to accompany us? We could try swapping you for some magic beans." "Have you ever considered how much waitress spit you've drunk in your time?" she asks, followed by an exaggerated laugh to reassure everyone she's joking. "It's okay, he's a friend. No, it's not too late to cancel your drinks orders." The café manager pops his head out of a hatch like a momentarily curious tortoise and says ominously: "Emma, could I have a word?" "Of course," she replies, "is it about a pay rise?" before trundling to the kitchen with her tail between her legs. Literally.

I see Emma three weeks later, now working at a different café. "Have you moo-ved on?" I ask. "Perhaps to Cow-ley?" Unsurprisingly, I have been unable to enjoy a frothy drink in a café since.

THE LIBRARY MOVE

Because not enough people demonstrated sufficient good taste to buy my latest book ("Hilarious. 5 stars." – *Psychologist Magazine*) I'm now back looking for casual work. Basically I am Ed Reardon – the only difference being that he is a fictional construct whereas I am very much real. Though how much longer I can sustain being real depends on finding imminent employment. My income streams have been dammed by the beavers of bad luck, my money trees gnawed down by the sharp teeth of fiscal reality, collapsed in on itself like an over-weighted badly constructed extended metaphor about beavers.

Hence I need to be an eager beaver and start beavering away. Unfortunately even the slightest of slightly paid jobs now requires a staggeringly indulgent application process and at least two academic degrees. The interview panel for one menial job wished to discuss my CV. This was made slightly awkward by the fact I did not have one. "I haven't got a CV," I announce. "Okay, if you had a CV," begins the lone female panellist perhaps more patiently than I deserve, "what would it say at the very top?" "Probably the letters CV," I reply. Thankfully she laughs. But not enough to offer me the job.

Two days later I have completed my CV. Under "achievements" I list: "(1) Snogged Katie Pearson at school disco (who everyone agreed was the hottest girl in Class 4B), (2) Narrowly avoided getting beaten up by Katie Pearson's brother." In truth I did not avoid getting beaten up by Katie's Pearson's boyfriend. Or Katie Pearson herself when she found out I'd told everyone.

I am quietly advised to remove this from my CV. This leaves precisely nothing under qualifications and achievements apart from "Wrote jokes for comedians." I am also told to remove this as writing material for top comedians it is not relevant for most photocopying roles. This surprises me, as a significant number of comedy writers tend to be expert photocopiers, given the necessity to augment their wages shortfall with clerical temp jobs.

One fellow comedy writer explained how he was unable to escape the daily torment of call centre work, even after his work was broadcast on national BBC radio. He also revealed that the minimum wages he earned in the call centre compared favourably to the remuneration per hour for writing comedy. He calculated that his call centre remuneration of £7.10 per hour worked out at approximately £1.20 per "p*ss off!"

Going for photocopying vacancies with a CV proudly declaring "I wrote the screenplay for Rupert Grint's last movie, supply material for Dara O'Briain, Hugh Dennis, Dr Phil Hammond, etc." doesn't help land clerical admin jobs. They suspect that photocopying may not be your first love, your undiluted driven desire, your impossible-to-distract non-divertible dream.

Sure enough, I attend an interview and am asked why I want to work as a clerical temp, i.e. photocopier. Unfortunately I flounder in my response, regretting that I never bothered to learn fluent bullshit. They say that in order to get on in the 21st century you need to speak a foreign language – preferably Chinese. This is not true. For the restlessly ambitious the most desired language to speak fluently is bullshit. Only when you speak it like a natural can you communicate with those in charge.

Next I attend an interview at an Oxford library. The job is full-time but only for four weeks. Nevertheless a full application and interview selection process has been deemed necessary. The three-person interview panel asks me why I want to do this job, what appeals to me about the role, and how its challenges and requirements are best suited to my skills. We all know the job purely involves carrying boxes up and down stairs. I am left to ponder silently how carrying boxes of books on staircases all day could possibly constitute anyone's dream employment vision. ("In my day, son, everyone wanted to be an engine driver – but today's kids uniformly aspire to be box carriers.")

Their deployed managerial phraseology contains a level of bullshit even the person who writes the tasting notes on M&S wine bottles would consider unnecessarily over-the-top, and advise, "Reign it in a bit, love."

"Obviously I'm attracted to lugging boxes upstairs all day in a library for the same reasons as everyone else: the glamour and the chicks. Especially the chicks. In the same way that I presume everyone is attracted to working in a hatchery for the chicks. And also the dispiritingly low wages," is what I want to say. Thankfully I restrain myself.

Unfortunately, increasingly red-tinted bills and final demands being shoved through my letterbox ensure that I do need to land this job, so I cannot risk appearing seditious in an interview.

Upon clarification, it becomes confirmed that the job (or "challenge and opportunity" – why is everything a challenge and an opportunity nowadays –whatever happened to problems?) does indeed consist of nothing more than carrying books up and down stairs. I am basically a leaf-carrying ant given a human form. "No," they say in a resigned tone revealing that they've answered this question already several times today, "there is not a lift." They ask me if I have an interest in libraries. I am shrewd enough to answer "yes" – they're not going to catch me out with that savvy psychological profiling question.

"Would you like a drink?" I'm asked. Experience has taught me to answer this question at job interviews guardedly. Never reply: "Yes, a Stella please." I ask for a coffee. White and no sugar. Five minutes later Sasha brings me a black tea with sugar. I decide not to complain, feeling a newly arrived frisson of unfamiliar confidence as I conclude, "Well she must have passed an interview to work here." The fact that Sasha is both ludicrously attractive and clearly very cold in her choice of tiny outfit is, in our hoped-for 21st century of meritocratic gender equality, an unconnected detail.

Since I am the only candidate cheap enough to say yes (or, more accurately, "well … I suppose so") I am given the job. Departing the interview I meet Handyman Pete, who informs me he's finishing a carpentry job today so I won't see him when I start in a fortnight.

On my first day I meet Pete again. "I'm definitely finishing up the job today," he informs me. The librarians brief me that I have to move all the books from Floor 3 to Floor 4, and relocate everything currently on the 4th floor to the 3rd. I consider swapping over the "Floor 3" sign with "Floor 4" and placing stickers on the lift buttons renumbering floors 3 and 4. This idea is rejected. So much for strategizing – and the "thinking outside of the box" mantra they seemed so keen on in the application process.

There is an intimidating amount of books to move. They are so dusty that I require both a shower and a bath after work each evening. After three weeks I have finished the job. On my last morning Pete pops in to say, "It's definitely my last day here too." Every single book since Gutenburg invented the printing press has now been carried either up or down the stairs by me. Sometimes in both directions, when directives weren't clearly given. There simply cannot be any books left unmoved. "Did I mention this office on the left has several book shelves, the contents of which require moving?" the librarian casually comments on my supposed last afternoon. No. No you didn't. I would have remembered that. This job has certainly won me over to eBooks.

A month later I return to the library to provide my bank details for payment. I am greeted by Pete who informs me, "I'm definitely finishing up today."

THE BANKER BETS

Like the overwhelming majority of the UK population, I have no idea what bankers do. But I still hate them. Obviously. Mark Twain said a banker is someone who will lend you an umbrella when it's sunny, but ask for it back when it's raining. He said that 125 years ago – probably nicked it from Barry Cryer. There's a clue about the venality of bankers within the title of their trade newspaper: *The FT* spells "*Theft*".

Remember all that spent rage and splenetic anger, now surely reappraised as misplaced, we used up on banks purely because of their insufficiently long pen chains? Bookmakers and Argos would benevolently allow their customers free tiny pens, but not the super-rich bankers. Their pens were spot welded to an infuriatingly inadequate length of chain, like a badly behaved dog.

Nowadays we're actively nostalgic about those old fashioned banks that just sent the occasional acidic letter enquiring about your overdraft, posing the not unreasonable question, "Dear Mr Smith. We've noticed the size of your overdraft, and just sought clarification as to whether you're still banking with us, or we are now banking with you." How we affectionately recall the anachronistic bank manager – whose welfare we used to refer to in casual conversation ("that'll cheer up my bank manager") whom I imagined was slightly avuncular and always wore pinstripe accessorised with a bowler – even in summer – and sensibly carried an umbrella.

Remember when professions such as bankers and journalists were respected as noble ones? (OK, you need to be quite old.) Those old school banks are now a Wetherspoons or a luxury hotel. One of Oxford's oldest banks became the latter – imaginatively christened The Old Bank Hotel. As did the house of banker John Parsons who founded it: Hawkwell House in Iffley. Indeed, he owned two houses, both of which became hotels (not something the average person experiences, unless playing Monopoly).

Recently two students from a High Street college drunkenly stole an ornamental bush from outside the hotel, and took it back to their college – leaving a continuous trail of soil that led along the street, through the college gate, across the quad, up the staircase and to their room. Mystified as to how their perfect crime had been detected, these master criminals were rusticated the next day. If only the tree they stole had belonged to the taxpayers and been worth £735 billion – then they'd have got away with it. And got to keep the tree.

One critical cause of the credit crisis rarely receives exposure and hence its deserved share of the blame: mathematical modelling techniques. Computer advances enabled banks to possess modelling projections, which led to huge rises in speculative funding. The three most common models are complex and prone to irrational performance; they are (in alphabetical order): Black Scholes Model, Markov Chain Model and Naomi Campbell.

Banks and building societies demonstrate a unique approach to customer service: they allocate all their resources into attracting new customers, and hardly any to existing customers. Imagine if supermarkets operated like that:

MANAGER: Is this your first visit to a Tesbury supermarket?

LADY CUSTOMER: Yes.

MANAGER: Have a gold basket and £25.

MAN CUSTOMER: Thank you.

MANAGER: Not you, scumbag.

MAN: But I'm a regular customer here…

MANAGER: Piss off, we're closed!

MAN: But that lady's…

MANAGER: … a new customer. Would you, Madam, like an introductory free i-Pod?

LADY: Gosh, yes please.

MANAGER: You, give her your i-Pod. Now!

MAN: Get off – I'm not authorising that.

MANAGER: Unauthorised debit? That'll cost you a £25 fee.

MAN: How did you get my wallet? That's my money.

MANAGER: I think you'll find it's our money – a common yet fundamental misunderstanding, Sir.

MAN: You can't give her my i-Pod.

MANAGER: God, I despise you regular, loyal customers; if you're too lazy to shop at other stores, you have to be prepared to sacrifice your i-Pod to fund our first-time customers.

MAN: But … I've been away, I haven't shopped here for a while.

MANAGER: Really? That'll be another £25.

MAN: Why?

MANAGER: Account dormancy fee.

MAN: This is outrageous. Now I haven't got any money left.

MANAGER: No money? That'll cost you.

MAN: How can not having any money cost me?

MANAGER: Not having any credit: £25 monthly fee. Besides, we need it: our policy of only selling to first-time customers meant we lost £90.9 billion before tax.

LADY: And after tax?

MANAGER: £90.9 billion. We don't pay tax – we're a big business.

LADY: Sorry, of course.

MANAGER: May I interest you in our banking services?

LADY: Tesbury have diversified into banking? Why?

MANAGER: So the government will bail out our £90.9 billion losses – they wouldn't do that if we stayed as a supermarket, would they?

THE EXPERIMENT

I am waiting in a room. It is located at the top of three tiring flights of stairs on a rather utilitarian staircase, which doesn't fit the context as I am in an Oxford college. This is the sort of dimly lit, undecorated stairwell ordinarily associated with rough tenement blocks, where no-one ever opens their door more than a few cautious inches, and when they do it is usually to inform the police "he ain't here".

Because of the impoverished writer's lifestyle I lead, my presence here relates to helping some graduate students with an Oxford University psychology experiment, for which I am to be paid £4. This matches the exact cost of my bus fare. Doh!

Although only just on time, I am the first to arrive. This indicates that my fellow experiment helpers will be students. Fully fifteen minutes later, the next people arrive and claim the remaining chairs. Then a punk-attired girl brashly enters and proceeds to start a conversation at a volume more appropriate to making yourself heard between rescue boats in a storm.

She spots another student and greets him. Loudly. "HELLO YOU. ARE YOU AVOIDING ME?" This long-haired male undergraduate, clearly avoiding her, denies avoiding her. "So," she booms at plaster fracturing volume, "do you like my latest impulse piercing? I've just had it, so there's still a lot of pus." The man next to me stops his coffee cup lift midway to his mouth, places it back on the table, reattaches the lid and pushes it away. It will be a while before any of us will feel like eating and drinking.

She turns her face towards her unsuccessful avoider and he immediately recoils. Which will make the next few seconds awkward if the piercing doesn't turn out to be facial.

"Err … it's good if you like piercings but I wouldn't have one myself," offers the unsuccessful avoider.

"That's 'cos you'll never be cool," she opines.

"I agree, but I think there are other reasons for that than piercings," he replies sagely.

"So are you coming to my birthday party?" she asks. "Not sure. There is footy on tonight," he stammers.

"What?! You'd rather be watching football?" "Err … actually, yes," he says, reacting like someone who has just discovered it is possible to tell the truth and plans to use this new-found ability more often.

Two student guys enter. One is freakishly tall and thin with a Beatles-like haircut, the other short and stodgy. Viewed from a distance, they resemble a mop and bucket. Then three undergraduate girls arrive, and I become increasingly aware that I am the only person in the room who is not an Oxford student. This appears to render me invisible as students continue their conversations around – and particularly above – me. The more brunette of the three girls surveys the now seatless waiting room, then stands invasively close to me – supporting my belief that I am invisible as a non-student.

She's wearing a short pink jacket the colour of strawberry ice cream. Noticeably, she is also wearing a pair of shorts so tiny that she evidently sourced them from a doll. Then washed them at a high temperature to ensure they shrank a bit more. Her friends have struggled into miniskirts and low sleeveless tops. Between them they are wearing just about enough clothes to dress one person. "It's not very warm in here," remarks one under-dressed Oxford-educated student to another. It's a mystery why.

"The reason I'm doing politics," Piercings Punkette informs her reluctant friend, and everyone else in the OX1 postcode area, "is because there is always something happening to discuss. Unlike your subject History which is dead. How can you discuss History? It's all done." Hmmm ... everything in the entire world that's ever happened – what a limiting subject for discussion it must be. Longhaired Guy pretends to be studying his phone.

We're ushered into a room full of computers. Helpfully, an A4 laminate declares "Computer Room"; otherwise – apart from the bank of 25 computers – we would have no way of working that out. We all pull a numbered ball out of a bag to be paired with a partner. I draw no. 23: away to Preston North End. Actually that's not true, the identity of the person we're drawn with is deliberately unrevealed.

Allocated a computer, we start the experiment. We are given £5 each, but told that if we choose to give any of it to our paired partner, then they will receive triple (£15); they can then decide how much to give back in return. Clearly we can both bag £7.50 each, rather than £5 for one and zero to the partner. So I allocate the full £5 to my partner. They give me nothing in return. The bastard.

Then the scenarios are played again, only in reverse. I assume they will present me with £5 thus transforming it instantly to £15, and I'll return £7.50. Sorted. After all, these are Oxford University students, so they will easily work that out. My partner keeps the £5 and gives me nothing. The double bastard. I want to know who my partners are. I suspect they're Tiny Shorts, Longhaired Guy and Foghorn Punkette.

A frozen screen means someone has failed to understand the most basic and rudimentary instructions. The idiot. Whoever they are, they are responsible for everyone being delayed. The instructions could not be clearer. The experiment controller walks over to my work station and points out it is me. An easy mistake to make – the instructions were ambiguous.

I am given a new partner and another £5, and reminded again I can give some of it away to become tripled. Maybe the £5 I gave away went to the girl next to me – she could use it to buy some bigger shorts. Again, none of the £5 is returned to me.

Outside, Tiny Shorts is chatting to Longhaired Guy. He's clearly mindful that Loudmouth Punkette will be coming down the stairs soon, so he needs to get moving to fulfil any wise ambition of avoiding her.

Her voice is suddenly audible, proven by panicked pigeons ascending en masse from rooftops, and Longhaired Guy abruptly stops texting and runs off in such a hurry that had he dropped his phone, he would not have risked going back to retrieve it.

Punkette appears, looks left and right several times like someone watching a frantically paced tennis rally, and then decides to go right in presumed pursuit of Longhaired Guy. He may need to get a disguise or Google "plastic surgeons".

"Oi!" I feel like shouting after all three of them, "you each owe me a fiver!"

THE PHOBIA EXPERT

My wife tells me that if I do this then I am the bravest man in Europe. I am not. The bravest man in Europe used to live in Liverpool, but now resides in Barcelona. He is Luis Suarez's postman.

I have been set a daunting challenge by Miriam. Miriam is a Dutch clinical psychologist. Evidently she is a very good one given she possesses her own spacious office at Oxford University. Recently she has contributed to several research papers and worked with the Dutch military returning from conflict zones. And she has achieved all this by the age of thirty. All I had completed by the age of thirty was my 1998 World Cup Panini sticker album.

She offers me a drink. "I don't drink coffee," she announces, "but I assume you make a cup with two spoonfuls?" She proceeds to deposit two heaped tablespoons of instant coffee into a small mug. One sip of that and the caffeine intake would ensure I spend the rest of the afternoon vibrating. It reassures me that someone with such conspicuous intelligence can still have knowledge blindspots. "Er, perhaps a bit less coffee," I advise.

"This is good," she announces. "I have learnt that English people say things are "fine" when they are not. In Holland we say what we mean. It is much more efficient." I soon learn that Miriam is abruptly and disconcertingly honest/Dutch. This takes some getting used to.

Miriam has read about my lifelong height anxiety in a feature I wrote for *The Guardian* and is keen for me to try her instigated radical therapy programme whereby she can counteract my acrophobia. My anxious brain has chosen to focus on the word "radical". I ask her what this treatment involves. "I am not going to tell you," she answers with the bluntness of a flattened butter knife. Er, OK. "I am going to expose you to situations that you will find very frightening. How do you feel?" "Fine," I reply. She gives me a look. I edit my response.

"You will have to trust me. Do you have any questions?" "Yes," I ask, "are you evil?" "No," she replies, "I am not evil. Any more questions?" "No, that's good enough for me."

Two days later we rendezvous in Oxford. Miriam announces: "We are going up Carfax Tower and will lean right over the edge. I have deliberately chosen a busy Saturday and the busiest time, to make you feel more anxious."

Queuing up for the tower, she asks me a series of questions, separating perceived fear from evaluated risk. Once we reach the roof I assume my default setting when on top of high places, and press my back against a wall at the furthest possible point from the edge. "Right," she orders, "you are going to walk to the edge. Now. Come on! Quickly!" At this stage I suspect she was sacked from her last job as a Sergeant Major in the Dutch army for being too bossy. If the clinical psychology career doesn't work out there is always dominatrix.

In fact she is cleverly using incremental steps of introduced familiarity. Or exposure therapy in psychology jargon. Gradually I reach the edge, sustaining my position for longer. My instinct is to be propelled back from the ledge with the force of two opposing magnetic polarities. Initially I flee to my safety place, but with Miriam's clever coaxing and applied CBT doctrine, I keep re-approaching the edge, each time for longer. Sticks ("Come back here") and carrots ("You're genuinely impressing me") are alternated as appropriate. I am encouraged to abandon my safety strategies and mirror Miriam's demonstrations of safe leaning.

"Can I remove my glasses as I fear they may fall off and smash to the ground?" "No," she orders, adding, "nice try, to stop your brain processing the imagery it's uncomfortable with." "Thanks," I say, completely busted. "And I can see your hand gripping the rail," she adds. "Which hand?" I enquire in my most innocent caught-next-to-the-empty-cookie-jar-with-biscuit-crumbs-on-face-while-denying-everything voice. "The one you're hiding from me." "Oh, that hand," I say unconvincingly, double busted.

At one stage she asks me to kick her. She did warn me it would be a radical treatment. "I will lean over the edge. Then kick me." She is demonstrating that she cannot fall as long as the majority of her weight is behind the edge. I am extremely reluctant to kick anyone, and suspect it may be a plot so she can claim self-defence as a justification for whatever she plans to do to me next. "Come on!" She chides me. I kick her very gently. She doesn't fall.

"How convinced are you that I won't push you over the edge?" she asks me. I answer: "100%". Though it's probably 80%, 85% tops. She enquires: "Why is your rational brain convinced I won't push you over?" "Because I haven't sufficiently pissed you off yet?" I respond. A laugh leaks from her adopted psychologist persona. Then she places my hand at the base of her impressively flat stomach – someone works out! "This is my centre of gravity – 50% of my bodyweight is below this point so I cannot possibly fall unless all of my body beyond here is over the edge." She explains Newtonian physics. And basically gives me a choice: I can select between the empirically proven laws of physics assembled by humanity's greatest minds versus my stupid amygdala.

Then I do it. I lean over the parapet with hands outstretched. And again. Only this time further. And for longer. She asks me to describe what is written on the wall I'm leaning over. I thought this was impossible only twenty minutes earlier.

This is proper making-a-difference psychology, improving people's lives. Done in just one session. But she tells me this is an inoculation – I will need a booster shot in a few months or my brain may slip back into its old ignorant ways.

We go for a celebratory drink. Later I see Miriam biking away on her elevated Dutch sit-up-and-beg bike. A wave of admiration for her floods through me. She has enabled me to do something in the last two hours that I had never been able to do in the previous forty years.

"So," observes my wife, "are you planning to spend another Saturday with your new sexy Dutch girlfriend?" "No," I answer. I'm not that brave.

THE PSYCHOLOGIST ON THE COUCH

I have spent the last five minutes trying to get the remaining foam out of my cappuccino mug. At £3.15 – a price that can only be set to ensure the staff run out of change by 10am – I am not prepared to leave an unfinished cup.

"It's only air bubbles," counters my café companion Helen. "That's as maybe, but I've paid over £3 for this air, so I'm determined to consume it."

"Funny," she says. Helen has an endearing quality of reacting to anything amusing by saying "funny" instead of laughing; it's almost as if she's too cool to laugh. Then she rises from the coffee shop couch to put on her jacket.

"You can't be a psychologist," I say, prompting a surprised tone in her response. "Why do you say that?" "Because," I explain, "we've been chatting for twenty minutes and you haven't asked me to fill in a single questionnaire."

"Funny," she says. Psychologists are indisputably fond of questionnaires, perhaps to the point of fixated fetishism; whether or not this constitutes an addictive behavioural loop is probably best left to a, er, psychologist to determine. They've probably got a questionnaire for that.

Having just said goodbye to Helen, a TV producer arrives promptly for our meeting. Before discussing work our conversation meanders:

"Who was the tall lady who just left?" he asks

"My friend Helen," I reply. "She's a psychologist."

"You ought to be careful talking to a psychologist."

"Why?" I ask.

"Because they're all obsessed with sex. Why did you become friends with her?"

"Because she's obsessed with sex."

"Really?!"

"No."

He doesn't laugh. Or say "funny". But he does say: "This script requires a lot more sex." He just beats me to the follow-up comment: "Don't we all!"

He warns me that psychologists will constantly evaluate me and, "They can read minds." I'm not entirely sure this is true. Two reasons immediately come to mind. If so, it would mean Helen had been evaluating me on her day off. Besides, if Helen could read my mind, it is extremely unlikely she would maintain a friendship with me. Especially when she peers into the vacuous and barren windy wastelands that constitutes my mind.

Psychologists get quite an unfair and prejudicial rap. Everyone appears socially suspicious of them. My personal theory is that this proves the multitude (and I'm including you and me in that collective multitude) must have something to hide, otherwise why would we fear paranoid exposure by a psychologist? If I was a psychologist encountering profession-based rudeness at social gatherings, I would invent some false terms as mock diagnosis: "That's fine if you don't want to talk to me. I can see you've got Idioticus Disorder and borderline Wotatwat Syndrome." And start sticking artificial pronouncements on them like I owned a diagnostic labelling-gun.

In my experience psychologists help create a better, healthier world. Plus a lot of our improved understanding of that same world has stemmed from psychological research. If ever there was one subject that stretched to cover all of the human condition – it is psychology. And no, they can't read minds. Obviously.

Psychologists are generally treated as outcasts, forced to socialise, date and marry amongst their own community. Unwelcomed by mainstream society, spurned and distrusted by the public, they are left alone to process their endless questionnaires. Okay, it's not quite as iniquitous as that. But…

Oxford University research psychologist Petrina informs me of this true anecdote: "My favourite encounter with the inaccurate depiction of psychologists was at the checkout in Sainsbury's. The cashier was dutifully making polite conversation and asked me what I did. I said I was training to be a psychologist and panic suddenly flashed over his face. He leant forward and whispered, 'Can you read my mind?'"

She also makes an insightful observation about Oxford's misevaluation of psychologists: "One of the main stigmas I have come across is that people don't think of psychologists as scientists, despite the fact that Clinical Psychologists have a doctorate. They think we just talk to people about their feelings and do not recognise that this is far from the case. I studied Psychology and Neuroscience and my peers who were studying biochemistry would consistently say that my subject was not a real science. Mind you, despite my degree being extremely experimental and research-based, with half of the course being shared with medics, I still came out with a BA rather than a BSc. Oxford isn't really helping us there!" She has a point.

One generally acknowledged Top Trumps category where psychologists score incontestably lower than the general population is humour. This following exchange genuinely occurred between a research psychologist and me when I volunteered to aid an experiment:

"Tell me about a recent personal experience involving the word 'glorious'"?

"I was watching the Commonwealth Games late last night. Like everyone else who was watching the Commonwealth Games late last night, I had lost the remote control."

No reaction. Makes note on pad.

"The commentator used the word 'glorious' and I thought surely there are more deserving recipients in our society to be described as 'glorious' than … oh, I don't know … Guernsey's third best tricyclist."

No response. Makes another note on pad.

"Inconsequential," says the psychologist.

"Bit harsh. I thought that was quite good for a spontaneous comment."

"No, the next word to use in a sentence is 'inconsequential'".

She makes a longer note on her pad. I resist a huge urge to get my own pad out of my bag and make a note.

"Can you repeat back to me the following ten digit number?"

"Are you giving me your phone number? If so I'm flattered."

Still nothing. Only this time she makes such a long note it necessitates turning over the page of her notepad.

"Sorry," I say. "Was that too Freudian? Sometimes I say the wrong Freuds … I mean, words."

The clock ticks with an invasive loudness. In the far away distance a fly coughs.

Eventually she breaks an indeterminate silence. "Have you any questions?"

"Is this thing on?"

A week later I meet Helen again. I tell her about the TV producer's attitude to psychologists and how he demanded my script treatment contained more sex.

She nods ruefully. "Quite a humourless lot these TV producers," observes Helen when I had completed reporting his occupational slander, "and they're all obsessed with sex." She pauses before adding "funny". And then emits a hearty laugh.

ABOUT THE AUTHOR

Richard O. Smith writes across many different platforms – like a railway station graffitist. He has written for BBC Radio 4's *The Now Show, The News Quiz* and BBC2's *Dara O'Briain's Science Club*. He's the principal screenwriter of *The Unbeatables* movie starring Rupert Grint, Rob Brydon and Anthony Head – and wrote the novel of the film *The Unbeatables* (Signal Books, 2015).

His book on stupid criminals *As Thick As Thieves* ("Made me think I should have considered a life of crime" – Hugh Dennis) achieved a no. 1 bestseller slot on Amazon.

Dr Lucy Worsley described *Oxford Student Pranks* as "a jam-packed jamboree of jollity" and German comedian Henning Wehn commented that his book on *Britain's Most Eccentric Sports* was "better than all 26 days of a cricket match".

He's the author of *The Man With His Head in the Clouds* (Signal Books, 2014) described by comedian Lucy Porter as "very, very funny." Telling the story of James Sadler, the first Englishman to fly, *The Man With His Head in the Clouds* is a non-fiction historical biography, candid autobiography and self-help psychology humour book. (Try finding THAT section in a bookshop!)

Richard is a Chortle award winner and a former National Football Writer of the Year Award winner. He has written for publications as diverse as *The Guardian, The Independent, When Saturday Comes* and *Oxford Times* magazine *Oxfordshire Limited Edition*.

He is Writer in Residence at The Daffodil Hotel, Grasmere in the Lake District.

Richard is available for speaking engagements. (Book him if you need an entertaining speaker – he's suspiciously cheap!) He describes himself "as a 'freelance writer' mainly because it sounds better socially than 'unemployed'. My passport 'profession' used to read 'writer', until a French passport official misread it as 'waiter'. He then asked me for two coffees. So I ignored him. Like a real French waiter."

ACKNOWLEDGEMENTS

Oliver Ledbury, James Ferguson, Tim Metcalfe, David Raymont and all the interviewees quoted in the book. Thanks to the people who allowed me to write about them in these stories for being such good sports. Especially Missy and Melissa (no, not their real names!) plus Sarah and Miriam (yes, their real names).

Some of these columns originally appeared in the *Oxford Times* magazine *Oxfordshire Limited Edition*. This monthly colour supplement was thrice garlanded with the prestigious Regional Magazine of the Year award. They are reproduced here with permission of the editor.

Special thanks to Oliver Ledbury who helped enormously with proof-reading and editing, feedback and advice, and Oxford comma usage.